W0254208

FEVER VISION

EUGENE HAYWORTH

Fever Vision

THE LIFE AND WORKS OF

COLEMAN DOWELL

PREFACE BY EDMUND WHITE

DALKEY ARCHIVE PRESS
CHAMPAIGN * LONDON

First edition, 2007

Library of Congress Cataloging-in-Publication Data
Hayworth, Gene.
Fever vision : the life and works of
Coleman Dowell / Eugene Hayworth. — 1st ed.
p. cm.
Includes bibliographical references.
ISBN-13: 978-1-56478-457-5 (alk. paper)
ISBN-10: 1-56478-457-6 (alk. paper)
1. Dowell, Coleman. 2. Authors, American—
20th century—Biography. I. Title.
PS3554.0932Z63 2007
813´.54—dc22
[B]
2006016859

Partially funded by a grant from the Illinois Arts Council, a state agency.

Dalkey Archive Press is a nonprofit organization whose mission
is to promote international cultural understanding and
provide a forum for dialogue for the literary arts.

DALKEY ARCHIVE PRESS
University of Illinois
605 E. Springfield
MC-475
Champaign, IL 61820

Design and composition by Quemadura
Printed on permanent/durable recycled, acid-free paper
and bound in the United States of America

Frontispiece: For a brief period in 1964, Coleman Dowell took work as a model to supplement his income. He wrote to his family: "I am now a model; three jobs in the past week, at 50.00 an hour." He appeared in ads for the *Wall Street Journal*, the Rambler, and the Jaguar.

FOR KEITH

CONTENTS

ACKNOWLEDGMENTS

I have had the great pleasure to talk to a wide variety of individuals who inspired and encouraged Coleman Dowell. Among them I would like to thank Dowell's colleagues and friends, Walter Abish, Martin Bax, Jack and Nora Beeson, Peter Glassgold, John O'Brien, and Maurice Sendak. I am especially grateful to Edmund V. White for his initial assistance in my research, as well as his ongoing support and his significant contribution to this book. A number of Dowell's relatives offered invaluable material by contributing family anecdotes, photographs, and letters, and I would like to acknowledge their help, beginning with Dowell's sister, Ruth Willis, his nieces Gayle Wohlken and Sandy Taylor, and Marty Dowell and Sherry Miller. Dowell's schoolmates, Dorothy Donnell Steers and Margaret Caudill, shared stories from their youth and copies of high school newsletters. I am also indebted to my editor, Martin Riker, for his fine editorial work, and to Marvin Taylor, the director of Fales Library and Special Collections at New York University for his assistance during my research there. Others who offered support, advice, or assistance include Esdras Lubin, Neville Atkins, and my colleagues Bud Coleman, Elissa Guralnick, Carol Krismann, and James Williams. I owe a deep debt of gratitude to Dr. Bertram Slaff, whose friendship and generous spirit sustained me for more than six years of this project. Dr. Slaff graciously shared vivid memories of his life with Coleman Dowell and provided full access to the letters and other personal papers I relied on to write the book.

I would like to make special acknowledgment to the libraries that granted permission to quote from material in their collections: Fales Library, New York University; The Howard Gotlieb Archival Research Center at Boston University; Department of Special Collections, Stanford University Libraries; The Houghton Library, Harvard; Rare Books and Manuscripts, New York Public Library; and the Rare Book and Manuscript Library, Columbia University. My research was funded in part by the Implementation of Multicultural Perspectives and Approaches in Research and Teaching (IMPART) Awards Program at the University of Colorado at Boulder, and a Coleman Dowell Fellowship in Experimental Work from the Fales Library.

On a more personal note, I would like to express my deepest gratitude to my mother, Patricia Hayworth, whose strength and compassion have always inspired me. Finally, I am especially indebted to my partner, Keith Waters. His wit, intelligence, and warmth never falter; without his encouragement and advice this book would not be possible.

PREFACE

Someone who commits suicide does not always produce the pity and terror in his friends he anticipates. The survivors feel at first a deep, shameful sense of guilt haunted by the words "If only . . ." If only I had been able to stage-manage a bit of literary success for him. If only I'd been more flattering, kinder, more useful. If only I'd simply been more present and not allowed him to withdraw from the world and from our friendship in particular.

Then another feeling sets in—of resentment, an affronted feeling of having been deserted or betrayed or rejected, for the flip side of "If only I" is "Why didn't he?" Why didn't he seek some professional help? Why couldn't he see that he was loved, appreciated, admired—if only by a cult?

When Coleman Dowell jumped to his death on August 3, 1985 from the fifteenth floor apartment he shared with his longtime lover, the psychiatrist Bertram Slaff, his suicide did not come exactly as a surprise to Bert or to me. I had seen Bert shortly before an event in Paris, where I was living at the time. I remember we were about to board the metro out near the Cité Universitaire and I said to Bert, "Are you prepared for Cole's death? You must get ready for it." He responded with a mixture of sadness and relief—sadness at my prediction, relief that I shared his apprehensions.

For years Cole had seemed terminally bored with his life—bored and anxious and disgusted. He regretted the loss of his looks and for years he'd worn a highly synthetic looking wig until he read something I'd written in *The Joy of Gay Sex* about how attractive a bald man could be if he knew how to take his baldness on board. From then on he was bald . . . flamboyantly, as he did everything else. Nevertheless he complained all the time about aging; too bad he didn't live into the era of the net, where even gerontophiles have their own site.

Like many artists he was a hypochondriac; most writers and composers and architects—those who are engaged in long-term highly demanding works that require years to pull off—fear they'll die or lose their minds or health before they are able to complete their masterpiece (which is always the project at hand). Cole was no different. He feared he had AIDS or leukemia or something else fatal. As if to tempt fate this sense of imminent doom did not make him work harder but rather drove him to fritter away his days cruising Central Park (which lay just outside his door) or the personal ads placed in magazines by black prisoners seeking pen pals and eventually lovers on the outside.

Or Coleman entertained, if such a frivolous word can be applied to something so grueling and (as I now know after reading this biography) something he so resented. Cole could turn a picnic supper into a Calvary, a tea-party into a martyrdom. His dinners were his form of traveling; as we learn in the pages that follow, he went to Europe only twice and never anywhere else, but he turned out complicated dinners of many courses that spirited the guest off to Brazil or China or France or Italy or Germany or Scandinavia. Even the table had come from a Spanish refectory. He agreed to come to my house only once and naturally I spent days preparing it. The main course was puff pastry enclosing salmon, rice and a dill sauce.

Like most alcoholics, Coleman alternated between grandiosity and self-hatred. His grandiosity took the form of lies—about his origins, his New York past, even his role in bed. His machismo required he present himself as the active, dominant male, which hardly made sense given that his partners were usually young black heterosexual men. His humble family he changed into the owners of Heaven Hill Bourbon; only in this biography did I learn that his father kept several grocery stores and was even a blacksmith for a time—and that he longed to own his own farm. In real life his parents and siblings seem painfully normal, but in Cole's fiction their stand-ins are never far from madness, cruelty and incest. In this biography we learn how much he resented the allowance he received from his lover, whom he accused of treating him like a servant. Bert might have enjoyed the elaborate dinner parties in his mild fashion, but wisely at midnight he always walked the dog and then beat a retreat to the bedroom (he had to get up at six A.M. for work). After midnight Cole's drinks would kick in, he'd begin to play the piano and sing his songs, especially the unforgettable "High Up." Then his mood would careen into hostility or self-hatred, for the other side to his grandiosity was a bottomless contempt for himself. His journal, apparently, is full of the umbrage he took during his dinner parties.

In his writing all these faults became virtues. His shifting and ever malleable sense of the truth in life became a postmodernist strategy in his novels. His moral ambiguity (for he was anti-Semitic but lived with a Jewish lover most of his life, just as he despised "niggers" but most of his adult affairs were with black men) got played out in his fiction in the self-degradation of a white character, Ivy, in *White on Black on White* or in the picture of "pushy Jews" in *Mrs. October was Here*. The ability to nurse a grudge over the years or to invent a baseless paranoid plot other people were supposedly hatching against him fed his fires as an inventor of "plots" in fiction. For instance, he thought that Carl Van Vechten had turned against him after the failure of Cole's musical based on the older man's novel. In fact, Van Vechten continued to love and admire Cole, but Cole was too ashamed to continue this friendship. The conversion of love into hate fed the central chapters of *Island People*, which are animated by ruthless satire. Life was not a large enough arena for Cole (especially since he'd shrunk its circumference through his alcoholic withdrawal from the world), but his elaborate novels with their shifting points of view and imbricated stories gave his imagination the scope it demanded.

Because I'd believed Cole's story about his rich family I never knew (until now) how much he suffered from his "failures." Most of Cole's literary friends —including Walter Abish, Gilbert Sorrentino, Thom Gunn, George Whitmore and myself—lived from hand to mouth. We were happy with our cult status and supported ourselves through journalism or by teaching. But Cole had a thoroughly unrealistic dream of making it big (through avant-garde fiction published by New Directions?). He wanted to bestow a fortune on his poor, widowed mother; he wanted to throw about his wealth and parade his popular success in order to justify all his years of struggle as a song-writer, television performer, model and novelist. I know the problem; though I'm in my mid-sixties and have published nineteen books, I still dream of earning enough money to buy a little house somewhere and pay off my debts.

Yeats said each artist must choose life or art; you can't have both. Though Cole killed himself because his life so bitterly disappointed his childish expectations of it, fortunately for his art he never compromised in order to succeed in any vulgar way. He wrote a muscular, unstoppable prose; he invented passionate, tragic characters; he created places and moods that are often chillingly gothic. He constructed his novels to resemble Rubik cubes. He tested the boundaries of morality and even decency. He understood passion in all its life-denying forms. He brought together the quite different influences of William Faulkner and the Icelandic novelist Halldór Laxness (another thing I learned from Hayworth's biography). He compounded his stories out of equal parts of observation and rhetoric, by which I mean the artesian flow of language he had merely to tap in order to be inundated by it.

Gene Hayworth has done his homework by interviewing surviving family members and friends and by reading early drafts and letters and everything unpublished that the estate has made available. He has a basic sympathy with a struggling artist, a victim of America's cult of success, a man who arose out of the working class and without benefit of higher education or family connections managed to make an indelible mark on the literary life of late 20th century America. This is a cautionary tale, perhaps—though what it mainly seems to be cautioning us against is a sentiment that overtakes most people with time: disappointment.

EDMUND WHITE

> I'll tell you how we went to sleep. We had a ritual. When we decided to go to bed, I would pick up Tammy, put her in my arms, and then Coleman would wrap himself around me and Tammy, and then I would be the first to fall asleep . . . And as soon as I was sound asleep, Tammy would get out of my arms, and get in between him and me, and then she would go to sleep. And Coleman would feel his family was now asleep. I was asleep, Tammy was asleep, and Coleman would go to sleep. I thought it was rather charming, informal but cozy.[1]

The American author Coleman Dowell described his first novel, *One of the Children is Crying*, as "a fictional farewell to [his] family."[2] By the time the novel was published in 1968, Dowell had moved far from his roots in southern Kentucky to establish a new home, in a situation completely different from the family of his adolescence. Unlike the impoverished Kentucky houses of his youth, the Eastside Manhattan apartment that he shared with his longtime companion Bertram Slaff and their cherished dachshund Tammy, reflected the identity he wished to create for himself as a cultured and cosmopolitan intellectual. Though Dowell never turned his back completely on his rural southern heritage, he believed that New York was his true home. The contradictory influences of the country and the city proved to be the greatest source of material for his complex novels and short stories.

Although Dowell was known for entertaining and had an extensive circle of friends, he also lived a large part of his life in isolation. For several years he vacillated between the Manhattan apartment and the quiet seclusion of a house on Shelter Island where his early novels were written. Social life stimulated him, but he was quick to take offense, often turning his harsh tongue against those in power over his career, first in the musical theater, and later in the world of publishing where he established a small following.

In interviews, conversations, and autobiographical writing, Dowell manipulated the facts of his life, in part to mitigate the feelings of insecurity that seized him when he was around others he viewed as successful. When asked what he did for a living, Dowell gave his occupation at various times as "composer," "lyricist," "poet," "playwright," "novelist," and "critic." He adopted multiple identities, best illustrated by the various names he embraced at different points in his life—school friends knew him as "Bobbie"; his sister Martha referred to him as "R.C."; he signed his letters home "Bob" or "Robert"; and adult friends knew him as "Coleman" or simply "Cole." In later life he developed an alter ego he referred to as "Frosty."

Dowell demanded respect and admiration from his literary friends, but he also sought out a series of uneducated, impoverished lovers, men he often paid for sexual favors. His relationship with these men meant more than physical gratification: Dowell took pleasure in adopting a passive role when he seduced them. The emotional trysts counterbalanced the otherwise placid home life he shared with Bert and Tammy.

Bertram Slaff met Coleman Dowell in 1954 and the two men became lifelong partners. Among their many shared interests was a love for the theater. Slaff had entered Harvard at the age of 16, studying government and pre-med, and shortly after graduation he enrolled in the Long Island College of Medicine in Brooklyn. In 1943 the medical school was taken over by the military and the students were put on the Army payroll. When the war ended, Slaff spent two years in Lexington, Kentucky, then he and a childhood friend took an apartment in New York where they hoped to write a play. One evening, after plying the playwright Bill Inge with martinis, Inge complimented them on the script, only to call the next day to confess, "I may have been a little optimistic."

Slaff developed a successful psychiatric practice and opened an office at 7 East 96th Street, but in 1954 he took a house on Nantucket to spend the summer writing another play. That summer he met Coleman Dowell at the Rope

Walk, a seafood restaurant at the end of Straight Warf with a view of the harbor.

"I bet I can guess what you do for a living," Slaff boasted. "You're a novelist."

"No, I'm a composer/lyricist," Dowell curtly replied.[3]

Though Dowell had already written music for television and would soon compose songs for several Broadway musicals, Slaff's intuition proved correct. Over a fifteen-year period Dowell published five novels and over twenty finely crafted short stories. *One of the Children is Crying* appeared in 1968, followed by *Mrs. October was Here* (1974), *Island People* (1976), *Too Much Flesh and Jabez* (1977), and *White on Black on White* (1983). *The Houses of Children: Collected Stories* was published posthumously in 1987.

Slaff nurtured Dowell's talent by providing a home and financial support. Four publishers encouraged his literary career. Dowell befriended James Laughlin, president and publisher of New Directions, Bradford Morrow, editor of the literary magazine *Conjunctions*, Martin Bax, editor of the British journal *Ambit*, and John O'Brien, who founded the *Review of Contemporary Fiction*. Each of these men played a seminal role in promoting Dowell's work. Sections of *Island People* were anthologized in *New Directions: An Anthology of Prose and Poetry*. New Directions also published the complete novel, *Island People*, as well as *Mrs. October was Here*. *Conjunctions* published much of Dowell's short fiction, including a reprint of *The Silver Swanne*, first published in *Ambit* and later published in limited edition by Grenfell Press. John O'Brien established the Dalkey Archive Press in 1983, and in 1986 began issuing original works. The press now publishes the Coleman Dowell British Literature Series. Through reissues of *The Houses of Children*, *Island People*, and *Too Much Flesh and Jabez*, Dalkey Archive Press has kept Dowell's work in the public eye.

From 1962 until his suicide in 1985, Dowell made it a habit to write daily. He developed a distinctive style, by exploring and experimenting with different facets of narrative technique. Unfortunately, the author has received little scholarly attention — Dowell is rarely mentioned or anthologized. With the exception of book reviews and occasional pieces written by colleagues, the critical response to Dowell's fiction has been sparse, even though he enjoyed the praise and friendship of authors such as Gilbert Sorrentino, John Hawkes, George Whitmore, and Edmund White. White continues to champion Dowell's work, regarding *Island People* as a postmodern masterpiece. Though ignored by mainstream readers, Dowell cannot be considered an obscure writer. All of his books were reviewed, and, though he was not often discussed in the media, he was featured on WGBS Radio in Miami with host Bev Smith,[4] filmed for a television documentary shown in Brussels, and interviewed for several leading literary journals.

The shift in his career from music to fiction came gradually. In 1957 Dowell met the novelist and photographer Carl Van Vechten.[5] Dowell wanted to adapt Van Vechten's 1924 novel, *The Tattooed Countess*, for the musical stage. When Dowell played selections from his score for the musical for Van Vechten, he obtained the author's approval. For almost five years the two men were in daily contact, discussing the musical, but also corresponding about the craft of writing. Their letters indicate that the two men developed a warm friendship, and both Dowell and Slaff were frequently invited to Van Vechten's home.

When *The Tattooed Countess* opened at the Barbizon-Plaza Theatre on May 3, 1961 it was panned by the critics and closed within a few days. "It played for exactly four performances," Van Vechten wrote in a letter to Edward Leuders, "each of which was ghastly."[6] Though Dowell continued to work on theatrical projects, he found that his notes worked increasingly more like fictional narratives. The plot of his next original play, *Eve of the Green Grass*, became the manuscript for an unfinished novel to which he would periodically return. The play opened at the Chelsea Art Theatre in 1965, starring his friend Kim Hunter. The show ran for only three nights. After this second disappointment, Dowell decided to give up writing plays and turn his complete attention to fiction.

Dowell's first published story, "Alte Frau im Garten" dates from this time; Ruth Landshoff York translated the story into German and submitted it to

Frankfurter Hefte for publication in 1962. Though this story is fairly uncomplicated, his later, more mature work draws upon many artistic and literary influences. From Faulkner he derives a reliance on southern culture and dialect, peppering his dialogue with expressions such as "I reckon" and "you figger." Like T. S. Eliot he uses shifting perspectives. Although he does not always provide a linear narrative structure, Dowell provides anchors: repetition of imagery, setting, and time serve to ground the reader. Specific techniques include narrative fragmentation, narrative within a narrative, multiple temporalities evoked by juxtaposition of varying verb tenses, and interior monologue.

Much of Dowell's work explores the psychology of the taboo in its evocations of incest, homosexuality, and pedophilia. His characters have been separated from society, and only through human contact can they find salvation. Core to his characters' relationships is the act of sex, which moves from oblique references to Millicent's lesbian lifestyle in *One of the Children is Crying*, through a pedophilic fantasy in *To Much Flesh and Jabez*, until it finally becomes the central theme in *White on Black on White*, the title of which Dowell explains in a quote from the book: "it's America fucking, twos and threes and mores, white on black on white."[7]

Even more than sexuality, the novels are concerned with the association between madness, creativity, and desire. They examine the power one person holds over another and reveal the multiple manners of human deception: by words, actions, and the failure to take action.

Some critics have situated Dowell's work in the style called "New Gothic," loosely defined as the evocation of psychological and spiritual horror and suspense, often brought on by history's effects on the present. This revival pays homage to the American Gothic of Edgar Allan Poe, Herman Melville, and Nathaniel Hawthorne, but has its roots in works by earlier British authors such as Charlotte Brontë. Dowell embellishes this tradition further by placing his emphasis on dreams and the imagination. Some of the themes of *One of the Children is Crying* reflect those of Poe's "The Fall of the House of Usher." By depicting the decline of an aristocratic family line, Dowell's characters Robin and Erin recall Poe's incestuous twins Roderick Usher and his sister, Madeline, who die as the Usher house collapses around them. Concepts associated with Gothic architecture and the visual arts also apply to Dowell's fiction, for his novels include elaborate patterns and ornamental, often ecclesiastical designs in the service of religion, such as his myriad Christ figures.

Dowell claimed to have written several of his early novels concurrently. This may help explain the fact that his aesthetic suppresses temporal continuity. "Even old movies," he said, "are interrupted by commercials and messages."[8] The result is a kind of collage—a painting that reveals perspective from multiple viewpoints. The same events and observations are reiterated by multiple characters, each of whom recounts the narrative through an emotional filter. Each interpretation suggests a variation—a way of evaluating the situation that is unique to the character's perspective. Some of the characters provide a literal interpretation of events, while others use language that reverberates with meaning. Still others present a deliberate misinterpretation of events known only to the reader. In each of the works there is always one character who possesses the ability to experience these multiple perspectives, to delve into the minds of each of the other characters, and to observe events as they occur over several points in time.

Dowell disrupts the traditional notion of authorial voice by creating characters who are themselves authors represented in the act of creating their own narrative. Every novel with the exception of his first examines the notion of fiction as a bridge between the writer and the imagined reader. The result is a series of narrative envelopes. The narrative unfolds in segments, offering multiple perspectives that do not provide factual insight, but add additional emotional levels, layer upon layer, serving, in Edmund White's words, as "nested, Chinese boxes,"[9] a term Dowell himself used in *Island People* to describe the fused consciousness of his main characters.

Although Dowell was reluctant to be considered a gay writer, since his death his career has been most widely promoted in the gay press, including biographical and literary pieces in such publications as *The James White Review*, *The Advocate*, and *Christopher Street*. Dowell lived through several decades in which he saw the metamorphosis of gay self-identity that culminated in the 1969 Stonewall Rebellion, and themes imperative to gay life flourish in his final two novels. Homosexuality appears first in a brief episode of *One of the Children is Crying* and emerges as one of the main considerations in *White on Black on White*. The gay characters are often artists, either writers, or, in the case of Millicent in *One of the Children is Crying*, an actress and model. Occasionally they are hustlers. In some cases the gay characters assume dual genders. Edmund White refers to these characters as "interstitial"[10] and Stephen-Paul Martin defines them as "androgynous."[11] All of Dowell's characters are complex individuals rather than stereotypes.

Though Stonewall liberated many gays and lesbians, Dowell shied away from depicting images of homosexual activism. This does not mean that his novels are not political: his examination of race relations, particularly in the context of gay relationships, illuminates social and cultural problems. Dowell does not merge politics and gay culture until his final novel, *White on Black on White*, when he turned to the pressing issues of race relations and inequality.

Several of Dowell's novels have been translated into Spanish and French, and in 1996 his French translator, Bernard Hoepffner, won the Prix Rhone-Alpes for his translation of *Too Much Flesh and Jabez*. The international reception of these works is one indication of their growing appeal.

The themes and characters of Dowell's fiction are intertwined with the fact and fiction of his life. Although some readers might find anti-Semitic, antifeminist, and anti-religious rhetoric in these works, Dowell asks us to look beyond those labels to examine the individual's role within these groups. Ultimately, he turned his animosity toward such group mentality. Social change can occur, Dowell suggests, not through any assembled movement, but only through individual action. He was not a gay writer, or a WASP writer, or a Southern writer—he was a *writer*. He struggled to avoid being categorized in his fiction as he struggled with it in his daily existence. If we could ask Coleman Dowell to make a distinction between the reality and the fiction of his life, Bertram Slaff, the man who perhaps knew him best of all, thinks he would say, "*You* could be bound by that kind of question. *I* am above it all. I don't share that frame of reference."[12]

FEVER VISION

Morda Dowell and Coleman, circa 1925. Coleman Dowell was born in the family house in Schley, about ten miles from Adairville, Kentucky, on May 29, 1925. His father Morda was a blacksmith who collected country ballads, which he loved to sing, strumming the guitar, singing with his eyes closed.

CHAPTER ONE

Kentucky and the War Years

In the winter of 1896, when his son Morda was eight and his son Marion was two, Robert Coleman Dowell, a preacher, disappeared from home. The facts are sparse and inconclusive. According to family legend, Dowell disappeared from the Lanston Saloon in Mount Vernon, Indiana. The following spring a skeleton was discovered near the banks of the Ohio River, but the remains could not be identified. The elder daughters were certain that the body was their father. Adding to the mystery, shortly after Dowell disappeared a stranger came to the family home with a coat draped over his arm, possibly the same coat the preacher was wearing the last day he was seen alive. Some family members believed that the stranger was responsible for Robert's death. However, not long after the coat was returned, Robert's widow Mattie took a new lover and suspicion quickly shifted to him.[13]

Robert had fathered five children, including three daughters, Octavia, Evie, and Callie, and two sons, Morda and Marion—whose twin sister Rose died at birth. Morda, the eldest son, ran away from home after his father disappeared. Later in life he told his children that a doctor had adopted him and wanted to send him to college, but that he had no interest in attending school. He returned to his birthplace in southern Kentucky, near the Tennessee border, where he met his future wife, Beulah Violette, at a neighborhood square dance. Beulah was pretty and extremely outgoing, and in 1906, when she was only 16, the couple married.

By all accounts both Beulah and Morda were storytellers. Their youngest son, author Coleman Dowell, must have heard the tale concerning his grandfather's disappearance on many occasions. The legend possibly gave him a penchant for the Gothic elements that he would later include in his novels and short stories. The art of storytelling, learned firsthand from his father, mother, aunts and uncles, enchanted him at an early age.

Coleman was the fifth in a family of six children that included Ruth, Pearl, James, Martha and Eleanor. Birth records and other documents indicate that the Dowells moved frequently. The two eldest daughters, Pearl and Ruth, were born on a farm in Oakville. By 1918 the family lived in Olmstead, where their first son James was born. Over the years the Dowells moved to Russellville, Schley, Price's Mill, Corinth, Gold City and Franklin. The houses were typical country homes, usually white with green shutters, a front porch and a picket fence around the yard.[14] One house, on the road from Price's Mill to Franklin, burned to the ground, and the family returned to the farm in Oakville for two years.[15] Martha's birth certificate indicates she was born in Oakville, Kentucky in 1922, and lists her father's occupation as "farmer" and her mother's as "housewife."

Robert Coleman Dowell was born three years after Martha, in the family house in Schley, about 10 miles from Adairville, Kentucky, on May 29, 1925. By then, both Pearl and Ruth were married and lived in homes of their own, but they would visit on occasion and Pearl would bring her family. James had also moved away, so Coleman and his two youngest sisters, Eleanor and Martha, were the only children left at home.

In an interview with John O'Brien, Dowell stated, " I was born in 1925 and so I grew up during the Depression. When I was five and six years old, the Depression was in full swing and all of this was all around us. People lived in tar paper shacks and cardboard boxes."[16]

By 1930, the family lived on another farm at 114 Franklin Road in Russellville, where Morda rented a house for seven dollars a month. That year their youngest daughter, Eleanor, was born. On the 1930 census Morda gave his occupation as "Blacksmith." To supplement the income he earned shoeing horses, he also soldered damaged goods for neighbors. One reason for the family's frequent moves was that each new home had a better blacksmith shop, one near farmers who could benefit from Morda's services. Around 1937, the family moved to Corinth, a tiny community between Russellville and Franklin. One of Coleman Dowell's first short stories, "Jenny Come Home," dates from about this time. Corinth had two stores, a Presbyterian Church, and Dowell's school, which was no more than 200 yards from his house.

In later life Coleman would recall depression-era Corinth with the exaggerated belief that everyone was happy then. He remembered people with smiles on their faces. He fondly recalled friends and neighbors, and described pangs of nostalgia, "almost a homesickness, for that innocent, simple existence."[17] These experiences were highly romanticized in his mind, represented by specific places like Miss Lassie's over the hill, the stile by Miss Ivy's, and the field of sweet peas beyond the ballpark. He also recalled fond memories of home life: his mother making chocolate pudding for dessert, and Miss Louise, dressed in a white chiffon dress, singing "When they ring those golden bells." The home in Corinth, which Coleman fictionalized as a setting called *The Trees* in his play *Eve of the Green Grass*, symbolized much of what he loved about the south, especially its gentility and hospitality. Much later, describing these memories in a letter to his sister Martha, he asked, "Was life really sweet then, or was it hard?"[18]

It was about this time that Coleman discovered sex. He confessed these first, traumatic experiences in an interview with John and Linda Kuehl, claiming that, at the age of five, he was raped repeatedly by a teen-aged American Indian handyman who worked for his aunt.

> In her large house filled with clocks and competing with the ticking of deathwatch beetles in the walls I learned to be afraid of what can happen to your body in the dark ... pains administered not by ghosts but by the terrible living ...[19]

In his novel *Island People* Dowell created a fictionalized account of the experience. The narrator describes the rapist as an American Indian boy, "an artificial cousin, an unadopted son of an aunt with whom I spent the summers."[20] The narrator in this account is raped repeatedly for a period of five years. The section of the novel is titled "First Person Biography" and like much of Dowell's fiction incorporates many autobiographical details. If the novel provides an accurate portrayal, by the age of ten Dowell had grown accustomed to anal intercourse and had developed feelings of love for the older boy.

After Corinth, the family moved to Price's Mill. By that time Morda Dowell had given up shoeing horses and owned a country grocery store where he enjoyed long conversations with the local farmers. This was the first in a series of grocery stores that Morda would own, followed by a business in Gold City, then another, Hopover Grocery, on Scottsville Road near Franklin. For a short time in 1942 Morda left Kentucky for Cleveland, Ohio, where he worked in a factory, possibly at Alcoa Aluminum, to help with the war effort. He lived above his daughter Martha and her husband Russell Cline in a house on West Boulevard. Beulah, Coleman, and Eleanor would sometimes visit, and Dowell remembered going with his father to the Roxy Burlesque Theater in Cleveland, where the two would "repair at church time on a Sunday morning, the one thing other than old music that [they] ever shared and enjoyed."[21]

By the time of Coleman's high school years, the Dowells lived in Franklin, Kentucky. Despite Depression-era poverty, the house was large and had an outhouse 100 feet beyond Beulah's vegetable garden. Coleman's niece Gayle remembered the outhouse as a "wee shed haunted by bees and . . . spiders." She also remembered the "nightly emergence of little beetles and moths that got inside the house," during the early part of the night while the family was settling into sleep, that "would pelt themselves against the walls."[22]

Fondly, Gayle recalled visits to the family home in Franklin:

> the fragrances of the weeds in the fields, Mother Dowell's bisquits [sic] baking in the oven, the smell of flour on her hands, the soft voice of Papa Dowell singing hymns as he opened the shutters to start a new day, the wooden floor under the heels of our leather shoes, tobacco twisted like rope, hanging from a hook, the bins of dried beans, the gun behind the store counter, the shotgun under the bed, the metallic sound of people peeing into the "slop jars" during night, the ghost stories just before bed, the voices all are there—the crows cawing the afternoon away in the graveyard beside the store, Uncle Cole and [his sister

> Martha] deep in philosophical musings, Mother Dowell snapping beans, talking about spells . . . The big moon, brushing our teeth under it by the edge of the garden.[23]

The family purchased goods through mail order and the children were often allowed to pick out items for themselves. A typical order included fingernail polish, slippers, toothbrushes, dress patterns, buttons, and batteries for the radio. Cousins, aunts and uncles would often visit. Neighboring relatives included Morda's older sisters, Octavia and Evie, and his brother Marion, who had four daughters and two sons. Beulah also had a large family. Her father, Samuel Harry Violette, was a farmer who, like Morda, also owned a store. He and Beulah's mother, Moetta Riggsbee,[24] had eight children that included Beulah, Bob Morris, Eugene, Virgil, Leonard, Viola, Madaline, and Pauline. The Dowell household was seldom without company and these early family gatherings served as the basis for Coleman Dowell's first novel, *One of the Children is Crying*. Dowell based many of the book's characters on his relatives.

Coleman, known to his family as "R.C." or "Bobbie," had a precocious interest in music and books and began reading Shakespeare at an early age.[25] Coleman's brother, James, and their father, Morda, ignored the boy, convinced that his passion for books and music was unmanly. In his turn, Coleman avoided the blacksmith shop, feeling unwelcome there. Ruth described life for Coleman as "just plain hell," since no one in the family seemed to understand him. But Morda did have a sympathetic side. He collected country ballads, which he loved to sing, strumming the guitar, singing with his eyes closed. Dowell referred to these ballads in *One of the Children is Crying*. He later said of these folk songs, "I think everything I write grows out of Kentucky ballads—even *Island People*. I grew up on folk songs, which my father liked to collect. . . . Folk music is the best, purest musical influence anybody can have."[26]

Morda sang hymns, but it was Coleman's mother Beulah Dowell who attended church. Warm and friendly, she enjoyed talking about the Lord and about the power of prayer. Beulah wanted one of her sons to be a minister. Since James showed no interest, she pinned her hopes on Coleman. He taught himself to play the piano by ear and subsequently played for the Sunday school. During the week he would play the organ in the Presbyterian Church for fun, while his sisters Martha and Eleanor would sing and his nephew Ed would preach. According to their childhood neighbor Bess Summers, Coleman liked to play the piano there when church was not in session. She said fondly, "R.C. could whip it up one side and down the other," despite having no piano lessons. Bess remembered that he was "cute as a button" and always said things that made the children laugh. Beulah Dowell liked to tell the story about how he often said, "I am so fatigued," even though he was too little to use that word and everyone else said "tired."[27]

Coleman attended several country schools. He attended school for the first three years in Corinth, in a three-room building that held grades one through twelve, with several grades grouped in a classroom together. His elementary teachers described him as "a bright boy," and "a sweet, well-trained little boy."[28]

Later Dowell attended Middleton and Simpson High Schools. He liked to insist that he studied Latin and Greek in a one-room schoolhouse, but neither his sister Ruth nor Bess Summers could remember any such classes, and Dowell himself sometimes attributed these early classical studies to his sister Eleanor.[29] Dowell exaggerated many aspects of his early education when he looked back on them as an adult. He told his niece Sandi, for example, that he would sneak his teacher's French books from the school and take them home to read. He said it was a mystery to him how he could read them since he had never studied French.

Dowell's education was simple but thorough, probably typical of rural education at the time. Classes in the school included algebra, biology, science, literature, and history. The biology class would go on field trips to a nearby pond in order to collect insects and mount them. The literature teacher assigned book reports. The children would practice scenes from different books in literature and perform them during Chapel, which convened one day a month. Each class would take turns leading the program, and there would be music, a Bible reading, war news, and jokes, and the program would conclude with a prayer. The school sponsored extra-curricular events like history contests and "Class Nite," and theatrical performances by the students. The high school broadcast a radio program which consisted of *Amos 'n' Andy*, tap dancing, vocal solos, and other numbers.

When it was wet and rainy and there were scarcely any pupils, school would let out early.[30] Diversions included music and square dancing, and games like horseshoes and stobs and rook. Other games included sugar lope town in the morning and keep away at dinner. Neighborhood events included hay rides and dances. The children shot firecrackers and they played basketball and often the boys went to Gordensville to play softball. At Aunt Evie's they could go swimming.

Town events included traveling fairs and an occasional motion picture like *On the Avenue* with Dick Powell, *Garden of Allah* with Marlene Deitrich and Charles Boyer, and Bob Steele in *Tombstone Terror*. Radio entertainment included programs like the *Lucky Strike Hit Parade*, which featured songs such as "Where or When," "A Sailboat in the Moonlight," and "It Looks Like Rain in Cherry-Blossom Lane." On occasion, Coleman attended the theater in Louisville, and recalled his "very first stage production, at the Louisville Amp[h]itheatre, VAGABONDKING—and how [he] sat there with [his] mouth hanging open at the splendor of the sets, stars, costumes, songs."[31] Exposure to such a wide variety of music, folk songs, country square dance music, the emerging big band sound of the radio, and theater musicals, would have a strong influence on Coleman's development as a composer.

And then there were the holidays: putting names on valentines, hiding Easter eggs ("They had 4 sacks!" Martha wrote on Easter, 1937[32]), and decorating the Christmas tree. Christmas was particularly memorable. In town they bought presents that included handkerchiefs, boxes of candy and bags of fruit, new dresses, and shirts. On Christmas Day, Pearl and Ruth would bring their families and Uncle Leonard and Aunt Sula would come for supper. It was this family holiday that Coleman chose as the setting for his first novel, *One of the Children is Crying*.

Sometimes Martha, Coleman, and Eleanor would perform minstrels, dressing in each other's clothes. They tap danced and sang, painted and completed puzzles. Sometimes they played school. Summers were full but life was not all play. Often Beulah Dowell was sick and Martha had to cook. Family meals were simple, with dishes such as cornbread and potatoes. Dowell remembered:

> the hunger staved off only by Pinto beans and corn bread, potatoes and canned peaches. Ah, those canned peaches, which mother fed me so hopefully for I had said they filled me up more than anything. It occurs to me now that my adolescent gluttony must have alarmed them, knowing the scarcity of food. I can recall now their eyes as I had helping after helping of food that was probably meant to survive into leftovers for another meal.[33]

Each of the children had chores, which included cracking walnuts, cleaning the house, helping with the wash and ironing clothes. Martha and Eleanor would sew their own dresses and embroider. The children often helped gather food. On July mornings Coleman and Martha picked blackberries and dewberries for pies. They helped pick cucumbers planted in the tobacco patch and bushels of small peaches and damsons. When there was ice and lemons they made ice cream and lemonade. Some mornings Coleman helped Martha wash, and then they would peel peaches until dinner. For their labor Morda sometimes gave them each a quarter.

When their parents were away, the children showed a fair amount of independence. Of these times alone, Dowell would later write,

> I recall a winter of great fearsomeness; I was a junior in high school and Eleanor was a freshman. Mother had gone to Cleveland to visit father, who was doing war work there... it was 1942. I carried her trunk across frozen fields on a sledge hauled by a mule; the sky was heavy and low, the temperature around zero. Mother was chipper and smart in a black suit and a necktie and a sort of fedora hat. She would be gone for two weeks. My mind skips—ignoring the days at school—to the nights in the bleak house, fireplace smoking (I have never learned to make a decent fire), the dreadful food Eleanor and I made: thick pancakes, all floury or doughy, fried liver—I don't think we ate a vegetable for those two weeks. The snows came, the winds came, the ordeal of existence was acute.[34]

If he struggled with his sexual identity during this time, Coleman hid it well. *The Middleton Monitor*[35], Dowell's first high school paper, linked him romantically with several neighborhood girls. The February 1943 *Gossip Page Extra* asked, "What certain senior boy is crazy about what certain senior girl in what certain school? Bobby Dowell and Ruth Dugan." Dowell escorted Dorothy Donnell, a member of the high school band, to the senior banquet.

Most likely these were casual relationships. In later life he discussed his early feelings of sexuality in unusual terms:

> I never had incestuous relationships, but I certainly wanted to. In my family—a really close and very beautiful family—there was a time, a free-ranging, free-flowing time when I would have gone to bed with my father and sisters in a second.[36]

Although probably intended to provoke interest in his work, the comment provides some insight into his lack of concern for social constraint. Dowell did have a fondness for his sisters Martha and Eleanor, but his relationship with other family members grew more aloof with time.

Dowell was an avid reader and the novels he discovered during his youth had a profound effect on his later career. He was especially fond of nineteenth-century fiction and read Proust, Flaubert, Eliot, Dickens, Hardy, and the Brontë sisters.[37]

His sister Martha was an artist who encouraged Coleman to pursue his own interest in writing, drawing, and music. Martha had attended Corinth, Russellville, Orlinda and Middleton schools. During the 1938–1939 school year she was the president of the Art Club at Orlinda High. At Middleton she was secretary and treasurer of her class and the principal artist for the school paper, the *Middleton Monitor*, which sold for five cents a copy. Like his sister, Coleman was involved in many school activities, writing and acting in plays, and playing the piano for school programs. Coleman was popular with the other students, and in September 1939 he was elected Secretary and Treasurer of his freshman class for the 1939–40 school year. Beginning with the December issue of the *Monitor*, each class contributed a cartoon to the paper, for a page called "Read 'Em & Grin." Dowell was the contributing artist for the freshman class and his sister Martha contributed the cartoon for the senior class.

Dowell's interest in song writing began about this time. According to the *Monitor* of November 1939, he and Martha composed the music and words for the school Alma Mater. The lyrics were simple:

Look! We see against the border,
Towering far into the sky,
Dear old Middleton's Alma Mater
As the years roll by.

M.H.S. we proudly hail thee,
Dear old school for thee we'll stand,
Middleton High School, we salute thee,
With uplifted hand.

That year the freshman class also organized a drama club and elected Coleman Dowell president. There were twenty-two members. The purpose of the group was to create the chapel programs. Dowell wrote the scripts and music and often performed in the shows with his classmates.

In September 1940 all the county high schools were consolidated into Simpson County High. Coleman left Middleton to attend the new school, where he played French horn in the band and the Brass Sextet, and served as the program conductor for the monthly class meetings. He participated on the staff of the new paper, *Simpson County Hi-Lights*, both as artist and as writer, providing cartoons and illustrations, gossip and jokes. *Hi-Lights* was a monthly publication selling for four cents a copy, sponsored by local citizens and advertisers from the community like Shugart & Hunt Drug Store, Jesse Mallory Jeweler, and Simpson County Bank. The first issue featured a cartoon entitled "Mr. Farris and Bobbie Dowell in Band."

The newspaper provided entertainment and social commentary as well as information. Dowell's sense of humor is represented in a series of cartoon panels he created. The cartoons also indicate his general attitude toward school—one depicts the coach teaching his kitten how to lunge, another shows Dowell's teacher Harold Spears, asking his fiancée, "Do you think you could live on my salary of $20 a week?" She replies, "Sure, Darling. But what would you do?"

But life was not all humor. The students were aware of the war in Europe, and the editorial section of the December 1940 paper carried a section called "Our Blessings," which read "Our Christmas pleasures are not dampened by the roaring of airplanes, the clatter of anti-craft guns, or the screaming of falling bombs." Coleman responded to the war effort with an illustration for the *Simpson County Hi-Lights* cover of November 1941, which shows an eagle, wings spread, a victory banner in its beak.

The Christmas issue provided a list of "Thanks" that had been submitted for the Thanksgiving holidays. Each item on the list began, "I am thankful," and contained items such as, "That I live in a still free U.S.," "That we are not yet in war and we don't have to make any great sacrifices," and, "That we don't have to live in bomb shelters as other children do and are not shot down because of difference of opinion." In the same issue the students listed their New Year's resolutions, which included flirting, doing better school-work, and learning more about politics. The teachers, Mr. Mayes, Mr. Harris, and Mr. Ferren wrote a letter that read, "Please keep our names away from the Draft Board." Other letters dealt with keeping loved ones out of the war or to bring those who were serving home.[38] The paper's final issue for 1942 said, "Remember America and buy War Bonds and Stamps today and everyday. Do everything possible to help the war effort."

By February 1943 the seniors had ordered their caps and gowns and many of the girls were engaged and preparing for marriage. The Easter issue of *Hi-Lights* featured a section on the *Ideal Girl and Boy*, and described the traits from each member of the graduating class that, combined, would make the ideal person. The *Ideal Boy*, it indicated, would have "Bobbie Dowell's music ability."

The final 1943 issue included the "Senior Class Prophecy," written by Evelyn Thurmond. In her prophecy, Thurmond predicted what life would be like in 1960. On an imagined visit to a cinema in Topeka, Kansas, she discovers, "There, realizing their life long ambitions . . . [were] Cole McDowell (Bobby Dowell to me), and others." The last page contains the signatures of the 26 members of the graduating class, under the heading "Senior Personalities." The message under Dowell's signature reads "Bright in Counsel." Other descriptions, like "Leader of an army," "Follower of Christ," and "Indomitable courage," provide some idea of the qualities and values emphasized at that time—chiefly religion and patriotism.[39]

After graduation in 1943, Coleman Dowell joined the U.S. Army Medical Corps. For a short period he was stationed at Darnall Hospital in Danville, Kentucky, where he and his friends practiced "brittle, witty repartee."[40] The employees at Darnall were both civilian and Army personnel. The hospital serviced enlisted and civilian patients, Veteran's, prisoners of war, and mental patients, and the facility held a neuro-psychiatric ward, a pharmacy, surgery, and a radiology department. In support of the staff of enlisted men and officers, there was also a post office, laundry and barbershop. Dowell, like most of the enlisted men, was probably stationed on the Fourth Floor, in Ward E-3, and would have received a copy of the "Hospital Regulations" H.R. No. 5-5 upon reporting for duty.[41]

While stationed at Darnall Dowell had one of his first homosexual experiences, with a black man he called "Booze," a patient who had "cracked up in the Army."[42] But he continued to hide his sexual orientation from his family. In a letter to his sister Martha he wrote:

> I have such a horrible hang-over this morning that I can't hardly see. I and a friend of mine, had a date with two lovely girls from two of the most prominent families in Danville. We met them at the U.S.O. and last night we made it a foursome in Lexington. We sent them identical corsages of gardenias which were really lovely.[43]

Soon he was transferred to the Philippines. He wrote that, though the weather was hot and dry, there was an occasional rain that left the air fresh and cool. Because of his poor eyesight he was passed over for active duty, but his skill as a typist secured him the position of officer's secretary. He served in the U.S. Army Medical Corps and in 1946, following the end of the war, he was promoted to the rank of Sergeant Assistant to the prosecution in war crimes trials in Manila. He was eventually promoted to the rank of Sergeant.

For holidays the family would mail him packages that included gifts such as cigarettes and shaving cream. His observations of the war probably served as material for his later novel *Mrs. October was Here*. Of his work in the war trials he wrote only, "Prosecution's side of the trial ended Monday at noon and since then I have had every afternoon this week off to make up for the extra time I have 'sacrificed'."[44]

During this period he composed music and attended classes at the University of Manila. In later life he spoke of taking courses in psychology, but in a letter home he wrote of his music studies:

> Did I ever write you about my daily noon-hour program of piano-styles? Anyway, I do have one —— broadcast, too! Old Impresario Dowell, they called me in them thar days. It's lots of fun and I have acquired a really casual attitude to the mechanisms of radio, thanx to my "Mike Technique" class at the U. of Manila. I have also attained a more or less polished technique with the ivories so that, with a glissando or two, I am quite able to cover up what I lack in musical background. My 'Manhattan Serenade,' 'Stormy Weather,' and 'Rum Boogie' interpretations are quite the rage and whenever I go to a club or something there is always someone trying to imitate.[45]

Though he was far from home, Dowell found inspiration in the daily life around him. Here he composed a short poem he titled *Awakening of A Bombed City*:

> Now the sun suddenly bursts over the rooftops,
> Glows yellowly through crevices in bombed walls,
> And silhouettes sentinel pillars against its fire.
> Taking a deep gulp of the fresh early air,
> I hurry away down the street, no longer vaguely and aimlessly

But with a definite goal in mind
A new day has begun.
The city is awake.[46]

The poem shows something of Dowell's eye for observation and his ability to capture descriptive detail. His interest in language is revealed in the contrast prevalent between the images of the sun and the silhouettes, and in the comparison of motion in the sudden burst of sunlight to the figure that hurries down the street.

The soldier entertained himself by writing verse and practicing piano. There was often official entertainment. Dowell described a few of these events in a letter to his mother:

> Monday night we saw a very good stage play — — — — "Kind Lady"; the first dramatic show we have had, having been on a strictly 'musical diet' ... Tuesday night we saw the movie 'State Fair' again, preceded by a thirty-minute broadcast by a well-known Filipino orchestra. Tonight there is a U.S.O. show at 6:30 and the movie "Stork Club" at 7:30.[47]

These experiences reinforced the fondness for theater and music Dowell had developed in high school and he began to draft his first musical play, *Haymarket*.

One candid letter home reveals what he hoped to accomplish once he arrived back in the States. The letter expresses his ambivalent feelings about life in Kentucky and the need to find more sophisticated friends:

> Quite by surprise a couple of nights back I met an old friend of mine who has been in the European theater— —France, Germany, Belgium and England. We have quite a few mutual friends and interests, so I awoke from the lethargy I have been submerged in for so long and really enjoyed a good conversation of 3 hours duration ... We talked food, wines, music, politics, religion, sex and every other conceivable subject ... That is the only world for me and the only one I fit in, which really sounds strange, I admit. But you know that I could never share any interests with the type of people we have always known. My word for them is provincial and I want, more than anything, to be a cosmopolitan. I have all of

> the requirements, all I need is the opportunity. My post war plans are quite different than they were previously and I will wait until I get home to discuss them. They are sure to arouse controversy, but when I want a thing I get it.[48]

This friend may have been Alec Nyary, a man who would play an important role in Dowell's early introduction to television. Nyary was born in Norwalk, Connecticut, and graduated from New York University. For a short time he worked for the New School for Social Research, and served in Europe during the war as an interpreter with the rank of Sergeant in the 4th infantry division. It is most likely that the two men met during this time.

In the spring of 1946, Dowell prepared for his departure from Manila, packing and assembling his manuscripts. He would be shipped back to a disposition center in the States, and planned to return from there to Kentucky. He hoped to be in the States by the end of March or the first of April, but did not know how long it would take to get out of the separation center. He was on a sulfathiazol diet and was taking sulfa tablets because of an infected tonsil which had almost closed his throat passage. He also had an infection in the axillary and pubic areas (probably a result of sexual activity), which he frequently covered with applications of talcum powder.

His harsh feelings about Kentucky were tempered by a genuine desire to care for his parents.

> I don't plan to do anything after I get home for at least a month, but just stay home. Then I will go visit people I've made promises to before settling down to LIFE. When I do, I intend to go like a veritable dynamo and make up for my lost years. I won't wish to impose upon you and Dad, so I want you to come to some sort of terms, weekly or monthly, for my best ——— shall I say 'board'? My status will be as a sort of paying guest, I won't be refused, so simply decide how much. And please don't feel hard about it darling, because I'm perfectly aware that until I am making enough to support you and Dad that you'll have to get along on the proceeds from the store. My greatest prayer to God is that He will keep you both well and safe until I am in a position to see you retire and let someone else take care of YOU for a change. There never need be any fear that I will get married, so everything that I become ——— financially, socially, will be

> shared by you two wonderful people. I can't help wishing that you weren't so far out there in the country. There's nothing to keep you from being lonely, and loneliness is something rather new to you after always having so many noisy brats around! Either yours or somebody else's![49]

This is the closest Dowell had come to revealing his sexual inclinations. He had confessed that he would not marry, and had probably come to terms with his homosexuality during his stint in the service. According to his memoir, *A Star-Bright Lie*, he had experienced another pleasurable homosexual encounter there:

> I had discovered the tactile shock of black skins and tongues and muscles . . . in the Army; a man twice my age had . . . seduced me in the middle of a moonlit Philippine field. . . . We continued our affair for months, and when we were sent home together, we made love in a gun turret each night and formulated our plans. . . .[50]

These experiences solidified his fascination with race and his passion for men of color that would influence his novels and culminate in his final work, *White on Black on White*.

Dowell's military service was followed by three years in Louisville before he made the final break with Kentucky. His plan to live with his parents rapidly changed. After he was discharged in 1946, he returned to live in Franklin briefly, until he was established in a job as a full-time member of the Kentucky National Guard in Louisville. Then Dowell moved in with friends, John and Miki, who promised to get him a piano and asked Dowell to stay at home and take care of the house and work on his music.

It wasn't long before Dowell set up house with his new lover, Mickey Berger. They found what Dowell thought of as the perfect place, a house on Cherokee Parkway, which he described as "the oldest and most elegant section of Louisville." Here they rented one wing of an English style house overlooking Cherokee Park. Dowell admired the house for the heavy exposed beams in its reception hall, the coat of arms in stained glass on the front door, a large tile patio, and about 200 steps curving up through the lawn and hedges. The apartment had four levels, a basement game room, a kitchen and living room, and a sun-deck overlooking the park and surrounding country.[51]

Dowell had difficulty sleeping and smoked heavily. He was earning very little from his clerical job and continued service in the National Guard. He was often depressed, but he had high hopes for his music:

> I have written a complete show with all new songs that is to be produced at the Memorial Auditorium here for the China Relief Fund, or some other charity. It is a fantasy in eight sets and is half musical comedy and half musical revue. It is called the "Haymarket Fantasy" and I have lined up the very best talent in Louisville including ballet dancers, tap dancers, radio singers etc. to take part in it. Miki is designing the sets and costumes, I have a leading Louisville ballet instructor to do the choreography and a radio orchestra to do the pit work. The title[s] of some of the songs are -
>
> Happiness Ain't an Easy Proposition
> Lilly is a Loo-loo
> We Have so Little Time
> Shopping for Thrill
>
> Life in the Rough- and many others. The titles will probably suggest something to you of the type of show. The plot (which a WHAS script girl is writing) concerns a group of escaped criminals, who have been wrongly accused, but are doomed to die. They are both men and women and the show is built around their realization that the twenty-four hours they can count on before being caught is all that they will ever get out of life, and they make the most of it. We have taken one character at a time and shown what happens—what is most important to them and how they achieve that particular thing. I have an appointment with a leading 'patroness of the arts' and charity leader here Wednesday and to audition the show for her, with a script reading, songs etc. wish me luck, darling.[52]

In his next letter he was even more certain about the future of the musical:

> it looks as if my Haymarket Musical MIGHT be produced! I have been holding my breath—wires have been coming from Cincinnati, Chicago, New York—from Henry Adrian, who produced "Young Man's Fancy," "Girl from Nantucket" and others—the latter being the biggest flop in theatrical history—

> $350,000.00 down the drain. His backer for the new show—which MAY be mine—is Alice Gurstenberg of Chicago who writes Little Theater plays and makes piles of money that way. The tie-up is this—Adrian is Nan Blakstone's husband's brother—I have been spending weekends in Cincy with Blakstone and hubby, writing her new material. They think I am sensational—a GREAT new talent et cetera and became so excited over my music for the Haymarket thing that they called Adrian and got him excited also. They started a publicity build-up on me that was simply out-of-this-world—Moody, melancholy etc. (beautiful child—me!) and I sent recordings of the songs, at Adrian's request, to his Chicago retreat, where he is staying with Miss Gurstenberg. Got a letter saying they could not make out the lyrics, recordings were bad. Etc., and DEMANDING that I make some professional recordings IMMEDIATELY.[53]

Other letters to his family were simply signed "Bob." He signed this letter, "R. Coleman," and wrote: "That will be my professional name—with Dowell on the end, of course. Like it? R. Coleman Dowell? It's my real name, and I think it's distinguished—don't you?"[54] His obsession over his name represents one aspect of what he conceived as the fragmented nature of individuals that he would later explore in *Island People*.

Dowell was working on his songs at a frantic pace. He composed "Love J'es Happens," "Take Love," "Play the Field," "I Hope You like It," and "Off to Paris in the Morning," all for the score of his musical. His songs were in the style of Noel Coward and Cole Porter, with clever lyrics and upbeat tempos, and he went so far as to ridicule Porter by composing a farce he called "You're the Bottom." He composed at least one song for Nan Blakstone, who had recorded an album titled "Nan Blakstone: The World's Greatest Interpreter of Sophisticated Song" in 1946. She had developed a reputation for singing bawdy numbers with titles like "Get Yourself a Past" and "Little Richard's Getting Bigger."

Dowell remained in the National Guard, and often traveled out to the various units, which usually consumed two days and nights a week. He spent the rest of the week catching up on work. Mickey was opening an interior design shop, a long-desired dream, and they worked on it together during free nights. Dowell wrote: "Bill W., head decorator for Stewarts, is one of our best friends and when he and Mickey get their heads together on something, then it spells success with a capital S. Everything in the shop is calculated and like most calculated things, very effective."[55]

Mickey felt comfortable enough with at least one member of the Dowell family, Martha, to whom he wrote a short note referring to himself as her "brother-in-law." Martha and her daughters, Carol and Gayle, would visit the couple on holidays.[56] Yet Dowell's relationship with Mickey was troubled. "I needed to have someone tell me they like the way I look," he wrote, "like my potential talents and, most of all, appreciated my hard-earned mind."[57]

Dowell had also contacted Alec Nyary, who was working as a publicist for DuMont Television, and the two men considered collaborating on a show. Dowell wrote that one of his songs, "Second Lovehood," had been sung at Chez Paree twice, and he hoped for an offer from a publisher for his music. He sent Martha the lyrics to another song, "I'll Keep You in My Heart," which he told his family had been recorded for Bluebird Decca Records.[58] That year Decca released two versions of a song with that title, attributed to the songwriting team O'Connor and Ridley. "I'll Keep You In My Heart" was recorded in August as the flip side to a Klenner/Hoffman tune called "Heartaches" by Vera Lynn with Robert Farnon and his Orchestra (DECCA F 8786 78), and again on November 10, 1947 by the Skyrockets Dance Orchestra (dir. Paul Fenoulhet HMV BD 5992). Neither song was attributed to Coleman Dowell. It is possible that Dowell collaborated with the composers on the tune but there is no way to know for certain. Dowell clearly wanted to impress his family with news of his success and exaggerated his creative efforts especially in letters to his sister Martha.

The National Guard was undertaking major reorganization, and new battalions and companies were initiated while the older units were either maintained intact or merged into new battalions. Though Dowell was still active in the National Guard he was desperate to pursue a career in music. One friend wanted to introduce him to Leonard Sillman, who had been involved in the theater as an actor, producer and director, with a series of musical reviews under the title *New Faces*. In 1948, Sillman produced the review for NBC radio.

For a short time there were plans for Sillman's agent to visit Louisville and hear Dowell's songs, but the radio show lasted only one year before going off the air, and there is no indication the two men ever met.

Other friends encouraged Dowell's songwriting talent and in 1949 an associate, a book salesman named Henry Staden, arranged an audition for Dowell in New York City. Dowell took his songs and the manuscript of *Haymarket* to the audition. He was successful enough to sign on with an agent. After his initial visit he decided to leave Kentucky. By December 1950, just as the National Guard battalions were alerted to hostile activities in Korea, Coleman Dowell was happily settled in New York.

CHAPTER TWO

The Promise of Television

On Derby Day, May 7, 1950, Dowell left Louisville for his first visit to New York, where he would stay for a short time with Walter Dowell. According to Coleman, Walter was "a titular 'cousin,' a man with whom [he] shared a surname but as far as [they] could tell no blood relations."[59] Walter played a part in setting up the audience. On the day of the audition he accompanied Coleman Dowell to Ben Crowell's apartment on East End Avenue.[60] Crowell was nephew to Alice Astor, and his guests at the audition included Ivan and Claire Obolensky, David McDowell, and Tennessee Williams. Dowell played a series of songs that included "A Chorus of Whores," and "Try Me," from his musical *Haymarket*.

One of the people at Crowell's apartment that afternoon was Audrey Wood, a theatrical agent whose clients included Tennessee Williams, Carson McCullers, and DuBose Heyward. Wood began her career reading plays for The Century Play Company, but had formed the Wood-Liebling Agency with her husband in 1937. The agency was responsible for marketing plays to producers, making contract arrangements, and assisting in casting and production. At the time she met Dowell in 1950, Wood had recently represented William Inge on a production of Inge's play "Come Back Little Sheba" at the Westport Country Playhouse and was involved in negotiations for a Theatre Guild production of Inge's new work "A House with Two Doors."

Haymarket, a story about a love affair between a black man and a white woman, was the musical Dowell began while in the Philippines. Although the original script is missing, the Coleman Dowell Papers at the Fales Library, New York University, contain a version of *Haymarket* dated December 29, 1958. The opening scene is a kind of dream sequence which depicts the Haymarket with

Coleman Dowell spent the summer months of 1955 in Calais, Vermont, working with John Latouche on Ah, Wilderness! *—the musical adaptation of Eugene O'Neill's play. He spent the weekdays composing songs for the show based on Latouche's book. By the end of the summer Latouche and Dowell were at odds and Dowell left the project.*

"furtive shadows [moving] about the stage, picking pockets, pantomiming knifing, making sordid love in doorways."[61]

After this opening the lights go out for a moment, then come up again on the farm-yard of James McLloyd, a "Scotch farmer turned Kentucky farmer."[62] McLloyd is preparing to take his produce to the Louisville Haymarket with his niece, Lily, who has come to America from the Isle of Skye. The farmer leaves his niece to run the stall at the market for him. Here she meets a stranger named Clay Davis, and they arrange to rendezvous in town later that evening.

Scene II takes place in a nightclub called the Sans Souci. Seated alone at the bar is a Negro named Cain. Dowell writes, "if one were struck by any single factor, it would be the variety of races represented: Armenians in colorful gypsy-like clothes, Chinese, Negroes and 'whites.'"[63] But the groups are segregated. The bar is frequented by prostitutes and customers are served by a waiter named Handy. One prostitute, Gilda, is the first character to introduce a theme important to Dowell's later writing. She says, "I come here straight from the farm—and I'm going back there someday, too."[64] This longing for the country and the conflict of values between city life and country life would recur in much of Dowell's later fiction.

Clay Davis brings Lily to Sans Souci where she sees Cain and compares him to Othello, explaining to Clay that she had once played Desdemona in a school production. Clay responds, "He's not a Moor. He's a Negro." Lily is not as innocent as Clay or her uncle believe. She tells Clay that she is no longer a virgin and that she knew his intentions all along. Her speech is interrupted by a brawl and the police come in and arrest everyone, including Lily, who, in the confusion, has moved against the wall next to Cain. When she asks the policeman what it is she has done, he gestures toward Cain and responds tersely, "This."[65] Her proximity to the black man results in her arrest.

The surviving manuscript for *Haymarket* contains many of Dowell's early songs. One, *A Lady Who's Shady*, is especially reminiscent of Cole Porter and begins:

> The crackling of a hundred
> dollar bill,

The taste of bourbon when
you're sick of swill,
A modest mention in a
codicil—
A lady who's shady
Has got to have some sun in her life.

Champagne is something that
can always please,
A sable lining for your
best chemise,
A tidy stack of new
annuities . . .[66]

The song list for the show indicates that there were two acts, but only the nine acts of Scene I remain in the book. A synopsis of the entire play, probably written by Dowell much earlier, reads:

> Lily arrives—meets Clay, who makes a pitch, telling her he is a stranger, lost and lonely. She falls for him. Nell's jealousy. Lily takes a job in the bar, meets Jemmy, who falls for her. Gilda arrives with a party of society friends, is taken with Jemmy, returns. Cain and Harpy lost in their delusions; Cain warns Lily about Clay—offers his protection. Gilda becomes an habitué of the bar (Try Me). Clay arranges to get Lily drunk, planning to seduce her (Sans Souci).
>
> Lily, having lost her innocence, dreams of Scotland and childish games (Riddle Song.) Nell plots to get Jemmy drunk enough to kill Lily (which will be planned as a mistake—he kills Cain instead.) Clay loses interest in Lily and he and Gilda decide they are made for each other (We'll Travel Together.) Jemmy asks Lily to marry him, but she feels she is not good enough (Two Of A Kind.) Play ends with Lily "crossing over" to the house, and the ghostly street sounds of a happier time.[67]

Wood must have found something she liked in Dowell's musical, for she signed him shortly after his audition.[68] Encouraged by the backing of an agent and the praise he had received for *Haymarket*, Dowell returned to Louisville and immediately sought release from the National Guard. In September 1950 he made his permanent move to New York. His romantic relationship with Mickey Berger ended on a positive note; later that year Mickey would drive to New York to visit for two weeks and the two men would remain friends for several years.

In these early days Dowell quickly made his way into a social circle which included the Astors, Mrs. William Paley, and Alec Nyary, the publicist for DuMont Television. His hopes for a successful career in the theater swelled. Crowell introduced Dowell to Bill Leslie, a writer and a curator at the Cooper Union Museum. Leslie was looking for a roommate and for a short time the two men shared an apartment in the mayor's house across the street from Gracie Mansion. The rent was only $30.00 per month. Dowell's half of the apartment consisted of two rooms—a living room and a bedroom—and the two men shared the kitchen and the bath. The apartment was let furnished, but Dowell asked Mickey to ship some of his own furniture from Louisville, including his piano. Dowell wrote home that he had found a job at a radio station and that his musical was set for production the next season.

When Mickey came to visit for two weeks Dowell took him to Connecticut, where they spent the weekend with Alec Nyary's family. There Nyary introduced them to the poetess, Isabella Fey.[69] According to Dowell, Fey's poetry and critical reviews had been published in *Partisan Review* and the *New Yorker*, and in a letter to his parents, he wrote: "She has the most gorgeous face I've ever seen with an incredible head of hair, set onto a rather short, chubby body. Her wit is colossal and her tongue, when she wants it to be, bitter and sharp. Only the most esoteric magazines publish her works and it's quite an honor that she should have been so impressed with my music."[70]

Fey wanted to write a lyric book for a play and have Dowell set the music. He described the collaboration this way:

> Our play, if and when we do it, will be set in New Orleans and centered about a colossal woman—7 feet tall, with 12 sons. She is the mistress of a gambling casino and eventually meets her death at the hands of a violent and jealous lover. The

ending is terrific — in the early morning when the mist hangs low and heavy over the river, she is placed on a bier, that is in turn placed on a launch and, with her twelve sons lined on either side, is sent floating away into the mist while the sons wail and chant.[71]

Together they plotted the story and devised a list of songs for the show, which Fey titled "The Tale of Annie Christmas (A Musical Folk Fantasy)." Fey wrote out a three-page synopsis for the first two acts, which took place on a New Orleans riverboat and featured Annie Christmas, "the legendary female Samson of early gambling days in the Mississippi."[72]

It did not take long for the young composer to gain visibility. Dowell's song *Anytime* debuted on national television early in 1951. A brief article in *Look Magazine* described Roberta Quinlan performing the song on her NBC musical variety show. *The Roberta Quinlan Show*, which had nearly 3,000,000 viewers, preceded the 8 P.M. evening news and featured Quinlan singing with Jan August and his orchestra. Originally, host Morton Downey Sr. alternated evenings with Quinlan, but after the first few months Downey left and Roberta Quinlan headlined the show all five nights for the next two and a half years.

Dowell wrote to tell his parents about the publicity:

> Mickey's cousin, Roberta Quinlan (the television star) and I posed for the cameras a full two hours, and the shots should be good. I'm wearing my plain old grey suit and my hair is as un-ruly [sic] as ever, so I should look natural. The story is all about how Bobby (Roberta) chose one of my songs to introduce on her program, and took me to a publisher (Mark Schreck, at Southern Publishing) who is in the pictures with us. There will be a nice little story of me, mentioning my musical, and the lyrics to the song that Bobby chose. It's wonderful publicity for all three of us, and should help me immensely.[73]

The *Look* article, titled "A Good Song is Hard to Find," reported that when Roberta Quinlan "complained that she had a problem finding 15 songs to sing each week, her audience helped out. Fans from all over the country sent her their original songs. At last count, the total had passed 7,000. 'Anytime,' a song by a young Kentuckian named Coleman Dowell, caught Roberta's fancy to such an extent that she sang it on her program, and started him on a Tin Pan Alley career."[74] As a result of the publicity, Dowell signed with music publisher Mark Schreck, securing a job to arrange songs.

By the time the *Look* article appeared in print, he had also accepted a job with DuMont Television. Founded by Allen Balcom in 1944, DuMont was the first broadcasting company to televise a commercial network program. During its short existence, it competed with NBC, CBS, and ABC, and was responsible for such original programs as *Captain Video*, *Court of Current Issues*, and *The Johns Hopkins Science Review*.

Shortly before his appearance on *The Roberta Quinlan Show*, while watching a rehearsal of the DuMont show *Starlight Time* with his friend Alec Nyary, Dowell asked whether or not a composer wrote the music especially for the show. Nyary suggested that Dowell compose something original for the producer, Bob Loewi. Although Loewi liked Dowell's music, *Starlight Time* went off the air in November 1950. Loewi decided to hire Dowell for a new show, *Once Upon a Tune*, a weekly evening comedy program that featured most of the original cast of *Starlight Time*. Dowell composed the theme song and added catchy, simple lyrics:

> Take a magic flight
> every Thursday night
> we'll show you a new way
> strap your dreams on tight
> for we won't be back
> until there's a new day
> never blue day
> dreams will come in view
> and we'll muddle thru
> till they all come thru
> you'll find your lucky star
> and we guarantee it will stay
> when "Once Upon a Tune" comes your way![75]

Once Upon a Tune made its debut on WABD at 9:30 P.M. on Thanksgiving Day 1950. For the first few months, *Once Upon a Tune* was broadcast from 7:30 to 8:30 P.M. on Thursdays (the first half opposite the Roberta Quinlan show), but it found a permanent time slot on Tuesday evenings from 10:00 until 11:00 P.M. The show's budget was approximately $3000 per week and, although it was performed at the Adelphi Theatre, there was no studio audience. To keep down costs, there were no painted sets or flats. Instead the producers used three-dimensional props and lighting effects against a scrim that stretched across the stage.

The Adelphi Theatre, at 152 West Fifty-Fourth Street (built as The Craig in 1928, renamed the Adelphi in 1934 and the George Abbott in 1965), had a television stage that had been used for a variety of programs, including *The Honeymooners*, and a re-enactment of the 1925 Scopes trial in 1952.[76] It had also featured a closed-circuit broadcast of the *ANTA Album* in 1955, the first telecast of an original theater production, jointly produced by the American National Theatre and Academy and the Cooperative for American Remittances to Everywhere.[77] DuMont leased the 1400-seat theater from the Shuberts until April 1957, when the theater reverted to staged performances.[78]

Dowell was excited by the chance to work in the Adelphi Theatre and by the opportunities offered by *Once Upon a Tune*. He wrote to his parents:

> I am now a full-fledged television writer. My songs can be heard every week on a program entitled "Once upon a Tune" and it's a full hour musical comedy type program, with my music. Last week I wrote two songs for a musical adaptation of the fairy tale "Beauty and the Beast." One is entitled "It's a Beastly Life" and it has created a minor furor in the New York music world. I have two publishers wanting to publish it and everyone is singing the song. I went down to the theatre this Thursday night and to my wonderful delight, the cameramen and stagehands were singing the song. I went into the restroom and someone in one of the booths was singing it at the top of his lungs to the accompaniment of flushing toilet. They flash a little picture of me on the screen at the end of the program while the announcer says "Original music written and composed by Coleman Dowell." It's a thrill, and I am being paid a hundred dollars a week right now for

> the work. The show is a budget show, which means that they sometimes run short and some week I might get fifty dollars, or even as low as thirty-five, but if they don't run over the budget, I will get a hundred. For that, all I have to do is write the songs, attend two rehearsals for about an hour each and that's all. I am as free as a breeze to come and go as I please, but the way it has worked, so far my days are booked as full as a day can be, often up until 2 o'clock in the morning. I'm also doing some work for the Southern Publishing Company, and if the songs go well I will get around 7,000 dollars for each one. This work is definite—no more speculation for me.[79]

Once Upon a Tune featured vocalist Phil Hanna and Reggie Beane on piano, Ed Holmes, Gordon Dilworth, Holly Harris, Charlotte Rae, and Sondra Lee. Dowell composed songs for the cast and for guest stars who would go on to achieve wider fame, such as Bea Arthur and Elaine Stritch. Each episode parodied a fairy tale, fable or book. Sid Frank wrote the scripts and Dowell composed the entire score, creating a wide variety of tunes from patter songs to beguines. Stritch appeared in two skits, titled "The Three Little Pigs" and "To Tamale and Back"[80] respectively; Bea Arthur appeared in one episode, "Gone With the West."[81] Of Arthur's performance Dowell later wrote, "I think she burped one of my songs; she made her professional debut on our show."[82]

Newspaper columnists in such publications as *New York World-Telegram and Sun*, *Tele-Talent*, and *Television Week* wrote admiringly of the show and the composer's talent. A long piece by Edmund Leamy in the *New York World-Telegram and Sun*, "Unpretentious Experiment in TV: Aiming High at Low Cost," called the show "the New York evolution of the so-called Chicago low pressure school of television."[83] Leamy complimented the "sole staff composer Coleman Dowell, who writes the original songs you'll find interspersed among the 12 to 14 on each performance."[84]

In his column "Behind the Scenes: Loewi Sings an Original Tune," Bob Rothstein expressed admiration for the "beautiful songs and singing . . ."[85] and in a follow-up story in *Television Week*, "Noted in Passing," Rothstein mentioned "some excellent original songs by composer Coleman Dowell." He continued: "Said music is probably the most ingeniously selected music on TV and is presented in astonishing variety, including blues, Calypso and light opera. It all seems to fit in with the story, too."[86]

These early years in the television industry helped shape Dowell's aesthetic. He composed nearly one thousand songs for the weekly broadcast of this show over its run, and developed an eye for short scenes and dialogue.

Home life was complicated. Though his relationship with Bill Leslie was platonic, there was an inexplicable tension between the two men that Dowell attributed to Leslie's drinking. Leslie was fifteen years older and found Dowell attractive, but he had recently left a failed relationship and had difficulty expressing his feelings for the younger man. In September, 1950 Leslie wrote Dowell a long letter which examined their relationship and discussed in depth Leslie's unhappiness with his own homosexuality. "Having—at least so far—circumvented what you so rightly called 'walking into calamity with our eyes wide open,'" he began:

> we have devised other, less formidable problems in solving one. For if we do not have the sexual relationship in common, we do not, as yet, have much more, save mutual friends, our love of music, and the household. I have a feeling, perhaps unjustified, that both of us are on guard, a bit uneasy, as if we were going through a probationary stage; we are palpitating each other for bruises with fingers not wholly sure of what they will find. This, I am sure, will pass, for though I am still as in love with you as I ever was, when that, through time and your own good offices, declines into affection, the more manifold sympathies that affection permits will fill out what is now a kind of vacuum. Love—for all the exalted slush that is written about it—has one object, sexual conquest.[87]

Such ideas disconcerted Dowell and for a short period he moved into an apartment on Perry Street with Kitty Marshall, an actress and secretary who also worked at DuMont. Audrey Wood continued to schedule auditions to promote Dowell's music and to help him find work as a composer; he also collaborated with Bert Stevens, composer of *Whistler's Mother-in-Law*, to produce commercial songs. These songs suggested the influence of Cole Porter and Noel Coward, who had both found huge success in the musical theater.

Like both Porter and Coward, Dowell's lyrics were suggestive, but his melodies were simple and less complicated. He had no pretensions about what to expect from his career at DuMont. Though television provided an income, he was still actively pursuing his dream of musical theater. In a letter to his parents, he wrote:

> sometimes this town gets on your nerves and you feel that you can't stand it another day, and then the next day something wonderful happens and you feel alive again—as if the whole, damn, big wild city belongs to you and everything's alright again. Most of my spare time is taken up with meeting the people I should know, who can help me or will be useful in some way. It's the sort of thing you have to do, even if it's unpleasant sometimes. When I go to the theatre, as I did last night, the people who got me the tickets saw to it that I sat next to an actress and her designer-husband, so that we could get more acquainted and perhaps work together. It's that sort of thing ——— you can't get away from it, and if you try to, or do, then you haven't a chance in the world. When you're trying to get ahead in the theatre every moment you're awake must be spent in figuring out new methods of getting ahead, and when you're asleep you dream about it ———— in other words, you live, eat, and sleep the business and you dare not let go for a moment.[88]

The final episode of *Once Upon a Tune* was broadcast on May 15, 1951. Jack Gould wrote a piece for the *New York Times* that called attention to the unpolished nature of the show, yet examined the need for producers to continue stretching the boundaries of the still novel medium. Gould understood the promise television offered for creativity and stated, "In terms of finished entertainment its departure cannot honestly be much mourned. But because of the type of television for which it stood—and for the problems which it raises for TV as a whole—its passing should not go unnoticed."[89] Even though the future of the show was uncertain, the success of Dowell's songs led to a feature article in jazz-oriented *Down Beat* magazine. Dowell enclosed the write-up in a letter to his sister Martha. He was proud of the fact his songs were being discussed in "the jazz-bible, which is quite the best publicity I've ever had and though it is not considered as nationally-read a magazine as LOOK, it is a much more important one for me, because the musicians now know who I am."[90]

According to the article in *Down Beat,* new episodes of *Once Upon a Tune* would "very probably be resumed . . . by popular request, but even if they aren't, the young tunesmith from Kentucky will have his time well occupied with two new network shows, his own Broadway musical, and the scores of two others."[91]

While Dowell waited to learn if television the show would resume, he continued to work on a series of projects. He worked with Philip Pruneau on the book for *Haymarket.* There were a few potential television assignments, and a chance at composing the score for another Broadway musical: an adaptation of the 1922 Austin Strong play, *Seventh Heaven* to star, possibly, Patrice Munsel of the Metropolitan Opera.[92] Arthur Lesser was working to acquire the rights to the play.[93] Dowell composed two songs for the musical on speculation and, though he was uncertain he would get to write it, he believed that there was a very strong possibility it would come through.

After learning that *Once Upon a Tune* would not be renewed, Dowell returned to Louisville for a short visit. Mickey was ill, and although Dowell had gone home to rest after what he called "a harrowing and draining season of pouring songs, week after week, into television's yawning maw,"[94] he found himself, instead, nursing his former lover back to health.

Back in New York, *Haymarket,* which Dowell had expected to go into rehearsals, failed to raise the necessary money. About this time Dowell met a man from Princeton, Hub Smith, Jr., a linguist who later became a travel agent. The two men shared an apartment at 37 Gramercy Park East, overlooking the park, the kind of place Dowell dreamed of finding when he first came to New York. It reflected "just about everything charming and gracious about this city," he wrote. "Gramercy Park is perhaps one of the most beautiful residential sections in this country—a little, locked and private square bounded on four sides by beautiful old houses. My apartment looks onto it from windows so big, that when they were opened, the whole bloody wall is out of the room and it's like perching on a balcony to sit at your own desk."[95] Mickey came to visit for a second time and brought him more furniture: two beds, a cocktail table, lamps, dishes, candlesticks and other items. Dowell was glad to see him.

Although he felt he belonged in New York, Dowell missed the comparatively easy going life of Louisville.

His relationship with Hub seemed to mirror his experience with Bill Leslie. Dowell wrote home that he planned to get rid of his roommate "because he drinks too much" and, Dowell reported, he had "plans for his apartment that don't include beer and whiskey bottles stacked to the ceiling, nor ruined furniture and rugs." He continued:

> [W]hen I give a cocktail party, it will be for conversation first and drinking second, and with people who know how to handle their glasses AND liquor. Don't frown, Mums. There ARE such people, and there is such a thing as social drinking—I've done it for three years and am no nearer alcoholism now than I ever was—It's impossible to live in this modern world, particularly in the theatrical world, and not take a cocktail or two. But there is also such a thing as carrying it to an extreme, and that's what my room-mate does, so OUT he goes.[96]

Despite the objections Dowell raised in the letter, he and Hub remained together for several years.

Work on "Annie Christmas," the story about the colossal mistress of a gambling casino conceived with Isabella Fey, was temporarily obstructed. He couldn't get along with his collaborator, a man named Chris who Dowell described as "a pompous ass and a rather untalented one."[97] But the primary reason there was no movement on the show was due to the quality of the book. Dowell and his partner auditioned the work for Audrey Wood but she decided that she would not handle it in its present form. Wood offered to arrange an audition for Dowell to play the score for Cheryl Crawford. If Crawford liked the work, Wood agreed to get another writer to write a book around the score.[98]

The New Orleans show was one of two big projects Dowell had in the works. George S. Kauffman, who had collaborated with George Gershwin, Rodgers and Hart, and Irving Berlin, was working at the time on an idea for a musical version of the Garbo film, *Ninotchka*, and needed a composer. Paul Bigelow recommended Dowell and, according to Dowell, Kauffman said he had heard Dowell was the best lyricist-composer since Cole Porter. Kauffman's wife, the actress Leueen MacGrath, also favored Dowell's music. Dowell wrote five songs for the show, and although Kauffman was in the hospital, Dowell met with MacGrath and a British director named Frith Danbury. Danbury told Dowell that one of the songs, Ninotchka's farewell to Paris, which Dowell called "High Up," "wouldn't get out of her head."[99] When Kauffman got out of the hospital, Dowell planned to play the new songs for him and, if that went well, would next play them for the producers, Cy Feuer and Ernest H. Martin. Unfortunately for Dowell, while Kauffman was still in the hospital, the producers signed Cole Porter to compose the score to the musical, now to be called *Silk Stockings*.[100]

During this period, Dowell began to visit psychics and palm readers. Throughout the remainder of his life he would rely on them for advice and encouragement. Rene Tilliard, one of the first psychics Dowell consulted, predicted he would have success, but that it would require hard work and conflict every step of the way. Dowell would complain that his associates were able to sail to Europe, and Tilliard would reply, "New York will be yours—NEW YORK WILL BE YOURS."[101] Tilliard encouraged him to think positively, and Dowell wrote to Martha about the practice, "The mind, as everyone knows, is the most mysterious and intricate organ in existence and the powers of the subconscious were unguessed by most people. Thinking positively entails saying, every day, all day—I feel wonderful; there is nothing the matter WHATSOEVER. You refuse to admit the possibility of failure and you keep at it constantly."[102]

Tilliard's prophesies proved to be highly exaggerated. Neither the Kauffman collaboration nor the New Orleans piece succeeded. Dowell returned to Kentucky for a short vacation in the summer to see his parents. He was deeply concerned about his parents' poverty and told his sister Martha, "I keep wanting to drive myself and others concerned with my creeping career, so that I can do something for them—make them independent, free to travel, a comfortable place to live—oh, so many things. They are my primary concern now, because I've my whole life ahead of me to do what I want to do."[103] But he was also concerned about his own lack of income, for he was not working and there was no movement on any of his shows. His letter continued: "I was so tempted to call you last night, but my phone bill is enormous and I don't dare go over a limit I've set. Hub has called Pittsburgh a couple of times and I've called Louisville once to ask Mickey how to apply a wall preparation etc. and the poor phone is so overworked that I just didn't dare. After the bill is paid, then I will be able to call you and chat."[104]

In 1953 Dowell met the Broadway producer David Merrick and he believed his success as a composer/lyricist was assured. Merrick talked about involving Dowell in many projects, among them *Hello Dolly*, *Destry Rides Again*, and *Gypsy*. In November of that year Dowell wrote to his parents:

> Things are so promising that I'm in a state of agitation from dawn till dawn. My career is gathering momentum at such a pace that, if it continues, it's bound to culminate in something wonderful, and soon. My show, which was a rather distant glimmering through the mist, has almost emerged in full light. My audition with Hollywood was impressive, and managed to impress. The important thing about that evening, however, was the presence of a Mr. Alfred Katz, New York's foremost publicist, who took more than a fancy to my music and is talking about me and it all over town. Monday night Mr. John Latouche (a famous writer you probably are not familiar with) held an audition for me in his home—Gwen Davenport (the Kentucky writer) was there, Mr. Katz again, and Carol Channing, one of the brightest Broadway stars (star of "Gentlemen Prefer Blondes"). Also my producer, David Merrick and his wife. This stirred up more excitement about me and if I'm to believe what everyone says, I have a very brilliant future indeed. Oh Mums, if you only had an idea of how exciting it is to have people of that caliber excited about my music. I've only been here three short years, and if this continues, my day is practically here. Good reports keep coming from Paris about my songs being done there, and the London show will open in about a month. Now, with the New York one looking so bright, and if God is willing, that farm and many other dreams of mine will be possible soon—soon—soon.[105]

Dowell did not give up television completely. He tried to negotiate a deal with NBC, where his old friend Alec Nyary now worked as Vice President of Publicity, but was unsuccessful.

Although Dowell was only 29, he had already had several platonic and romantic relationships. His life with Hub Smith was calm on the surface, but

Dowell continued to seek out other romantic interests. While he was in Nantucket in the summer of 1954, he met Bertram Slaff, the man with whom he would share the next thirty years.

By the time the two men met, Slaff had established a successful psychiatric practice in New York. He managed to blend his professional life in psychiatry with a social life in the arts. While working in St. Louis as an intern at St. Louis City Hospital in the 1940s, Dr. Slaff had met Leonard Bernstein, who was in town to spend two weeks as guest conductor of the St. Louis Symphony. Slaff invited the conductor to dinner at a restaurant and was accepted. Bernstein brought William Inge, then drama critic of the St. Louis *Star-Times* (later the well-known playwright). "We had a most enjoyable and festive dinner," Slaff recalled.[106]

Dowell and Slaff found that they shared many interests including theater and psychiatry. In Manhattan, they frequently went out on what was then called "The Bird Circuit"—visiting gay bars with names like "The Golden Pheasant" and "The Swan." Shortly after their first encounter, Dowell told Bertram Slaff that he had a terrible confession to make. "I lied to you when we first met," he began. "About my age. I'm not really twenty-seven—I'm twenty-nine." Dowell believed that he would have to make a career in the musical theater before he reached the age of thirty. By posing as a younger man, Dowell attempted to extend his chance to achieve greatness. He was so obsessed with the idea of youth and beauty that he often stated he would never grow old. According to Bertram Slaff, David Merrick had convinced Dowell early in his career that to succeed in the theater, he would have to do so before the age of thirty.

In 1954 Dowell's association with David Merrick had not yet soured, but it would be Bertram Slaff who helped him through his most painful experiences in the theater.

CHAPTER THREE

Ah, Wilderness!

Before meeting Bertram Slaff, 1954 was a quiet year for Dowell, the tedium of inactivity only periodically broken by trips to Kentucky or visits with friends. His producer, David Merrick, kept Dowell on the payroll, paying him $50 per week. Merrick periodically hinted at projects for the young composer, but they did not materialize. Yet Dowell had good reason to trust the Broadway maverick. Although he was only 43, Merrick had developed a reputation as an extremely clever promoter of his theatrical shows. His first musical, the 1954 production "Fanny," was a box-office hit, due in part to promotional stunts which included hiring a skywriter to scrawl "Fanny" in the sky over Grace Kelly's wedding in Monaco. Yet by the early 1950's Merrick had also developed a reputation for callous incivility. The playwright Sam Behrman called him "a mouse trying to be a rat,"[107] and Stan Freberg, another playwright Merrick courted, quipped, "Merrick is the Bermuda Triangle in a Brooks Brothers suit. He lures writers and playwrights in like naval air squadrons, never to be seen or heard from again."[108]

Eventually Merrick decided to use Dowell for a musical adaptation of the Eugene O'Neill's play, *Ah, Wilderness!* Unlike other, more tragic works by O'Neill, this play had a lighthearted atmosphere that Merrick felt would work well on the musical stage. Dowell composed ten songs for the show that he occasionally auditioned for potential backers and librettists. Merrick hoped to convince Sam Behrman to write the book, but Behrman was working on his own play, *The Cold Wind and the Warm*. When deliberations with Behrman stalled, Merrick signed John Latouche as book and lyric writer, and suggested the title "Connecticut Summer." Dowell hoped to begin work on the project

Bertram Slaff and Coleman Dowell shortly after they met in 1954. Slaff had taken a house on Nantucket Island for the summer. The two men met at the Rope Walk, a seafood restaurant at the end of Straight Warf with a view of the harbor.

immediately, but Latouche was busy with another production and Dowell had to wait. He wrote to Martha:

> My collaborator-to-be, John Latouche ("Cabin in the Sky" and others), has a new musical opening a week from Thursday, which is holding up our getting down to serious work on "Ah, Wilderness." It's called "The Golden Apple" (you've probably read about it) and is based on the Iliad and Odyssey, and set in Washington state at the turn-of-the-century. It has an operatic form, in that there is no spoken dialogue—all is sung. It's a fascinating piece of work—not high-brow, but wonderfully poetic and, on occasion, terribly funny . . . I'm going to Haiti for one week . . . and that will take care of my rest for a year or so. Latouche is going to Haiti with me, so it will not be all pleasure, as we will be working part of the time.[109]

The plans for the Haitian trip, scheduled for late summer, did not materialize. Latouche may have been preoccupied with "The Golden Apple," which opened in April 1954. Dowell kept busy writing letters to friends. His home life with Hub seemed good. Martha often sent them baked goods to help them get by on their small budget. Dowell spent some time in the summer with his family in Louisville, but spent most of his time in the apartment at Gramercy Park.

Dowell was charming and made many friends, particularly women with an interest in literature. Among them was Isabella Fey, the poet he had met at Alec Nyary's home in Connecticut. Fey was traveling in Denmark in 1954 and often wrote to Dowell to discuss her opinions about the books she was reading. One of the books she mentioned, Halldór Laxness's *Independent People*, may have provided some inspiration for Dowell's novel *Island People*. Fey wrote to Dowell in 1954 from Kolding, Denmark, where she was staying with her young son Esdras and her husband:

> Before we go further, let me tell you that the book, *Independent People* (*Sjolfstaed Folk* in Icelandic) has been one of me favorite books for years. I intended many times to lend it to you . . . It is one of the great novels of European literature. I've read it dozens of times . . . Remember the passage of the little boy who is destined to go away, and who will some day remember the song of the bird 'too monotonous, just the same he-he-he for a thousand years—yet someday he will

> want to come back and hear this same song, this same and no other—' or words to that effect? By this time you must have finished it. Can you ever forget the ending? And that incredible passage you quoted—I could not sleep after reading it . . .[110]

The novel must have struck a chord with Dowell, whose own early farm life mirrored much of how Laxness represented life in Iceland. Many of the novel's ideas, including the discord between dream and reality and the theme of independence, would later color Dowell's fiction.

In December 1954 Dowell visited his sister's family in Cleveland, then flew to Pittsburgh to visit Hub and Hub's family for Christmas. The Smiths gave Dowell a subscription to *The New Yorker*, monogrammed linen handkerchiefs, a new shirt, and $10.00. Hub also took Dowell to see Fred Burleigh, the local Pittsburgh impresario, and there was some discussion that Dowell might create a show for Burleigh in the spring.

Burleigh was a Yale drama graduate who later created a bawdy musical tribute to burlesque titled "Sugar Babies" with Ralph G. Allen. Since 1937 Burleigh had been the producing director of the Pittsburgh Playhouse Theatre. "Lend an Ear," one of New York's most successful reviews at the time, had its start at the Pittsburgh theater, often a showcase for new writers.

Dowell planned to compose a sort of "Peeping Tom" revue, and told Martha it would have an "opening curtain like an enormous keyhole, and then each sketch and song can show a different aspect of 'behind doors' activity. My opening number, which I've just completed, is called 'Our Town Is a Dawn Town,' and the rest of the show can follow that thought, showing what transpires at dawn in many parts of the city."[111] The concept of a revue, likely a result of his work for television, represented something very different for Dowell, whose ambition was to compose a serious musical. Nevertheless, he began work on the music after returning to New York, and hoped to have the material to Burleigh by February 15th.[112]

Dowell may have spent the beginning of the year working on the revue, but there is no indication that it was ever completed. In April 1955 he clipped a brief article from the *New York Times* and sent it to his sister Martha and her family. He had again been rewarded with the media attention he coveted. The note he attached read, "Here is my recognition—feel like I've been drinking champagne this morning . . ." The letter contained a brief notice by Sam Zolotow that read:

> Recognition has been accorded to a new composer to create the melodies for the song-and-dance transformation of Eugene O'Neill's play, "Ah, Wilderness!" He is Coleman Dowell. The book and lyrics are being furnished by John Latouche. The sponsors, David Merrick and Joe Mielziner, to present the offering around the first of the year.[113]

Another notice in the *Rialto Gossip* column a week later confirmed the news. "Coleman Dowell," Lewis Funke wrote, "has been asked to do the score for the musical version of O'Neill's 'Ah, Wilderness!' "[114]

Finally by the summer there was movement on the show Dowell had invested so much hope in. He spent the summer months of 1955 in Calais, Vermont, working with Latouche on the musical adaptation of O'Neill's play. He spent the weekdays composing songs for the show based on Latouche's book. Unfortunately, Latouche was working simultaneously on the libretto for *The Ballad Of Baby Doe*, which took valuable time away from the project.

"I'm up in Vermont—way up—with John Latouche," Dowell wrote to his parents. "writing like crazy."

> It's very exciting and wonderful to know that at last this is happening. The papers have had amounts of publicity almost every week since I sent you the opening announcement, and I will save them for your scrapbook, if you're still keeping it.
>
> So far, in advance money, I received about three thousand dollars—one thousand flat, from my producers, and 2,500 from the publishers. Makes me feel like a millionaire. I'll feel differently when tax time rolls around. Of course, this is only advance money. When the show opens, I should make about one thousand a week from box-office and double that from publishers, if it's a hit. Then we'll get that farm! The time draws nigh —— hold onto your hats.[115]

Often Dowell had indicated that when his finances were secure he would purchase his parents a farm. He hoped that he would soon have the income necessary to provide for their long-term security. Morda Dowell was ill, but

Coleman did not have an opportunity to visit. In his letter home he wrote: "I'm so happy to know Dad is feeling better. I was so worried, and had worked out an elaborate system of communication with Hub, whereby he was to open all your letters and if I needed to be reached, he could do it with expedition."[116]

The farmhouse in Calais, newly acquired by John Latouche and Kenward Elmslie, should have provided the perfect, isolated setting to concentrate on the musical, but there were many distractions. Latouche was also working on *The Vamp* and the house in Calais was often overrun with visitors that included his other collaborators, Douglas Moore and James Mundy, the novelist Carson McCullers, and Latouche's mother, Effie. Ruth Landshoff York, niece of the publisher Samuel Fischer, also came for a short visit. York had led a fascinating life, appearing in the 1922 film *Nosferatu* and acting on the stages of Berlin. After publishing short pieces in German magazines her first novel, *Die Vielen und der Eine* (*The Many and the One*) appeared in 1930. In 1937 she emigrated to the U.S., where she worked as a translator and playwright.[117] She wrote a poem for Dowell describing the Vermont Hills, which began:

> Vermont. Mont vert. Mont blanc. Mont La Touche.
>
> The crickets sound a breakfast bell
> The dragon mouth starts posing
> The sun has thrown his lightning spell
> And woodchucks trot a dozing
>
> Green grass surrounds the daffodils
> Green begets green in Vermont hills.[118]

Dowell assisted in running the household, often cooking for the group, preparing elaborate menus like cheese soufflé, sausage cakes and stewed apples ("I've turned out to be official cook," he wrote to Slaff in April, "since last night's soufflé was so successful.") He felt at times that Latouche was taking advantage of the situation, but he enjoyed being part of the cultured ensemble, and would often accompany them to Barre or Montpelier for movies and shopping. Dowell must have felt a sense of enthusiasm, for he was surrounded by people with a similar interest in music. Douglas Moore had composed *The*

Devil and Daniel Webster in 1938, and Kenward Elmslie, who would soon begin collaboration with Jack Beeson on *The Sweet Bye and Bye*, had already created the book and lyrics for his own comic opera *Caravan to Mecca*.[119]

During the weekends when Dowell could take time away from his work, Bertram Slaff would fly to Burlington and drive to Calais to visit. Unlike the other men Coleman Dowell had dated, Slaff could appreciate his need for recognition. Slaff had also had his share of publicity, as the first American patient of the celebrated Viennese orthopedic surgeon Dr. Adolph Lorenz, who had come to New Jersey in 1921 to open a clinic for crippled children. Slaff did not let his infirmity, clubbed feet, distract him from his ambitious goals. He graduated from Harvard in 1942 and by the time he met Dowell had already started a successful career in psychiatry in Manhattan.

The two men slept in a small one-bed house near Latouche's pond. Their relationship developed rapidly and when they were apart they exchanged weekly letters. Of Slaff's first visit Dowell wrote, "everyone was enchanted with you, and all said so without restraint. John reiterated that you were welcome anytime—and anytime can't be too soon."[120] Because there were so many people coming and going at the house Dowell and Slaff sometimes met in other places like Williamstown that were not too distant from Calais.

Dowell's letters to Slaff provide a vivid image of how the group occupied their time, working on the *Sunday Times* crossword puzzle, Kenward Elmslie and Coleman playing backgammon, occasional horseback riding and games of bridge. When Latouche did work on *Ah, Wilderness!* Dowell felt sure that things were going well. He would send the lyrics along to Slaff with notes about his progress:

> Mr. Latouche, who had a beautiful lyric for me, and a sunny day—the sort I'd hoped we would have together. After a rather sketchy breakfast, I wandered up the slope behind the house and found a tree, shaped like a rocking horse, and twice as comfortable, on the peak of the hill. From this vantage point, I surveyed my world and set the poem to music. It begins
>
> I watched the old moon
> through the wishbone of a mole

So you can see it was not the usual popular image, and did not call for a *snappy* melody.

Incidentally, It's a true poem, and very beautiful, in which Nora, the maid, (as a sort of Greek chorus) outlines the entire plot in a mystic Irish song. The six people are imagined as six white doves flying:

The first two doves
by a dream were lead (Richard and Mur)
The next two were tied
by a tangled thread (Lily and Sid)
The last two were linked
with a golden chain (mom and pop)
As they flew through the sun
And the rain.

And then she explains why they are in their various conditions. It's very beautiful and if David doesn't throw it out without a hearing, I think it will make both a charming and an unusual opening for a show.[121]

Another letter described the progress they were making:

John has finished the first scene now, and has improved so over the O'Neill dialog and awkward plotting that it's a pleasure to think about. There was a reading this morning for Helvitia and Ken, and I sang the first song when the time came. I'm happy to report that John more than liked it, and everyone thought it was exactly right. We called David (Merrick) about casting Imogene Coca as Aunt Lily, and he was in agreement. This may seem as off-beat to you as it did to me at first, but think about it and I think you'll agree that she has a perfect mixture of comedy and pathos called for. John wants Hiram Sherman for Uncle Sid, and again this, to me, is a good choice. Of course, none of these people can really sing, but that seems to be the latest trend in musicals. Coca could do wonders with Autumn in spite of her voice, and that is, I suppose, the important thing.[122]

Though he was preoccupied with the score, Dowell took a keen interest in Slaff's work as a psychiatrist at Mount Sinai Hospital. Dowell wrote to express his curiosity: "The talk at Sinai sounds very interesting—I want to hear about it if you feel like talking about it. I like it when you tell me what you've done, or what you're doing in advance, because then I can imagine you at the various places and seem nearer."[123] In the same letter he wrote that Latouche:

> has written a wonderful new lyric to 'Love is All Around Us' and the whole house is humming the melody, which is a very good sign. Work is slow, I fear, but I think he's purely an inspirational writer and it's no good pushing him. Last night I dreamed of the opening of 'Wilderness,' which I attended with you and three of my sisters. John asked how many sisters I have, and when I told him four, he said the three were the Three Fates, of course.
>
> Being up here has affected me strangely—there is an absolutely timeless quality about the days, but not in the good sense we have experienced together. I might have been here for two years, and I assure you that I'm not exaggerating. I seem to have lost my sense of proportion, or something. Anyway, such a usually ordinary thing as a phone call left me in a haze—and because it was you, the haze was doubly strange. I have settled into this peculiar routine like one of Paul Bowles's characters, and, when I think about it, it's only to have a faint, surprised feeling that here I am, and here I may be for the rest of my life.
>
> As I said in opening this, John has left for New York, supposedly for 24 hours, but no one believes he will return for several days. He left me well supplied with lyrics to set, however. Thank god for that.[124]

By the end of the summer Latouche and Dowell were at odds and Dowell left the project. Dowell's anger at Latouche was overshadowed by a more significant tragedy. Morda Dowell died on December 18, 1955. Dowell's mother, now alone, depended more and more on her children for support. Dowell did not attend the funeral, but his father's death would provide the basis for his first novel, *One of the Children is Crying*, a partially autobiographical story about a young man who returns to Kentucky for his father's funeral.

The Ballad of Baby Doe opened in Central City, Colorado in July 1956, and shortly after that Latouche died of a heart attack. "The show that I've been slaving over for three years is dead as a doornail," Dowell wrote to Martha, "among other things, John Latouche died in July[125] of a heart-attack. He was only thirty-nine, and although I had grown to sincerely hate him, I didn't want him to die."[126] The composer-lyricist, Robert Merrill took over work on the show. He read the play at David Merrick's request in 1957 and collaborated with

Joseph Stein in the summer of 1958. The two men created the Broadway hit for David Merrick, which they re-titled *Take Me Along*.[127]

Out of these early experiences in the theater Dowell developed an obsession with what he believed to be Jewish domination of the arts industry. This obsession lasted for the rest of his life. He struggled with feelings of anti-Semitism, reinforced by his relationship with Hub Smith, who once answered a phone call from Bertram Slaff and said to Dowell, "It's the Merchant of Venice."[128]

To some extent Dowell recognized that his feelings were irrational, yet this was just one manifestation of the contradictions he so readily incorporated into his personal philosophy. His relationships with both Merrick and Latouche ended badly for Dowell and he felt, as he would in many later relationships, that he had been a victim, cheated by Jewish composers who got the best shows and venues.

Slaff had moved his office to 1100 Madison Avenue, and he and Dowell shared a room there until they found an apartment at 58 East 83rd Street. Dowell also kept his room with Hub at Gramercy Park. They also planned a trip to Europe to get away from the stress of all that had happened that year. On the application for his passport, Dowell listed his occupation as "composer." Though the passport was issued in August, the trip to Europe was postponed.

In the summer of 1956 Slaff and Dowell shared an ocean side house. "My summer was almost perfect," he wrote to Martha. "I wish you could have seen the enchanting little house we had, right on the sea, made of glass, but sturdy so that it's stood up through hurricanes where larger edifices collapsed. We went deep-sea fishing, rode horseback, read, ate—everything but work."[129] He added:

> Let's see—where to begin—first, I'm not going to Europe until April. The trip was postponed two days before the sailing. I felt both disappointed and glad—glad because I couldn't afford it and would have come back to taxes, bills, and no funds to meet them with. Disappointed for the obvious reasons. It was to be a combination business and pleasure trip—that damn review Tenant Produc-

> tions have been after me about was the business part . . . My agent says things are bright, but I refuse to believe anymore of that. I'm still being paid weekly to do nothing, but I want a show, and not just the money.
>
> I have a new apartment! That's keeping me busy as hell, but it's going to be, in the words of the painter, "a show place." To begin with, the living room is 20 x 20, with a great bay at the end with eight windows in a semi-circle. The ceiling is almost 20 ft. high, and I've had the whole thing painted off-white. (It also has an enormous fireplace). My carpet, which will cover the floor from one wall to the other, is red—a nice subdued red and the draperies are the same shade of red. One chair is being upholstered in a deep plum and the window seat, which is 12 ft. long, will be in the same color.[130]

This apartment, like the ones before it in Louisville and Gramercy Park, must have meant a great deal to the young composer. He took care to describe each of these settings to his sister, possibly in part because he believed that his home reflected his success. *Place* became increasingly more important to Dowell, and the description of place, both in his theatrical pieces and his later novels, represented the physical manifestation of a character's psychological state.

Though Dowell remained on David Merrick's payroll, he was determined to make his own decisions about the future and found himself retreating from the producer's circle of influence. Though bruised by the collaboration with Latouche, he already had a new project in mind. Dowell paid his first visit to Carl Van Vechten in January 1957. The Van Vechten circle, which included many of the major literary figures of the Harlem Renaissance, offered a welcome alternative to the indifference of Broadway's callous avant-garde. Among Van Vechten's articulate friends Dowell found both confidants and rivals, and the encouragement he needed to pursue his new plans.

Portrait of Coleman Dowell by Carl Van Vechten, circa 1957. Best known as the author of Nigger Heaven, *Van Vechten was a photographer and friend of many Harlem writers and singers, and was Gertrude Stein's literary executor.*

CHAPTER FOUR

Carl Van Vechten's Protégé

The apartment on Central Park West that Coleman Dowell visited on January 7, 1957 must have produced an immediate impression on the young composer. His hosts, Carl Van Vechten and Fania Marinoff lived in the San Remo in a spacious apartment cluttered with sculpture, tapestry, and photographs. The entry foyer was lined with books and the walls of the drawing room displayed original paintings by Raoul Dufy, Diego Rivera and Giorgio di Chirico.[131] It was at the grand piano in this drawing room that Dowell first performed his music for Van Vechten.

Known to his friends simply as "Carlo," Van Vechten's achievements included renown as a novelist during the 1920s and a career as music critic and Paris correspondent for the *New York Times* that began in 1907. In later life he was an accomplished photographer who developed a reputation for stylish portraits of celebrities in the world of art, dance, music and literature. Dowell and Van Vechten had much in common, from their earliest provincial upbringings to their mutual love of salacious humor and bawdy songs. And, although Van Vechten was married, it was rumored that he took an intimate interest in attractive young men. Van Vechten may have been influenced in part by the young composer's appearance, for after this initial meeting he invited Dowell to sit for several photographic portraits.

Dowell hoped to adapt Van Vechten's 1924 novel, *The Tattooed Countess*, for the musical stage. That snowy January afternoon he performed a few of the songs he had composed for the potential musical. The novel, loosely autobiographical, had been made into an unsuccessful film called *A Woman of the World* and Van Vechten was reluctant to approve any further adaptations of his work. Coincidentally, Van Vechten had been entertaining a similar request from playwright and theater reviewer Robert Downing, who lived at 36 Gramercy Park, in an apartment in the building next door to the one Dowell shared with Hub Smith. In May, 1957 Downing wrote to Van Vechten:

> Thank you for writing me about THE COUNTESS. The main thing is to get the best possible production if it is all as good as it now appears to be—and to bring forward the skill of a new talent combined with the recognized merit of your own work. You know I could only wish the very best for you, the young composer, and this work which has been so very close to my heart for such a long time.
>
> It does not matter about my ms. now. I had hoped to bring it to you—completed—on your birthday. The Merman show and moving to the new apartment set me back a bit, but the draft was almost ready. I could only wish that it might have evoked the praise you have for Mr. Dowell's work—but since he also has the gift of music, I'd not stand a chance.
>
> Perhaps I may have the privilege of bringing his work to the attention of Jo Mielziner. Do you think this is possible? To have some part in producing THE COUNTESS would make the blow a little easier to sustain . . .[132]

Van Vechten must have enjoyed Coleman Dowell's songs: by the end of that afternoon. The author granted his approval for the project. The meeting was the beginning of an amicable collaboration that would last for the next three and a half years. Van Vechten spoke admiringly about the project. "I haven't had time to read the script yet," he wrote to Dowell on January 18, "but Fania was most enthusiastic about the lyrics." On February 6 he added, "I am immensely pleased." In May Van Vechten wrote to Downing, praising Dowell's preliminary score. According to Van Vechten, *The Tattooed Countess* contained "seven enchanting songs, precisely in the right mood, and with lyrics that Cole Porter or W. S. Gilbert might have envied."[133]

Dowell worked diligently on the musical adaptation and the two men became devoted friends. Suddenly Dowell found himself part of a celebrated circle that included Langston Hughes, Leontyne Price, Gloria Vanderbilt, Pearl Bailey, Tallulah Bankhead, Laurence Olivier, and Noel Coward. Although he could have been easily overshadowed by such company, Dowell was not one to conceal his own talents, and he occasionally composed songs for Van

Vechten's friends. One song was written in memory of Elinor Wilie who, according to Van Vechten, had never wanted to be told she was a great writer, just that she was a beautiful woman. Based on that offhand remark Dowell composed a song entitled "Beautiful."[134]

From 1957 until *The Tattooed Countess* opened in May 1961, Coleman was one of Van Vechten's favorite companions. He was often a prized guest at Van Vechten's salons, where champagne flowed freely and guests savored exotic treats of chocolate and candied ginger. On many of these occasions Van Vechten would ask Coleman to play music from *The Countess*. Dowell would perform the songs, rewarded with applause by the receptive crowd. But he did not enjoy everything about these gatherings. According to Bertram Slaff:

> The food was lousy . . . when we were invited to dinner, Coleman would say "why don't we have dinner here at *home* first, and then we'll pass up the okra." It was noteworthily bad. It really was okra . . . it was just slimy stuff. Coleman was a wonderful cook so that eating at Van Vechten's was just . . . and the okra, we wouldn't do it. But we would drink the champagne. For four years we really had a wonderful time there. It was grand. Van Vechten's wife was Fania Marinoff . . . they insulted each other with great wit. She would say . . . to the women, "now you women, you . . . you *whores*, don't you hang around by . . . my senile husband." And he would say very proudly, "that is my *Jewess* wife. You don't have to pay any attention to her whatsoever." And they would carry on like that—with humor. It was all done with great fun.[135]

Dowell was extremely productive in the early part of 1957, diligently composing music and trying to line up producers and backers for *The Tattooed Countess*. Although he retained much of the original novel, he attempted to weave his songs creatively into the narrative. In the original book of 1924, Van Vechten examined the influence of social hierarchy on a small Midwestern American town. The action of the novel takes place near the turn of the century. After a brief affair with an Italian named Tony, the title character, Ella Nattatorrini, returns from Europe in 1897 to her hometown of Maple Valley, Iowa, where she falls in love with a young boy named Gareth. She is received in a series of parties that culminate in a reception at the Opera House. To the staid citizens of the town (including her sister Lou and Gareth's teacher Lenny Coleman), concerned with outward appearance and manners, the Countess represents shocking, revolutionary ideas. She wears make-up and smokes cigarettes and believes that the things kept hidden (like her tattoo) should be brought to light. But modernism has limits: her aesthetic lets her appreciate the opera, theater, and arts of the old European world, but she dismisses the Impressionists and praises an earlier French tradition. For Gareth, the Countess represents the promise of spiritual escape; she helps him fulfill his yearning not to be bound by social conventions. Her world is one propelled by passion, which sends "her staggering and spinning down the rough but exciting erotic highway."[136] Ultimately the Countess and Gareth seduce each other—his goal is freedom, and hers is the conquest of his innocence.

The musical had potential for box office success. The Midwestern setting, used to great effect in Rodgers and Hammerstein's 1943 musical *Oklahoma!* and Meredith Wilson's 1957 hit *The Music Man*, offered an arena in which to explore the small town naiveté made popular by such musicals. The works had appeal on two levels. In post-war America such representations of character celebrated patriotism and the wholesome spirit of the nation, but to more self-assured New Yorkers, these musicals provided undertones of social hierarchy that confirmed their own status as sophisticated intellectuals.

Dowell's work on the theater version of *The Tattooed Countess* underscored those social themes. Periodically Dowell shared information about his progress with Van Vechten in letters. In February he wrote:

> Between Monday and yesterday, I wrote a really wonderful song for Ella to sing when she thinks of Tony—it will be much more effective at that time than "The Right Life," which should come before, when she and Lou are together. Apropos of Lou and Ella, you mentioned a scene between them that is missing in this version—I can't imagine which it is, unless I failed to give you some pages. We can clear this up when I see you Sunday . . .
>
> I have planned more of Albert Coleman, and will expand the idea for your approval or disapproval when we are together. I've written another song for him in the second act called "Come Walk With Me" which he would sing to Lou. I

thought, if it were not too far fetched, that he might be the device with which to soften Lou up a bit—no definite romance or anything like that, but, because I like her, I'd like for her to have a little more masculine attention.[137]

Dowell's original schedule for completing the musical by April was unrealistic. He had completed several songs prior to his original meeting with Van Vechten, but he intended to write the book as well. He had many ideas for staging the production, including a fireworks display. He wrote:

I am working, and if things continue to flow as easily as they are at this time, I should have it well finished before April 30th—and I hope that will include revisions too. I've added two new songs, which the story seems to demand, bringing the total up to 18—but I don't see anything wrong with that—my feeling about most musicals is that there is a dearth of music. Do Iowans indulge in fireworks displays on the 4th of July? I thought this would be colorful, and would furnish a background for certain histrionics at the conclusion of Scene I, Second Act. I've kept thinking over what you've said about Iowans not boating, and am trying to find another reason to have them all congregated on the river banks.[138]

Dowell's agent, Harold Freedman, tried to convince Dowell that almost every successful show on Broadway had taken at least two years of writing. Freedman also assured Dowell that before any writer created an adaptation it was standard procedure for the originator and the adapter to negotiate a contract. Dowell was in agreement and wrote to Van Vechten, "If you don't mind another personal note, I think this is correct and proper, for very selfish reasons. A great sense of security goes along with written approval—or permission."[139]

Leonore Merrick and May Freedman wanted to produce the show, and Mrs. Merrick indicated that her husband might co-produce. David Merrick thought the show could provide an interesting vehicle for his new star, Mary Martin. After the initial arrangements were discussed, Freedman, who also represented his wife May and Leonore Merrick, agreed to contact Van Vechten's lawyer, Arnold Weissberger, to arrange the contracts. But there was some trouble negotiating an agreement able to meet the needs of all parties involved. In April Dowell wrote to Van Vechten to explain that the Merricks wanted a four-year option on the show. Leonore Merrick "said she had talked to David . . . He assured her that he had had a four year contract on 'Fanny'—that Rodgers and Hammerstein had had a four year contract on 'South Pacific'—ad infinitum."[140]

Neither Dowell nor Van Vechten would agree to such terms because they were anxious to see the show go into production. Harold Freedman asked Weissberger to draw up an alternative plan since he was most familiar with Van Vechten's desires, but the lawyer refused. Freedman responded by sending a standard contract, but that was unacceptable to Van Vechten.

Dowell was anxious to get an agreement with the producers on paper in order to secure backers for the show. In April he invited Ivan Obolensky, the son of Alice Astor, to hear the score, and he asked Van Vechten to attend. "I thought I'd better write you," Dowell told Van Vechten, "as I haven't your phone number with me and I will not be at home the early part of the evening. If this arrangement is displeasing to you, I could put them off until I return from Kentucky. However, any pledge of money would be all for the better. Please let me know how you feel about this, and I will abide by your wishes."[141]

Final arrangements for all involved depended in part on the performers. Dowell hoped to sign Anthony Perkins in the role of Gareth and wanted Van Vechten's friend Eileen Herlie for the role of the Countess. Perkins would not be free for an October production because of filming commitments. "I believe . . . he would not be free before spring,"[142] Dowell wrote to Van Vechten. Initially Herlie agreed to take the role, but because of extensive delays she signed to perform in *Take Me Along* instead. Coming on the heels of his involvement with that show (the musical version of *Ah! Wilderness*), the news must have been especially painful to Dowell. Herlie's letter, which indicated her change of mind, hinted that there were other problems plaguing the production:

> I never, for one moment, dreamed that Chuck Bowden hadn't been keeping you completely up to date with regard to "The Countess." Forgive me for disappointing you. There were many reasons which I shall explain to you some time.[143]

Despite the legal issues, indecision about the cast, and no guarantee that there would be money to produce the show, Dowell continued to develop the book.

> I don't know what your feelings are today (about the play, of course) but I feel a bit better. We had a reading of it, for timing purposes, last night—and the same friends who had crucified me for the first draft second act were deeply moved by the present one, and they are, believe me, as jealously guardian of your novel and its mood as anyone. Anyway, the whole thing—with music—ran for 3:10, so when you refer to it as an Opera, you're right![144]

June 17, 1957 was Van Vechten's 77th birthday. In honor of the event Dowell sent a birthday card, illustrated with a smiling cat, that contained the message "Happy Birthday, Tiger. Love, Cole." Dowell also included a fictional piece he had written specifically for Van Vechten's birthday, titled "A Fable, For Carlo's Amusement." Though brimming with personal references, the story reflects Dowell's love of language and playful, Joycean use of vocabulary, as well as his interest in period settings. It began:

> In the tyme of delphinius, in the rain of remembrance, one reigny afternoon in October's blue still wetness, the Layde Morticullus walked in her garden between the borders of rue and time and brooded on Gallavar out of the east, whose steed lightening, out of the west, had carried him northward to the polar regions where he was wont to gambol amongst icy pinnacles with his slithery hooves striking sparks so that peoples the world over, seeking the flash of firey flickerings, would say to one another, with noing nods and nodding knows "Tis lightening."

And ended:

> "It's not the end!" said Layde Morticullus and Lochinhad, taking her in his arms, shouted with the bells—
> "It's only the beginning!"
> *The beginning*[145]

Dowell's use of circular time, the Christmas setting, and the thrush song were ideas he would explore in greater length later in his career as a novelist.

The wordplay (reminiscent in the beginning paragraph of Lewis Carroll's *Jabberwocky*), and archaic spellings are examples of Dowell's interest in period pieces that draw attention to the text.

In the summer of 1957 Dowell and Slaff took the first of two European vacations together. Dowell was no longer on David Merrick's payroll and the chance of a steady income seemed slim, so prior to the trip Slaff gave him $1500, a gesture that insured him pocket money. Just a day before their departure Dowell received his International Drivers Permit and on July 4 they arrived at Orly Airport in Paris, France. From Paris they traveled to Strasbourg, then on to Grimsel Pass, Switzerland. The vacation lasted eight weeks. In August they traveled to Germany and Italy, where they visited Venice, Milan, Florence, Rome, Naples, the Isle of Capri, Portofino and San Remo. Dowell wrote to Martha from Italy:

> I have seen famous cathedrals, famous paintings and famous people. I have seen operas, plays of which I understood not one word, but loved anyway!, and have sat in cafes sipping an aperitif and watching the world drift by. This city is beyond description, so I won't try to describe it.[146]

Bertram Slaff was anxious to show Dowell the cathedral in Sienna, which he felt was the most beautiful cathedral in the world. Unfortunately when he said, "I'm really looking forward to showing it to you," Dowell replied, "I've seen enough cathedrals."[147]

They stayed on the Isle of Capri for five days, absorbing the sun, a welcome change after the cold weather that had greeted them in Paris. Dowell thought Capri to be one of the most beautiful places he had seen, the blue water of the Mediterranean and the town of Capri rising out of it:

> high, high up so that, to get from the harbor up to the town, you have to take a *funicular*, which is a little cable-car I always thought would crash each time I got into it. The houses are built, leaning, against the sides of the mountain so that it's difficult to understand how they keep their dizzy perch century after century. There is a little square, called a *piazza* where everyone gathers each evening to sit at tables and sip wine and watch everyone else go by. It's always crowded like a New York subway and everyone makes an entrance. Because the island is small,

> when you've stayed there for 5 days you recognize each face. When I was there, there were only three other Americans, two Englishmen and the rest were French and Italian. People wear outlandish clothes and go "native" with a vengeance. I went barefoot the entire time, with rolled-up trousers and a sweater slung around my shoulders, because as soon as the sun dips behind the mountain, the air is cold—It's amazing to feel hot one moment and then, bang! goes the sun and with it, all the warmth. Tropical by day and mountain-cold by night. Quite a place.[148]

Though he was physically away from work on the *Countess*, Dowell could not put the play or Van Vechten far from his thoughts. He wrote to Van Vechten frequently, and mentioned the play on several occasions.

> When I said "preoccupation" a moment ago, I find it continues just that and neither time nor tide can still its intensity—only production. Don't fret over the less-than-second act—I'll make you eat crow yet—and Miss Marinoff, too! The solution . . . lacks only a typewriter to prove itself.[149]

For entertainment Dowell read *The Autobiography of Alice B. Toklas*, in which Van Vechten figured prominently. On an undated postcard to Van Vechten from Portofino Dowell added, "always one step behind the Countess, but I glimpsed her slender ankle whisking from a carriage this afternoon—the rest of her was somewhere else—maybe tomorrow . . ."[150]

In early September the two companions arrived in London. To Martha, Dowell wrote, "The trip was both business and pleasure. I had to be in London by the 28th of October for business—a show that I have music in there and discussion of another one."[151] He did not care for London, though he admired its antiquated charm. From there they traveled to Scotland, which he described to his mother in great detail:

> Scotland (this was my first time there) was oh, so beautiful and our name is to be seen everywhere on shops, restaurants, private houses etc. so, without a doubt, we are Scotch! I discovered the small section that all of our family must have come from some time ago—it's called Oban, and the name Dowell, McDowell and MacDougall are the only names to be found there. The Scots treated me as a native son returned and when I would go into a bank to get a traveler's check

> cashed, they would keep me talking for half an hour at a time. The moors are wild, going up toward the Isle of Skye, and the hills are high and brooding. The heather was in full bloom, and this is a sight that would thrill you, I know. A blaze of purple as far as the eye can see—no houses whatever for 60 miles at a stretch, and the only living things to be seen are sheep munching heather. Every now and again, there will be a wild whirl-pool formed in a basin at the foot of a rushing mountain torrent, and there is always a palpable vapor hanging over the whole scene—it looks other-worldly and rather disquieting. We arrived at Loch Lomond just as the sun was setting—beautiful and serene. We didn't have a place to stay and were rather worried—finally came upon a little ramshackle inn and asked for rooms. Sorry, they said, but you can have the chalet. As it turned out, the "chalet" was about the size of a dog house with two small beds in it. My head touched one wall and my feet the other. But we stayed there and loved it, with the sound of cows going to the bath-room outside the window all night through![152]

The Scottish landscape and the culture suited him. Dowell felt an affinity for the people he met, and took delight in a feeling that he was exploring his family's lineage. He would later incorporate what he defined as his family's Scottish heritage in his first novel.

The two men returned to the United States on September 8, 1957. Dowell had not yet told his family about his relationship with the psychiatrist—the letters he wrote home about his European travels did not mention his companion by name. This may have been because he had not yet ended his relationship with Hub Smith. Although he listed his new 83rd Street address on his application for the International Driver's Permit, he told his sister to write to him at the Gramercy Park address when he returned to New York.

While Dowell labored over *The Tattooed Countess*, Bertram Slaff was gaining wider recognition for his work in adolescent psychiatry. Shortly after their return from Europe, Slaff co-authored "A Brief Analysis of the Nature of Psychotherapy" with Abram Blau, which was published in the *New York State Journal of Medicine*.[153] Slaff had moved his office to 1100 Madison Avenue, his practice was growing, and he had made several smart investment decisions that allowed him to support his companion. Dowell may have been embarrassed by the situation for he claimed, if asked, that he had inherited family money as a descendant of the Heaven Hill Bourbon family.

The days passed quickly. Dowell settled back into work on *The Tattooed Countess*, and his collaboration with Van Vechten continued smoothly, much as it had been before his vacation. There had been difficulty finding backers for the show, but Slaff agreed to invest $10,000 and David Merrick offered to handle distribution of the shares once a star has been chosen to everyone's satisfaction. Both Van Vechten and Dowell felt that Mary Martin did not have the scope to play Ella. In November Dowell invited Van Vechten to attend an audition for Margot Moser, who had played both Julie and Carrie in "Carousel," Laurie and Ado Annie in "Oklahoma," and Tuptim in "The King and I." Dowell said of her, "she is an enchanting thing—pretty as a picture, with a big, clear voice. She is about thirty, but can project the older songs with warmth and understanding of the lyrics."[154] During the audition Dowell planned to sing the men's songs, primarily to save time and money, but also to allow Van Vechten to concentrate on only one new person. Joe Moon would accompany on the piano.[155] Moon had already read the play, and, according to Dowell, "called today to say that it's the most—(his words)—magnificent musical play he has ever read. . . ."[156]

Margot Moser was perfect for the part, but three years passed and by 1960 she was working as a chorus girl in *My Fair Lady*. In June she replaced Lola Fisher as understudy for the leading role, and by January, 1961 she had replaced Pamela Charles in the role of Eliza Doolittle.

In addition to Moser, Dowell and Van Vechten discussed other actresses who might fit that part. "I think Patricia Morrison," Dowell suggested, "who has elegance and enormous warmth, would be a marvelous Ella—and also Greer Garson! It would be practically the story of Miss Garson's life!" He continued:

> Anyway, we are working on the auditions, and Sunday night we will put ourselves through the paces, and Miss Moser and I will try the duets. Joe is making some

> special vocal arrangements to bring out (or point) the songs, without making things sound too contrived and polished, which would be somehow wrong at this early date. I have great hopes.[157]

For unsubstantiated reasons Dowell felt that his favored position in Van Vechten's circle was being usurped by James Purdy, a writer Van Vechten had also photographed in 1957. Dowell was also jealous of Purdy's attentions to Bertram Slaff. When Van Vechten wrote to tell him, "Purdy . . . asks: 'Does Bert Slaff know that he is destined to be captured by vampires?' "[158] Dowell replied, "I'm getting worried about Mr. Purdy's excessive interest in Bert's future. That young man should be advised that, if there are any vampires in the picture, I have priority, a sharp tooth and (for rivals) a silver bullet! Also a sharpened stake, wolf's bane, hen's bane and garlic—so there!"[159]

Dowell began to compose short fictional pieces and plays that had an experimental nature similar to those Van Vechten admired by James Purdy. In a letter dated January 10, 1958 he wrote, "I have been working on 'The God-a-Mighty-Bird."[160] This play was never published but Dowell used a similar title for a short story he eventually published as "The Great God-a-Mighty Bird." Van Vechten was especially fond of Dowell's short story, "My Father Was a River." He referred to the story in a letter to Dowell:

> Your metaphysical story about the papa who was a River, a Fox, and a lion, and his incestuous son is your masterpiece, perhaps ANYBODY'S masterpiece. IT held me spellbound in its terrific charm when I finally found time enough to read it last night.[161]

It may have been their friendship that encouraged him to pursue fiction, but Dowell did not let these efforts impede his work on *The Tattooed Countess*. His agent, Harold Freedman, suggested revisions to the play, but there was still no definite commitment from Merrick to produce it.

Dowell was hired for a brief time to work with jazz drummer Louis Bellson on an ailing production called *Portofino*, then playing in Philadelphia. The show starred George Guetary and Helen Gallagher. Richard Ney, songwriter, producer, and director, planned to move the show to the Adelphi Theater in

New York in February, 1958, but the Philadelphia premier did not go well.[162] Dowell met with Bellson and offered suggestions, but Ney rejected the assistance and ultimately the show flopped.

Dowell was also concerned about his mother, but grew increasingly impatient with her requests for money. Beulah Dowell had sold the family store after Morda's death and was living on what remained from the proceeds, but it was a meager income. Although Coleman had given her reason to believe that his financial situation had improved and sent her money as often as he could, his only income now came from Bertram Slaff, who had hired Dowell to work as his private secretary. Though this arrangement allowed Dowell to support himself, it would also become a point of contention between the two men. In January 1958 Dowell wrote to his mother:

> My trip to Europe was paid for—that included hotels and transportation. I had to pay for my food and drink and other expenses. Though it didn't come to a heck of a lot, it was still enough to drain my small resources dry. I have the greatest potential of any of the family to help you, but again I must repeat that the road is long and arduous, as you should be aware of by now.[163]

The frequent letters Dowell sent home accompanied by news clippings about his success had given his family the impression he was quite wealthy. His brother James suggested Dowell support their mother and use the expense as a tax write-off. Dowell felt that no one in his family could truly appreciate the sacrifices he had made to develop his talent. Sometimes his anger turned to sarcasm:

> The "Tattooed Countess," of which you read a page or two, has taken me almost a year to write thus far, and I'm still making revisions as they are suggested by my agent. There are several producers interested, and this one should actually come off, if I persevere and manage to keep old man depression away. But it still entails an amount of work beyond the comprehension of anyone who hasn't written a show. If any of you doubt it, then get paper and typewriter and set about writing a play. You will be just as well equipped as I was when I first started. The fact that I have developed a technique is beside the point—so could the rest of you, if you tried hard enough.[164]

Another letter reflects Dowell's hope for the show's success, and his growing bitterness and uncertainty:

> I am much involved in my play. Things are going extremely well—I hate to say more than that, but I have gotten further this time than ever before. We are working up our auditions, and there are a great many people excited by it. If things continue in this vein, I should be in a position to send you a decent sum of money before very long. I'm keeping my fingers crossed, and please do the same...
>
> I haven't anything else to say. I'm working very, very hard, and now I must begin rehearsing the singers for the auditions. As I said before, things are really looking good, but past experience has taught me not to count too much on appearances. I'll keep you informed of progress.[165]

It is not surprising, given the urgency of Dowell's letters and his need to impress his family, that they mistook his situation. In April Dowell took time to visit his family, and when he returned to New York he wrote:

> Thank you, thank you for a really splendid time. I got (or so it seems) some lovely rest, which I needed—came back to New York in 1 hour 35 minutes, to find that my mailbox was filled with telegrams telling me of a meeting immediately upon arrival. It's a wonder to me that they didn't have a police escort waiting at the airport for me! Anyway at 4:20 I was sitting in conference with almost all of Paramount Studios (I realize I kept saying Warner Bros. to you, but it was my mistake), the upshot being (as of yesterday (how many parenthetical phrases can you employ!))—that they agreed upon the merger, throwing in the old movie version for our use if we want it etc. They did ask, however, for a percent of the gross rather than the net, and this slight change threw my producer's lawyer into a tailspin from which he has not recovered. It may result in the percent coming off my share, which is dwindling before my eyes, anyway. However, the point is to get the show on and pray. Day before yesterday had a session with Tony Perkins—I imagine that will thrill the gals.[166]

Shortly after returning from Kentucky, Dowell got a call from the police. His old friend, Walter Dowell, had died alone in his apartment and Coleman was the only person the police knew to call because his name was in Walter's personal address book. Other friends were in poor health. Coleman remained on friendly terms with Hub Smith, who drank heavily and eventually succumbed to liver damage. Alec Nyary, Dowell's friend from DuMont Television, suffered from hepatitis and died August 31, 1957, after a brief illness. Slaff also suffered the death of his mother.

Though the loss of these friends must have saddened him, Dowell's grief could be tempered by the knowledge that he had someone to share it with. If his own family sometimes made him feel bitter or insecure, Slaff's relatives made him feel he was part of the family. That Easter Dowell prepared a holiday dinner for them.

The two men led an active social life. Dowell used his influence with Merrick to get theater tickets, and occasionally took Van Vechten to see shows such as "The Bridge of San Luis Rey." The fate of *The Tattooed Countess* now rested with the producers. "As you probably gather," Dowell wrote to his friend, "since the 'Countess' is now in other hands, I am having a marvelous spree of re-reading Van Vechten. 'Firecrackers' last week, 'Parties' and 'Peter Whiffle' this week—'Blind Bowboy' and 'Nigger Heaven' rising on the horizon like the bright man-made moons that they are."[167] Dowell also spent part of the summer, in July, in Water Mill, Long Island.

Bertram Slaff and Coleman Dowell accompanied Leonore Merrick to the opening performance of *Gypsy* on Thursday, May 21, 1959. The show, directed by Jerome Robbins, had a libretto by Arthur Laurents and music by Jule Styne and Stephen Sondheim, and a set design by Jo Mielziner, who was to have been co-producer for *Ah, Wilderness!* The musical starred Jack Klugman as Mother Rose's boyfriend and Sandra Church as Gypsy. From their seats in third row center orchestra, beside the theater critic Walter Kerr, Slaff distinctly recalled the exciting moment when Ethel Merman entered from the rear of the theater and bellowed, "Sing out Louise!"[168]

Gypsy had been one of the musicals Merrick considered for Dowell, but in the end was just one of the successful shows that had somehow slipped through Dowell's hands. By now it was also clear that neither Merrick nor his wife Leonore would be involved in any aspect of *The Tattooed Countess.*

Bowden, Barr and Bullock announced the scheduled opening of *The Tat-*

tooed Countess sometime in "the early fall" of 1959.[169] There was still no production contract, but it was finally signed on July 2, 1959, between Dowell, Charles Bowden, H. Ridgely Bullock, Jr., and Richard Barr as producers.

Other projects occupied the composer while he waited for the producers to move forward with the show, including the score for *The Crystal Tree*, by Doris Julian (later scored by Duke Ellington), and *Beautiful Dreamer*, which was announced November, 1959:

> "Beautiful Dreamer" is promised for Broadway. James Morris will be starred in the musical, based on the life and songs of Stephen Foster. The libretto will be provided by Coleman Dowell and the music by Isaac Van Grove. The production will be directed by Ernestine Perry. The sponsor is the Wickland Company, of which Joseph Moon is the supervising producer.[170]

Brief, periodic announcements about *The Tattooed Countess* continued to appear in the *Times*, suggesting some of the difficulties Dowell faced. There were frequent problems with the producers, Bowden, Barr, and Bullock, and the directors, cast, and others involved with the show changed frequently. In March, 1959 the *Times* announced that "'The Tattooed Countess,' Coleman Dowell's musical, has impressed Peter Glenville, director. It will be done as soon as Mr. Glenville is available."[171] In June the opening was postponed until "sometime in 1960,"[172] and a year later, in September 1960, the *Times* indicated that the musical was planned for off-Broadway, "to arrive in late December, with Mr. Barr directing."[173]

In December, 1959 the painter, Balcomb Greene, offered Dowell and Slaff the use of his house at Montauk Point. Greene was in Paris until June, and the house would provide a getaway from Manhattan, where Dowell could work uninterrupted on the Stephen Foster play, *Beautiful Dreamer*. He and Slaff attempted to spend Christmas there and headed off with champagne, chestnuts, bourbon, and a goose for Christmas dinner, only to discover upon arrival that there was no fuel for heat or hot water. Shortly after the trip back to Manhattan Dowell wrote to his niece Carol, "I . . . have just finished the second act of the Stephen Foster play . . . From my 17th floor eyrie I look down on white rooftops and a still, half-snowbound world . . ."[174]

Although Dowell completed the libretto for *Beautiful Dreamer,* he found himself embroiled in controversy over the show. Ernestine Perry, the director, planned to open the show in December, 1960, at the Madison Avenue Playhouse, starring James Morris as Stephen Foster. Dowell believed there had not been enough preparation, and asked to have his name removed from the bill.[175]

Once again Dowell focused his energies on *The Tattooed Countess.* The producers had delayed the show several times and Dowell, worried that Van Vechten would not live to see his novel staged, insisted that it open. Bowden, Barr, and Bullock were dropped from the production and Dick Randall and Robert D. Feldstein took over as producers. In addition to Eileen Herlie several other actresses were considered for the leading role, including Mary Martin and the opera singer Gail Manners, but the new producers settled on Irene Manning. Manning had been away from the Broadway theater for fifteen years, when she had last appeared in the 1945 production of *The Day Before Spring.* In addition to Manning the producers signed Carolyn Maye and Coe Norton. Manning proved difficult to work with, writing lengthy letters to Dowell demanding changes in her script. The actress tried to influence many aspects of the show, especially in her self-serving suggestion that she and the male lead should be the only attractive actors in the cast. In March 1961 she wrote a patronizing letter of advice:

> My dear Cole:
>
> Well, it looks as if "THE TATTOOED COUNTESS" is really going to be put on after all—and I'm sure you are pleased with that!
>
> Before we go any further, however, my dear, there are a few bits of advice I'd like to pass on to you (as writer to writer).
>
> You are going to have FANTASTIC PRESSURES put on you before we 'open'—to make all kinds of CHANGES that each person feels "will help the show"—but in fact, is only a single-purposed re-action to aid and abet that particular person's part without due regard for the over-all picture of the show itself.
>
> In the first place: *PLEASE REMEMBER YOUR ORIGINAL INTENT AND PREMISE OF THE PLOT*! (i.e. That the *COUNTESS* and the *BOY* are the only ones at-

tracted to each other sufficiently for him to decide to go with her.) If—in the casting—THIS IS LOST SIGHT OF—THEN THERE IS NO REASON FOR THE SHOW!!!!!!!!! And people and critics will say "why did he write such a show?—The boy could have stayed at home and been with either Lenny or Clara. He must be out of his mind to go off with the older woman in such a case."

Do you see, Cole, what I'm trying to say?

That—in the book and your original play—the TWO MAIN CHARACTERS were the ONLY ATTRACTIVE PEOPLE in the SHOW. That is the ONLY REASON he goes off with the Countess.

Now—again—as to casting your play—one does NOT ask if the person will "please the bald-headed men"—nor—that we "ought to have *some attractive people on stage* to please the audience." One usually casts "according to the *CHARACTER IN THE PLAY*" . . . in relationship to the others in the cast or plot.

I beg you, Cole, to think this through (above) before deciding on EACH CHARACTER in the show. And—DO NOT LET ANY ONE (especially 'johnny come lately') deter you from your ORIGINAL IDEA of the people.

Also since there may be many times when we are all excited and want you to change things on the spur of the moment. DON'T DO THIS. Always say YOU MUST THINK IT OVER—AND ONLY MAKE A CHANGE when YOU HAVE HAD SUFFICIENT TIME BY YOURSELF —with no PRESSURE FROM ANYONE—(including me)—to THINK EVERYTHING OUT CAREFULLY!

Just remember *you* have written this play—and music & lyrics—and it has been 'your baby' for THREE YEARS. Don't let it suddenly 'get out of your hands' and be changed into something that you don't intend! A good suggestion is to put a little sign on your bathroom mirror—and every morning read it and remember—"It is MY SHOW—I must keep to my ORIGINAL INTENT or PREMISE!"

I write you this just in case I don't get the chance to talk with you privately. I think you have a *fine show* that could be a *success*—providing *casting*, etc. is *RIGHT*! It is *UP TO YOU* to see that it is!

Affectionately—and the opposite of the Countess's tattoo—I DO CARE what happens. . . . Irene.[176]

The new producers agreed to open without trying the show on the road first. Because they had not yet raised enough money for the production, Bertram Slaff purchased a 5 percent share for $2,500 in April of 1961. As a venue for the musical they first considered the Cricket Theater on 2nd Avenue, but the Company eventually negotiated arrangements with Georgia Gersene to use the Barbizon-Plaza theater for eight performances, commencing on May 2nd, 1961.

Dowell had faith in the show and friends continued to encourage him. Kenward Elmslie wrote:

> It's an enchanted score, "High Up" of course echoes and echoes; I'd forgotten songs can re-appear, so involuntarily, in memory, should re-appear—but then the gift of writing luxurious melody that speaks directly and immediately is RARE.
>
> "Rolling Stone," "Fin de Sickle," "Glow" (ah!)—each song creates its own landscape so deftly—I can't tell you how happy it made me to hear theatre songs I could enjoy once more; I long to hear them again, to see them on-stage, to play them on records—and all this I hope happens without difficulty, for any sensible audience should adore them.[177]

The Tattooed Countess opened at the Barbizon-Plaza Theatre on May 3, 1961. The production was staged by Robert K. Adams, and William Hargate designed the costumes. The set design by Robert Soule, an elaborate side-view of a Victorian home with other houses situated in the distance, stretched across the length of the stage. The cast included Irene Manning, John Stewart, Carolyn Maye, Virginia Payne, Coe Norton, and Travis Hudson. Prior to the 7:30 curtain Van Vechten sent Dowell a telegram which read, "My love and devotion / Is as deep as the ocean."[178] Telegrams came in from friends across the country, wishing Dowell all the best for opening night.

Manning delayed the opening by 45 minutes. Although the audience, made up in large part of friends and acquaintances, applauded warmly at the end of the show, critics were not as kind. Some considered it an amateurish production. The show had not gone through previews and there was no occasion for rewriting. There were acoustic problems and the orchestra overshadowed the vocalists' numbers. At the end of the performance David Hollister, who had arranged and orchestrated the music, went over to the piano and played a strain from the *Funeral March*. Early the next morning he wrote a note of apology:

> I know only too well what a modest and sensitive person you are and feel you are probably taking most of the blame for the weaknesses of this production on your own shoulders. Don't. You deserved better than you received at the hands of all of your collaborators, including myself. I can only say I did my best. I hope I didn't disappoint you too much, because I know how much you expected. I will always appreciate the faith you have shown in me . . .
>
> Well, I am already going on too long. My parting thought will be to be glad the "Countess" is produced. Don't waste time on post-mortems, and least of all should you be disheartened or discouraged. Your talent and great gift show through in so much of "The Tattooed Countess" that it cries out for you to simply learn from the mistakes without underestimating the successes—and go on to the next project with vigor and creative zeal.[179]

Howard Taubman, of the *New York Times*, published a scathing review of the play in which he said "Coleman Dowell's new musical, which opened last night at the Barbizon-Plaza Theatre, makes the worst of the possible worlds available to it . . . Mr. Dowell catches little of the spirit of Mr. Van Vechten's novel, and he has failed to establish a consistent style."[180] Other critics were similar in their attacks. Jack Gaver wrote:

> A primary trouble is that, after 37 years of changing mores and morals, about the only excuse for doing anything with Van Vechten's story on the stage would be to use it as the basis for a satirical jibe at what might be called the 'Peyton Place' syndrome. Dowell doesn't begin to approach this concept, and, offered straight, it is just dreadfully dull.
>
> The production suffers from a jerky sort of presentation due to the use of many scenes in a limited stage area. Director Robert K. Adams probably did the best anyone could under this handicap. Robert Soule created the undistinguished period sets: Bill Hargate did better with the costumes.[181]

And Judith Crist of the *Herald Tribune* added:

> Suffice it to say that both book and lyrics are done in a leaden prose style and the music varies between the reminiscent and the monotonous. The four-piece band does, however, succeed in drowning out a good part of the dialogue and lyrics.[182]

The following day Van Vechten wrote to Coleman, "there is nothing to say, nothing to do, except that we feel very badly about this . . ."[183]

The musical closed within a few days, after only four performances. Friends tried to cheer Dowell. Ruth Landshoff York wrote, "Don't be too sad Cole there were lovely songs in it."[184] Notes and letters from those who had worked closest with him on the show reflected the warm feelings and regard they held for him. Virginia Payne, a member of the cast, wrote:

> Thank you so much for an "Enchanted Evening." It was so good of you to add one more happy memory to the "Countess" company. Despite all the travail, there was so much good and worthy in the work and the people, that we loved being together and appreciating one another. Please place me high on your list of admirers. You are such a fine and generous, giving person—the real mark of the true artist—and I am ever grateful for the privilege of working with you and knowing you. Here's to the next—and make it soon! God bless and deepest thanks.[185]

Van Vechten took the reviews in stride. "It played for exactly four performances," Van Vechten wrote in a letter to Edward Leuders, "each of which was ghastly."[186] And on May 5 Van Vechten wrote to Mark Lutz:

> Well, it ended like a giant firecracker all at once with a big BANG. The audience was brilliant; the applause was staggering. The notices were the worst I ever read. Fortunately not a single word of mine was used. Also fortunately Cole repeated this fact endlessly to every one. I am not unhappy about the failure except for Cole who is deeply injured.[187]

Although Dowell owed a great deal to his relationship with the older man he could not bear the embarrassment he felt. Though Van Vechten's feelings for Dowell were not diminished by the show's failure, Dowell abandoned the friendship. He would later spoof Van Vechten and his social gatherings in *Island People* and write disparagingly of their relationship in *A Star-Bright Lie*. Van Vechten felt the loss deeply, expressed in letter to Dowell several years later:

> After I sent you a bottle of champagne for your birthday, instead of a letter of thanks, you sent me a very snippy letter of acknowledgement. For MY birthday,

> and it was my 83rd, you did not even send me a card. So I decided that you had had enough of me.[188]

The Tattooed Countess closed just a few weeks before Coleman Dowell's thirty-sixth birthday. He was no longer David Merrick's golden boy or Carl Van Vechten's crown prince. From the musical theater he had garnered harsh lessons. After three and a half years of work on the *Countess*, its failure brought him close to despair. But Dowell had also begun to develop an individual style for writing fiction. He had drafted several strong stories including "My Father was a River," and he had already begun submitting them to publishers for consideration. Although none of the manuscripts were accepted for publication, editors encouraged him. Dowell would complete one more theater piece before turning his full attention to fiction.

CHAPTER FIVE

The Death Fund

After the failure of *The Tattooed Countess*, Coleman Dowell experienced severe depression and contemplated suicide. During his career in television he had suffered one mental breakdown, and the stress of life in the theater had taken an additional toll on his self-esteem. He tried to fight this depression by tackling new projects. He wrote to his sister Martha:

> [T]he future, bless it, is still as bright as ever, but the present is sometimes unbearable. In brief, my biggest head-and-heartache is this . . . a sort of deadlock that won't allow me to write—since last May when my show closed I have written only four songs, which was my weekly output before. It's a sort of mental & spiritual constipation and I don't know the medicine to take for relief. I'd give a lot to be able to see you—that, I think, would be a part-cure. I feel so cut-off from everything. I live by a sort of thin gauze curtain that allows me to see and hear, but not to touch the important things.[189]

He may have experienced difficulty composing songs, but Dowell had no trouble finding inspiration for other forms of writing. During the three years following the close of *The Tattooed Countess* he completed two plays, at least three short stories, a script for a television show called *The Doctors*, and the first draft of an autobiographical novel. "I am up to my ears in writing," he admitted to Martha in April 1962, "but just paused to send mother a letter, and ask you to do the same."[190]

Early in 1962 Dowell and Slaff moved to a new apartment at 500 East 83rd Street. After they were settled Dowell made a resolution to spend more time with his family. He made periodic visits to his sister Martha in Ohio and trips to Kentucky to see his mother and he was excited by the fact that, after eleven years in New York, he would finally host some of his family in his own home,

Coleman Dowell in Vermont, circa 1955. Although he considered Manhattan his true home, Dowell never fully escaped his longing to be in the country, and thought back fondly on the time he spent in Calais.

first his brother Jim, and then his nieces Carol and Gayle, who planned to visit that summer. A letter negotiating the arrangements contains one of the first mentions of Dowell's novel:

> [*I*]*f* my publishers come through with a sizable advance for the book before June, than I will set you and Gayle and your friend up in a nearby hotel; chic, of course; in the meantime I will try to find someone with room enough or—unlikely thought—someone who will be away while you are here.[191]

In April Jim arrived for a visit from Texas and Dowell took him to see Kim Hunter in Frederick Knott's mystery play, *Write Me a Murder*, at the Belasco Theater. Dowell had met Kim Hunter through Bertram Slaff's best friend Joel Katz, whose wife May had been Hunter's best friend since childhood. After the show Coleman and Jim attended the cast party, and Dowell wrote to his mother that the actress found Jim very charming. Coleman and his brother had a volatile relationship that Dowell later wrote about in a short story titled "Wool Tea." This visit was one of the few meetings with Jim that he recalled fondly.

Dowell spent a great amount of time reading, and during April completed *Ship of Fools*, by Katherine Anne Porter. To his niece Carol, who had asked for suggestions, he offered a list of his favorite books, including J. D. Salinger's *Franny and Zooey*, Oscar Lewis's *Children Of Sanchez*, Peter Feibleman's *A Place Without Twilight* and Harper Lee's *To Kill A Mockingbird*.[192]

Letters to his family suggest the pace with which he wrote:

> I have been working fiendishly. Finished the play in January; the agent said she could sell it. She has gotten a copy to Katherine Hepburn and we are waiting for a reply. My first story was published April 2nd—in German, in Frankfurt, Germany. I will send you a copy of the magazine so you can at least see my name in print! Lippincott has accepted my novel for publication, but I'm still writing on it and Lord knows when I will finish. It started out to be a short one, but it grows and grows. I hope to finish it before we leave for Europe on June 29th.[193]

His agent at this time was Flora Roberts, who was working hard to sell his new play *Eve of the Green Grass*. His short story "Alte Frau Im Garten" ("Old

Woman in a Garden"), had just been published in *Frankfurter Hefte*.[194] The magazine paid Dowell $24.97 for the story, which had been translated into German by his friend Ruth Landshoff York.

Although "Alte Frau Im Garten" is only three and a half pages long, this early story exhibits many of the characteristics of Dowell's more mature fiction. Detailed observations of nature give the story a realistic quality, yet there is tension between this outer world and the inner life of the old woman who sits meditating in her garden. A bee alights momentarily on her bonnet, a grasshopper settles on her skirt. The old woman watches as an apple falls to the ground. The story shifts subtly from the present to the past as these natural images move her to remember the pig she loved as a child, her parents, and her marriage. Her thoughts move from observing the white of her wedding dress to the recollection that white is the color of a shroud.

Images of death pervade the story. The old woman considers the solitary act of lying in a coffin, gravestones, the cemetery separated from her garden by a hedge of flowers. We learn that she has received a letter, but the contents of the letter are not revealed. Smoothing out the paper, her thoughts turn to her son, Tom. The proximity of the act to the thought leads the reader to conclude the letter concerns him. The story ends with the old woman waiting for tears to form—the letter, then, brings sad news. The suggestive nature of the story is an important aspect of Dowell's fiction—the reader must puzzle out the character's emotional state and ponder the symbolic meanings of natural images to draw conclusions about what has or has not occurred.

Though publication of the short story must have cheered Dowell, he was disheartened by a minor disagreement with his mother. He wrote to his sister Martha in May:

> Thanks for sharing my pride in the published story. I spoke to mother, who had received a copy, and I quote her verbatim; and my replies:
>
> "What on earth is this thing you sent me?"
>
> "A story I wrote."
>
> "What language is it?"
>
> "German."

"But, dear, you know I don't read German."
"I know, but you can read my name, can't you?"
"Well, yes I can do that. Has it been accepted?"
"*What?*"
"I said has it been accepted?"
"What the hell do you think *that* is, an audition?"
"I mean — — — did they pay you for it?"[195]

Even after the press he had received for his work on Broadway, Dowell still struggled for recognition from his family. He may have exaggerated when he wrote that Lippincott had accepted the manuscript of his first novel, which he planned to call *The Grass Dies* or *The Other Side of the Air*. He described the book to Martha in November, 1962:

> It is about the death of a father and its effect upon his wife and six children. It is set in Kentucky, thirty miles from Bowling Green in a town I choose to call Roseville—or actually on a farm seven miles from there. Any resemblance to persons living or dead is strictly intentional, but I have taken the license of art (and mine is art until proven otherwise, and I don't mean by the critics) to interchange personalities, invent fictitious backgrounds and so on. One or two incidents are mainly true; the rest is extension, distortion, invention. It is a very cruel book.[196]

Dowell also solicited advice from contemporary authors, among them John Howard Griffin, the author of *Black Like Me*. Dowell had written to Griffin after the publication of *Black Like Me*; the two authors shared a mutual friend, an Army buddy of Griffin's named Charles Criswell who had recently died.[197] Dowell hoped Griffin might consider writing a blurb for *The Grass Dies* once he found a publisher for the book.[198]

Work on short stories and the novel alternated with work on the play, *Eve of the Green Grass*. On May 15 he wrote to his niece Carol:

> Sorry to be so long in answering your letter but I have been (will it never stop!) in such a dither about the play that I could not put typewriter to paper for fear it would create more havoc. Now perhaps it will. There is a plot afoot to 'try' the play out at a summer theatre—a growing practice nowadays with wary produc-

> ers—and if this comes to fruition, it will mean that I will be away from New York from June 1st to the 22nd at least, which would shoot our plans to hell. It might also mean that I could not go to Europe on the 29th but would have to take a plane over later.[199]

The European trip that he mentioned was another vacation with Bertram Slaff, to visit Switzerland, Denmark, Vienna, Greece, Italy, and Lisbon. Dowell's new passport was issued on May 17, 1962 and on June 30 Dowell received his International Drivers Permit. Stamps in the passport indicate that the two men arrived in Rome on July 18, 1962, traveled to Lisbon, then Switzerland, where they stayed in Zurich with friends Madeleine and Tommy Aman. Madeleine was the daughter of the man who founded Swiss Air. Bert had met her during an earlier visit, and she invited them to stay. After Switzerland they continued south to Denmark, then to Vienna, Austria.

Vienna was a highlight for Slaff, who was anxious to visit Sigmund Freud's house. Unfortunately, Dowell wounded his knee and while they were walking in the city one afternoon the couple had a vehement argument. According to Slaff, Dowell said, "Let's take a taxi because my knee is hurting." Slaff remembers his reply:

> I said "*no*." I was very cold. I said, "We are *not* taking a taxi. This is the city of Freud. We're going to 19 Berggasse." Which is Freud's studio, and his office. And I was absolutely cruel to him. I really would not agree to take a taxi. He said, "Well fuck you, I'm going home. I can't stand you anymore." And this is the background to this story. I was born with clubbed feet. I was a cripple child. And I was the first American patient of the great Viennese orthopedic surgeon, Dr. Adolph Lorenz, father of Konrad Lorenz. So it turns out I was living out something of my own, in my cruel behavior to Coleman. So, he is *mad* at me, and I'm *furious* with him for being mad at me, and I'm saying, "*No*, we're walking to Freud's house. . . ." We finally take a taxi to our hotel, and he's packing to leave. And all of a sudden it dawned on him that I'm behaving in a crazy way. Cole . . . said it dawned on him, he said, it doesn't have to do with Freud, it has to do with Lorenz, that this is the Viennese surgeon, and I was not going to allow his telling me his knee hurts when my feet were an issue. In the end it dawns on *him* what's going on between us. That I was being cruel to myself, by saying "we're not tak-

ing a taxi." I was saying this was Freud's town, but it was Lorenz's town, and suddenly this . . . all of this hatred of me evaporated because he was suddenly aware I wasn't being cruel to him I was being cruel to *me*. And then we made up completely. He was full of sympathy, and warmth to me. . .[200]

It was just after their return from the trip that the couple decided to add an additional member to the family, Tammy, a dachshund puppy. The dog delighted Coleman and he and Bertram Slaff welcomed her warmly into their home. Dowell referred to Tammy often in his letters, and once indicated that he based all of his female characters on her. Both men lavished the dachshund with affection.

Dowell finished another play, *The Indian Giver*, which he hoped to have produced in Germany. In July he received a letter from Stefani Hunzinger at Fischer Verlag, who wrote:

Would you please be kind enough to grant us still a little more time for reading your manuscript, THE INDIAN GIVER? We are interested in it and, therefore, would like to pass it to a friend of ours, a German theatre man, for his consideration.[201]

The publishing company sent him an advance of $300 for the short piece. For several years the staff at Fisher Verlag continued to offer hope they might place *The Indian Giver*, but there is no indication that they succeeded in finding an appropriate venue for the show.[202]

There was other good news toward the end of 1962. In November Van Vechten announced that he would be including Dowell's letters and manuscripts in a collection to be donated to Yale University. Dowell wrote to Martha:

Off and on . . . I have written stories and fables for Carl Van Vechten's birthdays, in addition to adapting 'Countess'. These stories and fables, the several versions of 'Tattooed Countess' and my German story, along with an early version of my current play-making-the-rounds, repose in the library at Yale University as part of 'my' collection. Also my hundreds of letters to him. He has set up these collections for every writer he has considered worthy of attention, starting with Gertrude Stein, whose writings he introduced to her native land.[203]

Dowell could not withdraw completely from the world of Broadway for he still held out hope to have a show produced and did not want to abandon his contacts. On Friday, October 26, 1962, he escorted Flora Roberts to the wedding reception of Harold Prince and Judith Chaplin. Prince was a Broadway producer whose shows included *A Funny Thing Happened on the Way to the Forum*. The couple married in the home of his parents, Mr. and Mrs. Milton Prince. The reception, on the St. Regis rooftop, numbered 2000 guests. Dowell found himself at a table with Richard Rodgers, Rita Hayworth, Gary Merrill, Farley Granger and Mary Martin, who, according to Dowell, "were all being vitriolic about the marriage, giving it six months, if that." Dowell "proposed a toast to the bride and groom and *forced* them ... to stand up and acknowledge it or face a scene."[204] The next day Flora Roberts told him that the guests thought he was "a *very* bitter young man."[205]

The following year his mental state had grown even more despondent. He wrote few letters and there is little of note in those that remain from 1963. One indication of Dowell's state of mind, in a letter to his niece Gayle, underscores the difficulty in relying on his letters, diary, and interviews as fact. He freely admitted that he was prone to exaggeration:

> About your depressions—try if you can, to ride *with* them; dramatize them excessively so that, by contrast, they won't seem so bad. I've been doing it all my life. If I am depressed, I say that I'm dying. In contrast to dying, depression seems preferable.[206]

By the end of 1962 Dowell had completed the first draft of his novel *The Grass Dies* and was sending copies around to friends for comment. For Christmas Slaff bought him a new IBM Select II typewriter, and, still anxious to achieve his financial independence, Dowell began another project which he hoped would bring in a large windfall.

> I am now working on a series of television scripts for the show called "The Doctors," a soap-opera that goes on at two-thirty in the afternoons, five days a week. Good money, if I can just keep from being bored to death. At this point in the writing it is sheer drudgery, not helped any by my failure to master this type-

writer, Bert's Christmas gift to me . . . *If* I start making $2500.00 a week (which is what the "soaps" pay writers) I will send you Santa Claus himself for next Christmas.[207]

Dowell was in analysis three times a week and he had started a journal in which he recorded his cheerless observations. The first extant entry, dated January 9, 1964, provides a detailed description of his thoughts about suicide:

> This morning . . . I was transferring a sleeping pill from the bottle in the bathroom into my private death fund (df from here on) . . . The idea of the df came to me two nights ago, and it seems a sensible and simple solution. I don't know why I hadn't thought of it before—actually I do know. It was my usual selfishness that has always kept me from the long view. As much and as long as I have wanted to put a stop to my life, I have been unable to look past the moment in any practical way—to save up for the future (and simultaneous end of it). Getting a night's sleep has always seemed more important to me at the moment than the larger issue of a lasting sleep. But when I came back from Geva's Tuesday night, after all that talk abut my writing and my talent and my future, I was clear enough in my depression to see that something had to be done, finally. So, instead of taking the three pills, I transferred them to another box and yesterday morning I put them in an empty medicine bottle of Tammy's and spent a long anxious time looking for a hiding place. Red pills red hiding place. This morning two more pills. Five now. In a couple of months, unless I find I have to accelerate it by getting prescriptions from Brown and Gershberg, I should have enough. This time it will work and the only thing I dread is the inevitable moment (comparatively) of panic and regret after I have taken the pills, while I am waiting, when I will be forced to think of Bert and, of course, Tammy. She loves me too and it seems especially brutal to take from her anything that she loves because no one can ever explain to her where it has gone, or why.[208]

Even though he was writing at a breakneck pace, Dowell had little income from these pursuits and relied on his position as Bert's secretary more than ever for his livelihood. He had finished another short story, "In the Mood," which he sent to several potential publishers, and thanks to his friend Yetta Arenstein (one of the three people to whom he would dedicate his first novel), a new literary agent, Lucy Kroll, was considering his work for representation. About these attempts he wrote bitterly:

> On Tuesday "In the Mood" came back from Harpers Bazaar with a rejection slip. I said to hell with it, without emotion, but later emotion caught up with me—a sick and cold fury and I imagined Alice Morris consumed with every conceivable cancer. Four years ago when I sent her two juvenile stories, I got an effusive letter calling my talent 'powerful' and 'original'. In the letter she wondered about my 'cryptic symbolism' and where it left the reader, but asked that I send her anything else I had written and assured me that she looked forward a great deal to reading more Dowell. Since then, as my ability has grown, I have tried that magazine twice more to the tune of two rejection slips. Is she tasteless, is she insane, does she exist? Purdy says that she is stupid, but he says that about every editor. Tracy Brigden still writes me personal letters, though they have shrunk to notes and no longer request more of my work as they once did. Roger Angell has grown abusive, using words such as 'affected, irritating, gloomy, terribly heavy'. I am no longer in touch with Flora and Lucy Kroll is reading my novel only because Yetta asked her to, and, I imagine, it was the request of a dying woman. Yetta wanted to give her the play, also, but Madame Kroll refused to read it, adjuring Yetta to use her—Kroll's time 'wisely' because there was 'so little of it'. Oh, parasites. What writer, I wonder, has not been made to feel scaly-dirty by the cold scorn of these ten-and-up-percenters?[209]

"In the Mood" represented an important step forward for Dowell. The story was based on an account Slaff shared with him regarding a patient who felt his life had no meaning until he came to believe that he was Glen Miller. Dowell's story explores issues of war and faith, and in it Dowell incorporated Christian symbolism through the characters of Martha, Mary, and Martha's son Johnny. Concerning the story he wrote to his sister:

> I congratulate myself that you missed hardly a trick in my (let us admit it) very difficult story. Fact, you got more of it, by a long shot, than anyone with the exception of Bert (and the Paris Review? They STILL haven't said yea or nay.) The philosophical point you question is not mine, remember, but that of a boy whose mind is failing—a boy who was brought up as a strict Catholic, who has believed that he directed his prayers to the source of all power, and when he finds him-

> self praying to the enemy (as soldiers actually do . . . they don't say "Oh God, let him miss me"; they say "Miss me this time"), then it must be the enemy who is the source of all power—and indeed is, in time of war, holding the power of life and death quite literally in his hands. Therefore, when he kills the enemy he has killed God . . . At least, my effort was to project myself into the failing mind of a religious boy in a foxhole with a dead Jap. A major clue to Johnny's readiness for madness is in the long passage about his never having known fear, and Mary's speculations about this, equating fear with poison etc. Also, he was a boy who never really had ANYTHING except his faith (though I never stated that he *had* faith; it has to be assumed). If you recall, I tell about how he used to fight to capture the hands of girls 'for the melancholy of reading (on their bracelets) engraved names other than his'. He hadn't even THAT proof of his existence. Also, his older brother was obviously the apple of most eyes (we learn this through Martha's talk about the two boys); the one person who cared for HIM was Mary, whom he almost never saw, so that when he asked even for understanding, it had to be from a person at a distance—like God, in a sense. The fact that Martha was too busy to SEE them as children must have been felt by Johnny, the weaker of the boys, and so was another proof that he existed only in his communications with God. He kills God (the enemy) and ceases to exist as Johnny. The last record of Johnny is destroyed. . . Actually, I can put it simply: when he killed the enemy, who was God, he killed himself . . . I daresay that long before Johnny 'killed God' he had, because of the fear that 'God' would kill him, lost the comfort of his faith. He couldn't believe any longer that "We" don't kill because killing was going on all around him and by him.[210]

The madness represented in this story, caused by a loss of faith, would become a theme Dowell repeated in almost all his later fiction.

The author was growing more isolated from his friends and those he continued to see affected him in different ways. As a diversion, he studied French with Yetta Arenstein, who had been diagnosed with cancer. Arenstein's interests matched his. She had worked as a book, newspaper and magazine editor. During World War II she had served as editor-in-chief of the English-language publication *Pour la Victoire*, the Free French weekly published in New York. She had worked as a sales manager and translator for the Continental Book

Center, and as editorial assistant for the George Macy Companies, publishers of the Limited Editions and Heritage Club books. She lectured at City College and at Hunter College while working for a Ph.D. degree at New York University, and she was a contributing editor to the *Saturday Review*.[211] Of her Dowell wrote:

> Yetta touched me. . . with her tenacity for life: how in contrast to my tired eagerness to be shed of it! I can't help wondering, as I have before, if I would be so doggedly anticipating the end if the seeds of that end were planted in my body and on the verge of bloom, as they are in hers; indeed, the figure of speech falls short of truth because she had come to bloom several times and has been pruned; if cancer-pruning works the same way as cutting-back plants does, then her final blossoming should be spectacular: one perfect bursting of the bud, one blazing flower that lives and dies simultaneously.[212]

Dowell had not yet cut all ties with his theatrical life, but he had severed at least one of them. He spoke disparagingly of his relationship with Carl Van Vechten, whom he no longer considered a friend. Slaff tried to convince him to keep up the friendship, believing that Dowell's feelings of rejection were based on paranoia. Dowell wrote:

> My last letter to Van Vechten gave him the ball to carry, allowing for no more arguments; he would either have to write and say, "Let's see each other" or stop writing. It looks as if he has chosen the latter course. Silly old man, I'm sorry I wrote him at all—letters full of lies. "A tragedy of errors" indeed! I meant to cut off any relationship with him, and why I let sentimentality rise like a turd to the surface I cannot imagine. Yetta's eloquent words about his 'last days' or something, I suppose. The truth is he will probably outlive everyone. Not that I want it otherwise—except in the sense that news of his death would at least be news. [213]

Dowell was beginning to take on a more secretive life, involving afternoon trysts. His taste in lovers gravitated toward Hispanics and African Americans, and he began to bring these men to the apartment he shared with Slaff.

> At sometime or other the desire to have someone in this house with me began to overwhelm me—I think it was after the mail came and there was neither

acceptance nor rejection; and after time enough for a phone call about the damn television thing had come and gone with silence. Anyway, I ran the streets, searching faces for the seeds of "yes" that might be there. How extraordinary a thing it is to want so desperately, and yet to be so choosy—to continue to specialize; today I knew that it had to be a Puerto Rican; all other faces were bypassed: the "das" the "ouis" the "yeses." It had to be a "si" and I did not find it. All day I ran the streets and I did not find it. I got into the service elevator at 4:30 with a delivery boy for East End Cleaners (we don't go there anymore) and spoke of the cold, and spoke of how nice a drink would be, and asked him to have one with me. He did. He is coming back for another in fifteen minutes. His name is Sterling and he is sterling. A most sterling Negro Sterling. Once he was here, sitting with me on the couch, I was so calm and easy that I forgot he was a stranger and might be thinking strange thoughts. I relaxed so completely that I could have slept—ideally, with my head on his shoulder. His shoulders are broad, his eyes are mild, his smile is very sweet. I adore him. Sterling. I have no notion of whether or not I will make a pass at him. It seems terribly unimportant. He trusted me enough to come here; he was curious enough (I really can't say he liked me enough because I've no way of knowing) to say he would come back. After he had picked up the Hannon's clothes he rang the bell here and asked—so nicely conspiratorial!—if I had some chewing gum for his breath. Why do I feel that the time until he comes back is unbearable? Why do I depend upon him so for comfort? Am I totally mad—at last, or have I always been? This is one question that will never be answered, you know. Yes, I do know.[214]

As Coleman Dowell grew more dependent on these liaisons, the conflict between his tender feelings for Black men and Hispanics and the occasional harsh epithets he used to describe them in his journal and letters intensified. Perhaps a measure of his mental illness was manifest in these contradictions: his partner was Jewish, but Dowell wrote disparagingly of Jews; his lovers were Black and Hispanic, but he vilified these minorities in prose.

When he was not involved with his friends and lovers, Dowell's hopes were focused on the television script his agent had submitted to NBC. In February, he wrote to his niece:

I'm pretty much on edge waiting to hear from the television people about *The Doctors*. The director loved my script but the producer may hate it. It went to

> him last Tuesday (a week tomorrow) and no word yet. I did send it through my agent, and she did say that Levton is notoriously slow about saying 'yes' or 'no'. My eagerness is based upon the money involved, and not any sense of artistic achievement—which would be impossible to find in the world of soap opera, I think. However, I do like my script, and so we shall see. Anyway, I've begun writing for television (I mean, thinking in terms of the camera) and so I'll go on doing it; my agent suggested that I try something for *the DuPont Show of the Month*. Why not?[215]

By November 1964 he had found another way to make money. On a whim Dowell accompanied his friend Terry Greene, a fashion coordinator, to a photographer's studio to gather first-hand atmosphere and details for a short story. During the visit Greene introduced him to the photographer and his staff and Dowell observed the photographer at work. As he was leaving, someone from the agency, mistaking him for one of the models, told him to report for work at 10:00 the following morning. The next day Dowell returned to the photographer's studio. He proudly shared the news with his family:

> I am now a model; three jobs in the past week, at 50.00 an hour. My first job was to advertise the *Wall Street Journal*, the advertisement to be in *The New York Times* and *The Herald Tribune* any day now. My second was to advertise the Rambler—twelve other models and I posed in front of the St. James Theatre from 12:30 at night until 2, with traffic stopped and crowds gathered (they thought we were shooting a movie); the air was icy and the photographer drunk. My third assignment was to pose as a chauffeur in a Jaguar. I already have two dates for next week and am being signed by an agency. Point: if you see in magazines or papers a man who reminds you of your uncle, it is.[216]
>
> I leave for Montauk tomorrow morning, instead of Wednesday night, because Terry (Balcomb Greene's wife) has arranged an 'on location' modeling date for me and six other male models—— we will pose in sports clothes on a fishing boat. She thinks they may want to use Tam—if they do, she will be paid too: $10.00 an hour. Anyway, I will be in Montauk until Sunday night, just for your info. Incidentally, posing I did for Jaguar will be in both *Holiday* and *Fortune* magazines—as usual, the Agency is not sure *when*.[217]

Dowell's first assignment appeared in a Christmas ad, a self-promotional piece for the *Wall Street Journal* which appeared on Thursday, November 12, 1964. The ad caption read: "Honestly, wouldn't you appreciate it?" After seeing the ad in the *Wall Street Journal* his friend Jeannette Gilbert exclaimed:

> COLE? Imagine my delight to see your face glancing superiorly from behind lenses grotesque and the perfect "prop" for your image as a typical Madison Avenue executive . . . Now, added to your talents as writer, composer, poet and cook we can include superb dramatic eloquence in emoting the "look!"
>
> No playwright/composer ever looked so elegant, composed, so charming or handsome—you have missed your calling, darling boy—why not compete with the Cary Grants of the theater and become an actor? You are marvelously photogenic, you know.[218]

Dowell did not let modeling interrupt his writing. In December he was making plans for a production of *Eve of the Green Grass*:

> Kim (Hunter) just called about my play; she and the director are getting together tonight to discuss ways and means. I wish I felt more delighted about the prospect of a production, but all I can think of is the necessary re-writing and I am not remotely confident that I can, or will, do it.[219]

Gentle Laurel was Dowell's first title for the play, which he changed to *Eve of the Green Grass*. Although the play differed from his earlier musicals, this was not Dowell's first attempt at drama. A letter from playwright Bill Inge indicates that Dowell had been working on another dramatic play as early as 1959: "you have written a darn good play," Inge wrote, "and if you want me to recommend it to anyone for you, I shall be only too glad. I'm not saying it'll be an easy play to get produced, for right now, there seems to be a general feeling that the issue of homosexuality has been discussed enough on Broadway stages. But you never can tell."[220]

On February 1, 1965, Yetta Arenstein died of cancer. Dowell spoke at the funeral service the following day. Later that month he attended the opening of *The Queen and the Rebels*, a play which starred another close friend, Tamara

Geva, the first wife of George Balanchine. The show opened on February 25, and Dowell claimed that he had "unofficially re-written the play"[221] for the production.

He had returned, momentarily, to song writing and submitted two—"Love Just Happens" and "I Haven't a Thing to Wear"—to the Library of Congress with an application for copyright. In a letter to Martha he indicated that he was again composing songs and hoped to have one recorded by Frank Sinatra:

> contacts have arranged for Mr. Frank Sinatra to hear my words and music via record, so I spent yesterday recording professionally (first time that way for me); draining the Suez Canal single-handedly could not have tired me more. Vast studio, control room behind glass, lights blinking signals—I wasn't so much scared as jellyfish boneless and slept with (by) futility. Some hours later, at the end of the session, I was running a temperature—I've been doing that intermittently, anyway, so perhaps there was no connection.[222]

Dowell was also in communication with Barbra Streisand's agent, Ted Brooks, to whom he wrote in March, 1965:

> Here is the song we spoke about: LOVE JUST HAPPENS. I find that I have only the transparency; I had given Miss Streisand the one copy I had.[223]

Bertram Slaff had heard Streisand sing when she was only 18, at a large theatrical party given by his friends Harvey and Sis Korman. The Kormans arranged an evening gathering with Streisand where Dowell auditioned a few of his songs. Later in May Dowell and Slaff entertained Streisand and Elliot Gould at a private dinner party. On May 24 Streisand sent a note that read, "Dear Bert and Cole, Can't wait for a rainy day! Many thanks and best wishes."[224] She liked Dowell's song "Autumn," which had been published by Chappell. According to Slaff, she wanted Dowell to rewrite it so she could have it re-published by her own company before she recorded it.

That month Dowell and Slaff rented a house on Long Island Sound. They had the house until the end of September and planned to invite a series of visitors. Dowell was concerned about his weight and began dieting, and was also trying to establish a writing routine. In August he received another rejection notice, a letter from MacMillan with a reader's note suggesting that he limit the scope of *The Grass Dies* and "tell the story of only one or two characters instead of six."[225] Slaff was planning a trip to Europe, and Dowell also had an invitation to travel to Vermont in August to visit Ruth York.

In October 1965 *Eve of the Green Grass* opened. The play was presented by a nonprofessional group at the Chelsea Art Theatre, St. Peter's Episcopal Church. The performance-reading, directed by Sherwood Arthur, starred Kim Hunter. Dowell's friend, Lady Elizabeth Kinnaird (who wrote under the name Elizabeth Eliot) sent him a letter regarding the performance:

> If you want any suggestions: I have only one; which is, that I took some time to work out that Morda Sheridan (Angel's husband) had "laid" (layed) Ivy (in the churchyard) *before* he married Angel.[226]

After seeing the performance, Dowell decided to abandon his career in the theater. Without any pain, without the mourning that the failure of *The Tattooed Countess* had induced, he came to the conclusion that he was not a playwright. To Bert he said, "I'm going to write novels from now on."[227]

Dowell described his response to *Eve of the Green Grass* this way:

> My own reaction was one of total horror. I could hardly live through the play and had a 'fit' afterwards, so that my friends later reported they felt as if they were talking to an "icy cold stranger . . ." I have decided that even if we get an offer for production, I won't go through with it . . . I think the play is dishonest, and I think critics would see that and crucify me again, which I would not survive.[228]

Elements of the play recall the work of Tennessee Williams. Dowell may have believed that imitating Williams assured success. The setting is southern: the imaginary town of Roseville, Kentucky (which was also the setting for *The Grass Dies*). One character, Ivy, is slightly mad. Ivy and her sister, Angel, have married Morda and Cliff, brothers the girls have known all their lives. After a tragic accident involving her husband Cliff, Ivy has vanished, but returns sixteen years later to confront the damage she has caused her sister, her son, and her brother-in-law. In his note on the setting of the play Dowell indicated, "The important elements of the setting are freedom, space, and an overlying, brooding sense of the past . . ."[229] This Gothic treatment of the past as a physical element hovering over the present appears repeatedly in each of Dowell's later novels.

The play also provides the first example of Dowell's fondness for nesting one narrative within another. The children, Laurel, Willow, and Royal, are planning to perform a play for their elders, and the dialogue of their rehearsals is intermingled with the outer plot of the play. As the narrative proceeds, it is the inner play which ultimately reveals the secret of the story and provides the resolution for its conflict, for the children re-enact the tragedy which forced Ivy to run away. Dowell had a special fondness for these characters, and they returned in other guises, including the short stories "Willow's Story" and "Willow Sheridan Rode Voltaire."

His final produced play closed after three performances. He continued to submit short stories to literary magazines, but no editor accepted them. Neither Sinatra nor Streisand recorded his songs. By the end of 1965 Dowell had once again succumbed to a series of professional defeats. Rather than retreating, he turned his full attention to his novel, *The Grass Dies*. His agent, Lucy Kroll, was working to find a publisher for the novel, and his friend Lady Elizabeth Kinnaird recommended that he send the manuscript to her British publisher, Cassell.

CHAPTER SIX

Agents, Editors and Royalties

One of the most memorable things about Coleman Dowell's friend Lady Elizabeth Kinnaird was her habit of speaking in doubles. According to Bertram Slaff she often repeated sentences. "I'm reading your book," she would say to Dowell. "I'm reading your book."[230] This habit annoyed some of the people she knew, but Dowell found her charming. Lady Elizabeth had published several novels of manners by the time they met, among them *Alice* (London: Cassell 1949), *Henry* (London: Cassell, 1950), and *Cecil* (London: Cassell, 1952), and a non-fiction work titled *Heiresses and Coronets: The Story of Lovely Ladies and Noble Men* (New York: McDowell, Obolensky Inc., 1959).[231] It was Lady Elizabeth who recommended Dowell send the manuscript of his first novel to Cassell, her publisher in England.

Kinnaird's and Dowell's many mutual acquaintances included Ivan Obolensky, who had established the publishing house of McDowell, Obolensky Inc. in 1957. Obolensky was Mary Astor's son, and Dowell had known him since his early days in New York. Obolensky's partner in the publishing venture, David McDowell, had been a close friend to James Agee, who, upon his death, left McDowell an unfinished novel about the effect his father's death had had on his childhood. McDowell turned Agee's manuscript into a novel and published it as *A Death in the Family*. Like William Faulkner's 1930 work *As I Lay Dying*, Agee's book takes place in the south and examines the psychological effects caused by the death of a loved one, and questions the rudimentary principles of Christianity in understanding such loss.

Agee's posthumous novel won the Pulitzer Prize in 1957. Ten years later Modern Library reissued Faulkner's *As I Lay Dying*. By then Coleman Dowell was writing his own novel based on similar themes.[232] *The Grass Dies* was

Coleman Dowell at the Montauk Point Lighthouse. In December, 1959, the painter Balcomb Greene offered Dowell and Slaff the use of his house at Montauk Point. Greene was in Paris until June, and the house provided a getaway from Manhattan, where Dowell could work uninterrupted on the Stephen Foster play, Beautiful Dreamer.

Dowell's initial title for the novel, a story loosely based on his own family and his father's death in 1955.

The work took several years to complete. Its publication followed a series of contentious disputes. Dowell's literary agent, Lucy Kroll,[233] marketed the manuscript but had no luck finding a publisher. On June 6th, 1966, upon the recommendation of Lady Elizabeth, Dowell sent the manuscript to Desmond Flower at the British publishing house of Cassell & Company Limited. He appended a letter that indicated he was working on revisions, and he noted that, if Dr. Flower was interested in the work, he would submit the final revisions as soon as they were completed. Dr. Flower acknowledged receipt of the manuscript in a letter that stated "I note what you say about the deletions which you are planning, and we will keep this in mind when reading the book."[234]

In April Dowell and Slaff took a summer house in East Hampton, between Gardiner's Bay and Three Mile Harbor. Dowell described the house, which they would occupy starting June 15, to his sister Martha:

> [F]our bedrooms, two baths, a dishwasher—no fireplace, but thermostat-controlled heat, a damn good thing to have, even in the summer, because the water is about thirty feet from our sundeck and on cloudy days it can get mighty cold. We have it from June 15th through Labor Day . . . We are going to buy another sailboat, so we will have two. The one we have now is like a tub—very safe, because it is unsinkable, but not very fast, so that Bert wants to get a small, fast one—a Sunfish or Sailfish.[235]

The house provided a refuge from the city and a place to write without unwanted interruptions. In addition to revisions on the novel Dowell began another novel tentatively titled *Too Much Flesh and Jabez*,[236] and a short story called "Singing in the Clump."

That fall a representative of Cassell, Edward Twentyman, sent Coleman Dowell a letter expressing his appreciation for the manuscript and making an offer for publication.[237] Dowell accepted the offer in a letter dated October 10th and signed the contract on October 31, 1966. A few weeks later Dowell wrote to Desmond Flower and Twentyman, advising them that the final manuscript was being sent under separate cover. He explained his revisions in detail, welcomed their comments and suggestions, and expressed his hope that the changes would be welcome.

Although Dowell was in direct communication with the publishers, Lucy Kroll solicited the assistance of another literary agent, Peter Janson-Smith from the London office of Elaine Greene Limited, to represent Dowell's interests abroad. Janson-Smith was to deliver the final contract to Cassell. On November 25th, 1966, Nicholas Flower, Desmond Flower's son, replied to Dowell's letter concerning the revisions, to say that he would not read the final manuscript until the contract had been received. Although Dowell had signed the contract nearly a month earlier, Janson-Smith had not delivered it.

For several months Dowell revised the novel, but the editors at Cassell were unhappy with the changes. Dowell communicated with the publisher through Lucy Kroll and Peter Janson-Smith. Nicholas Flower, displeased with the revisions, insisted on publishing the original, unrevised manuscript. He felt that the new version was too long and lacked the power of the original, and he wrote to Dowell, "It is after all your book—you wrote it and you obviously like it the way it is or you would have done it differently."[238] Lucy Kroll responded:

> Mr. Dowell wrote and likes the revisions and that is why he wishes you to publish the revised edition. He is the creator and I hope you would defer to him, as I do. The fact that you like the unrevised version does not satisfy Mr. Dowell. He feels that the time and effort which went into these revisions presents his novel in the form in which he would like the reading public to receive it.[239]

Part of Flower's objection had to do with the fact that he had not assisted the author with the revisions and Dowell was now working on the manuscript with Lee Wright, an editor at Random House. Random House had originally rejected the novel, but accepted it for publication in the United States after it was taken by Cassell. Flower was not interested in ceding control of the changes to another publishing house.

In January and February of 1967 Dowell worked with Lee Wright on the revised version of the American edition, which had a set date for publication of February, 1968. Wright requested minor changes that she felt would improve the book. Lucy Kroll wrote again to Nicholas Flower with that hope that Cassell would "publish this final version as then it would make for no complications for the reading public on both sides of the Atlantic."[240]

Disagreements extended to the title of the novel. Wright suggested changing the title to *One of the Children is Crying*, a line from a critical scene in the book. Lucy Kroll asked Dowell to send a letter to Cassell's publicity department with this recommendation. Other titles proposed included *Parents and Lovers* and *The Family of the Late Lamented*. The Cassell staff disliked the new suggestions, and the sales department insisted on *The Grass Dies*. On May 16, 1967 Dowell met with Lee Wright, notifying Random House about Cassell's decision to keep the original title, and offered his own agreement on *One of the Children is Crying* or *One is Crying* for the American title. Dowell himself probably preferred the original title, for he wrote, "England has finally insisted—and won the battle—upon the original—'The Grass Dies'. Hail, Britannia!"[241]

Meanwhile, Cassell had assigned an editor to work with Dowell on the British edition of the book. In a letter dated June 8, 1967, Laura Ford, of the editorial department at Cassell's, wrote to ask if he had received permission to quote a Hart Crane poem, and continued:

> I believe you are worried about the usage of WHICH and THAT. I'll certainly keep an eye open for this, but the point is that in England we so often use WHICH, when you would use THAT—which seems to complicate things all the more!
>
> I wonder if you would have any objection to my changing GOTTEN to GOT when not in conversation? Also, it is definitely against our House practice to use the word, FUCK, or F___, as an alternative. So far, I have noticed it twice (page 37, line 13, and page 71, line 5 from bottom). Could you suggest an alternative or an adjustment to the sentence?[242]

Dowell sent copies of the manuscript to Martha and to his brother Jim. During his attendance at a meeting of the American Academy of Child Psychiatry in Dallas, Texas, Bertram Slaff had taken time away from the conference to visit Jim Dowell and his family. Slaff was intrigued with the opportunity to observe the family who figured so prominently in Coleman's novel. Although

Martha praised it, Jim's response was less commendable: As Coleman Dowell described it:

> I'm sorry that poor Jim found the sex in my book sickening, almost as sorry as I was to discover that he really has no manners at all. I am most of all sorry for any pupils to whom he is supposed to impart an understanding of literature because literature and weak stomachs are antithetical; I'm afraid that a man whose stomach collapses at my little allegorical-sexual recovery of a schizophrenic girl could never withstand the horrors of Emma Bovary's self-destruction.[243]

Most of the people who read the manuscript offered words of encouragement and praise, but Dowell was growing disillusioned with other friends he had once trusted. His relationship with Lucy Kroll was waning, and his friendship with Elizabeth Kinnaird had turned sour. Dowell had intended to dedicate the British edition of the novel to her, but he grew increasingly upset over her claim that she was his English agent and on February 21, 1967, Dowell sent a letter to Lady Elizabeth indicating this was not the case. He wrote caustically:

> When I asked if I might have your permission to dedicate my novel to you, I was regrettably ignorant of how complicated a procedure it is. I did not know that a familiarity with Burke's Peerage was a, if not the, sine qua non—all those articles!: The Lady Elizabeth etc.—though that would be, of course I now see, in abominable taste.
>
> [W]hen I made my request it was as friend to friend, and not as client to agent. That is, my New York edition (if there is one) will certainly not be dedicated to Lucy Kroll, so I do not think it would be fair that my English edition (if there is one) should be dedicated to my English agent, which you informed me and my other guests a number of times you were.[244]

Dowell decided to dedicate the book to Bertram Slaff and Tammy, and to the memory of two deceased friends, Hub Smith and Yetta Arenstein.

Cassell set the publication date for January 18, 1968, just one month before the American publication. Random House meanwhile announced their publication of the book with a press release in the form of an invitation that read, "The McChesneys have gathered for their father's funeral . . ." After all of the confusion and contention both editions of the book were published on schedule. With the exception of minor editorial changes[245] there are few differences between the two texts.

This early novel is one of Dowell's most accessible books. It was widely promoted with newspaper reviews in Boston, Denver, Hollywood, Houston, Louisville, Milwaukee, Sacramento, and Tulsa. Reviews of *The Grass Dies* also appeared in England and Ireland. "Dowell is a born writer unafraid of blood and anguish and the darker passions," wrote Don Robertson for the *Cleveland Plain Dealer*. "His novel is at once complex and profound, melodramatic in the best sense, a creation of horror and beauty and awful grief."[246]

The characters in the novel are loosely based on Dowell's siblings; after its publication, his relationship with several family members was severely strained. Nor were there large financial rewards. On January, 23, 1968 Lucy Kroll obtained Dowell's advance from Cassell for 67 pounds 6 shillings ($161.26) The check represented the total amount of 75 pounds minus the commission to Peter Janson-Smith of 7 pounds 14 shillings. In February Kroll sent Dowell the final payment of the advance. After subtracting the agency's ten percent, Dowell received $145.13.

In May, 1968, shortly after the publication of the book, Dowell returned to Franklin, Kentucky, where he visited family and friends. One high school friend, Dorothy Donnell Steers (the girl he had escorted to the senior prom), invited him to her home for a small gathering. Dorothy recalled telling Dowell at the time that if *he* hadn't written that book she wouldn't have read it—she thought it was "trashy." "Dowell told me that his editor insisted that he include the *trashy* part early in the book," Dorothy remembered. "Books about homosexuals were few and far between then," and she "was disappointed that Bobby had written such."[247]

In an interview with John and Linda Kuehl, Dowell described the book as "a fictional farewell to both [his] family and to any religious belief or feeling."[248] The novel opens on Christmas Eve 1962 with the death of Murdoch McChesney, the father of a prominent Southern family.[249] The family's children struggle to understand the complex nature of their relationships with their father and with each other. Murdoch's death is a catalyst for the sequence of events that lead each of the main characters to self-examination and discovery.

Like Agee's book, *A Death in the Family*, the action of the novel takes place over the course of the next 24 hours. It reveals through flashbacks the pain Murdoch caused his wife Eula Marie and their six children. The McChesneys are haunted by the past—specifically by their parents' infidelities and the perceived class structure that has alienated their maternal and paternal families. Also similar to Agee's book is the way Dowell's novel explores the weight of family dysfunction and the death of religious fervor. In its description of the difficult, nearly impossible act of communication and the fragmentary nature of the subconscious, it is related more closely to Faulkner's *As I Lay Dying*.

One of the Children is Crying displays the control Dowell maintained over his themes and his intricate use of form to support them. Although the organizational structure of his later works became more complex, this first novel contains all of the elements of experimentation Dowell would employ throughout his career. Like Faulkner's work, the novel takes liberties with voice and verb tense—and although the present action occurs in a brief span of time—the narrative moves back and forth between past and present.

Although critics damned the book for its exploration of incest, no acts of incest occur in the novel. Erin is drawn to her brother Robin by sexual attraction, but Dowell explains, "Robin and Erin never penetrated each other—if they had, I wouldn't have had a book—and their repression was what made them take over the role of parents."[250] Erin's attraction is echoed in Aunt Antonia's feelings for her own brother Murdoch, who Antonia describes as "her son, her dream lover."[251] Priscilla reveals that the one act of incest described in the novel, between her and her brother Spur, is in fact a story she invented to repel her husband.

The novel suggests that the concept of "self" is a composition of multiple identities. Dowell called them "fragments." He makes this idea concrete by creating some division in his individual characters, through their names, psychological makeup, memory, and interpersonal relationships. Jasper is also known as Spur—these two names represent two sides of the same man.

Priscilla is schizophrenic, Erin is caught between her past and present, and Robin feels as if he and Handy have shared each other's skins. This idea is symbolized in the novel by mirrors or reflections, often used to represent self-reflection. Erin's reflection is "watery." Priscilla sees only a part of herself in the mirror. Rhoda avoids "the cobwebby mirror." The mirror cannot reflect the entire image, for none of the siblings is whole. In a biographical entry on Dowell for *Postmodern Fiction*, Maria Vittoria D'Amico links such mirror imagery to the compulsion to write about the act of writing, a *narcissistic* view that emphasizes "a peculiar aesthetic intercourse between creator and creation."[252]

The novel is divided into three parts: *The Gathering*, *The Clan*, and *The Leavetakings*. Part one, *The Gathering*, is composed of five subsections, and each section introduces one of the McChesney siblings: *Robin*, *Priscilla*, *Rhoda*, *Spur*, and *Erin*. Dowell may have modeled the structure of the book on Faulkner's *As I Lay Dying*, which interweaves the interior voices of several characters and alternates their perspectives from chapter to chapter. The lives of Dowell's characters are in varying states of disintegration and their return home for their father's funeral renews unresolved family conflicts. The subsections interweave their interior monologues, dreams, memories and desires, creating multiple voices within a single narrative frame. Facts and situations revealed by one sibling are clarified and refined by another, and the reader is left with a picture of unspoken misunderstandings. Dowell vividly describes the relationships of the youngest siblings, Rhoda, Spur, and Priscilla. All three are married, but each couple suffers from a lack of intimacy. Dowell is careful to balance the siblings' perceptions with those of their partners, who offer outside perspectives on the family.

The main action occurs over the course of Christmas Eve and Christmas day. Past and present actions are intermingled in a montage, focusing on particular memories of the summer Robin left home. Dowell uses the structure to reinforce his themes: the tripartite division suggests the holy trinity, underscoring the fusion of Robin's role with that of his father, and the notion that Murdoch's ghost continues to haunt them. The final section of part one, *Erin* (the 'mother' of the story), moves from consciousness to consciousness, suggesting that she is a "container" for the other members of the family. As a result of these shifting perspectives, Dowell creates a sense of disharmony that represents Erin's eventual descent into madness.

Although the initial subsection is titled *Robin*, the novel begins from Erin's perspective, with a telephone call to her brother. Dowell combines Robin's point of view with Erin's to suggest that they share one consciousness. Erin and Robin are the two eldest children and their parents, exhibiting the same weaknesses Faulkner's parents displayed in *The Sound and The Fury*, have ceded control of family matters to Erin and Robin, who have assumed their parents' roles. To Robin, Erin is "more mother than sister"[253] and one Christmas he considers giving her a doll that says "Ma Ma." Priscilla, the youngest, refers to Erin as Spur's "mother." Spur thinks, "For a moment Robin and his father had been one man."[254] Rhoda recalls Robin and Erin coming to console her when she tells them that she will not graduate from college, and Ed, Priscilla's husband, describes their visit to calm Priscilla after she learns of his affair with Nonie. Dowell says of Erin and Robin that their "crime was not overprotection but fostering confusion about who their parents were."[255]

When the novel opens, Robin has been away from home for three years and Erin manages the house and continues to care for her mother and father. Her one desire has been for her brother to return. With her father's death this wish is fulfilled, and Erin thinks, "With Robin here, love would once again be possible."[256] But Robin knows his presence can only have dire consequences: shortly after leaving home he had written his sister a letter that explained, "we should not take roles not meant for us."[257] Robin states this most clearly at the end of the novel, when he realizes that his siblings are "the children they had maimed in unimaginable ways because [Murdoch] had maimed them first, his two oldest children, handing on to them blindly the blind traditions and myths and distortions of the country he had never understood."[258]

Sexuality shades every aspect of the novel. Murdoch has fathered at least one illegitimate child, an unnamed boy who attends the funeral with his mother Weezie at the end of the novel. Robin reveals that Millicent is also illegitimate, the daughter of Eula Marie and a farm hand. (The novel's form emphasizes the fact that they are not part of the family—unlike the other five siblings, Dowell names no section of the novel for Millicent or the boy). Dowell uses two key metaphors to portray sexuality. Most of the siblings describe sex in terms of animal imagery. According to Spur, his wife Bonny has "a feeling for animal sex."[259] This association recurs often: Rhoda thinks of sex like "two animals in a field"[260] and on the train Robin feels "the man's stirring animal nature."[261] Even Eula Marie says of Millicent, "she had watched men looking her daughter over, in the flesh or in magazines, and had seen their britches stirring as if they carried live animals in their pockets."[262]

Occasionally Dowell applies the language of agriculture to sexuality. When Robin discusses the farm, his father's mind goes from ripeness of wheat to the breasts of young girls. And again, when he confronts his father with a letter from Weezie, announcing that she is going to have Murdoch's baby, his father says Robin has "wasted his seed" and asks, "How many bellies have you ripened in your lifetime?"[263] These images of sexuality stand in stark contrast to the idea of romantic love, most fully realized by Rhoda's husband Andrew, who does not understand how the McChesneys can hide from each other. He believes that if his children see the love Robin and Erin share, they will get a more balanced picture of what family means. He is unaware of the unfulfilled but perverse nature of their love.

Part two, *The Clan*, focuses on the gathering at the McChesney homestead. In this section Dowell develops the relationships and interactions of the siblings as well as the maternal and paternal families, and explores the theme of faith and its effects on the family. This section introduces Murdoch's sisters, Editha and Antonia, who came from Scotland with their parents before Murdoch was born. After their parents' death Murdoch was raised by Antonia, "instilling in him the facts . . . of his ancient lineage and blood rights . . ."[264] This primitive view conflicts with what the children know about Christianity. Priscilla indicates that her father "didn't believe in God."[265] She is countered by Aunt Antonia, who fabricates a story of Murdoch being baptized "like an infant . . . the infant Jesus."[266] Robin, like his father, is associated with Christ throughout the novel—symbolized by the wounds in his hands, by his association with his father, "whose place he had taken in life,"[267] and by the actions of his sister Erin, whose thoughts about betraying Robin echo Judas: "Am I going to be the one?"[268]

The final section of the novel, *The Leavetakings*, more closely examines the siblings' interpersonal relationships. This section also puts the family in a larger context by depicting the town of Roseville and its class structure. Flashbacks make up a significant portion of this section, interwoven with present day scenes leading up to the funeral. Many of the events involve other members of the community and key relationships outside the family are revealed, including Robin's friendship with Handy, Millicent's date with Luke, and Weezie's marriage to Hollis. Other scenes reveal the dissolution of the McChesney family; Spur leaves town for five years, intending to enlist, and both Rhoda and Millicent leave home for school. Robin takes a job in a nearby town, and shortly after that a letter arrives for Murdoch McChesney marked "Personal." Erin gives the letter to Robin by mistake (again Robin assumes his father's role). The letter is from Weezie, the young girl carrying Murdoch's child. The ensuing confrontation between Robin and his father convinces Robin to leave home.

In counterpoint to the family story is an exploration of race relationships, epitomized by the friendship between Robin McChesney and his black friend Handy. Like the encounter between Rufus and his black nanny in *A Death in the Family*, the relationship between the two characters in Dowell's novel carries with it the full weight of the relationship between the races in the South in the first half of the twentieth century. It is a theme that Dowell would explore in much greater detail in his final novel, *White on Black on White*.

One portion of *The Leavetakings* appeared in print separately, as a story titled "Handy," and Handy's presence runs like a recurring melody throughout *One of the Children is Crying*. Roseville boasts signs of racial prejudice such as *No dogs and Coloreds Allowed*. There are periodic feuds between the Baptists and the Catholics, and all dislike Negroes and the "snakecharming hillbilly." Prejudice has penetrated the McChesney family. When Robin explains to Spur that he and Handy " had shared experiences that made them each a part of the other,"[269] Spur replies, "Even if I was a draft dodger, I wouldn't own up to looking like a nigger inside."[270]

Each narrative of these relationships alternates with scenes from the funeral home. Erin doesn't want anyone to leave until Robin arrives. She sees his return as an act of resurrection. The climax of the novel occurs when Handy brings Robin to the funeral parlor. When Robin enters Erin kneels to take his wounded hand—she bows her head to his feet and says, "Let us be together in our loss."[271] Robin, who has been drinking steadily throughout his trip, "heaved and the vomit splattered her with bits of old food, and of Scotland."[272] According to Dowell, this is both a "baptism" and an "ejaculation."[273] Robin shows contempt for everyone and continues drinking over Erin's body until Handy takes the bottle away, places Erin on a cot, and tries to clean her. Robin addresses his father's corpse, "I condemn you to lie fallow without seed and the rain to fall on you and erode you and carry you away grain by grain."[274]

The final sections of the novel move quickly toward the end. Erin has gone into shock because she has recognized Robin's "soul-deep self-condemnation."[275] At home, Robin continues drinking and Bonny (Spur's wife), joins him at the table, trying to think of a way to make him put away the bottle. She asks who will look after Erin (the one thing she imagines might have an effect on him), but Robin replies he will look after Erin as he always has. When he goes up to her room to soothe her, Erin thinks that she is talking to the wind. By allowing herself this misunderstanding, she is able to confront her feelings and state things she would normally keep secret. She says that she does not dream of the wind as such a thing so masculine, "Especially a thing so prodigal with its seed."[276] Erin is beginning to face her emotions, but can only do so metaphorically.

By 8:30 on Christmas morning the family is assembled for the funeral service. Robin tells the family that Erin will not be ready in time. "His last act of protectiveness to the family had been to lock Erin in her room and lie about her condition."[277] Robin realizes that his sister is facing the pain she has kept locked inside and he cannot bear it; he downs a bottle of whiskey and finds another to share with her.

At the funeral hall, Hollis Ward begins his eulogy by announcing that his wife, Weezie, will not be able to attend the service. Deftly Dowell interweaves scenes of the service with scenes of Robin and Erin. Though Erin bares her soul to Robin he realizes "he would never be drunk enough to listen to what her eyes were trying to say."[278] Weezie appears at the church door with Murdoch's son, and she sees the outraged faces of the McChesney family. The widow "had seen Murdoch plainly in the boy's eyes and understood that her husband's blood was endless and indestructible."[279] Meanwhile, Erin and Robin, still drinking heavily, make their way outside to walk around the family grounds. Robin tries to coax her back to a happier time and asks Erin if she has plans to marry. Finally Erin finds a way to express what she has kept hidden: "You are forbidden me by the law of the land, but you are the law, you are the land, so I will marry the land."[280] Robin, now completely drunk, and Erin, lost in the past, lie in the snow and fall asleep, finding the ultimate escape in death. Robin's death is a kind of crucifixion—he dies for his sister's sins. The religious symbolism is enhanced by the knowledge of Murdoch's young son, who will take his father's place.

After the publication of Dowell's first novel, he received a letter from James Ethridge, inviting him to send biographical information for inclusion in the reference encyclopedia *Contemporary Authors*.[281] As a part of the entry, Dowell included information about his motivation as a writer:

> My motivation as a writer is refutation, so strongly so that my writing frequently rejects its own plots, themes, focal characters, emphases, before the midway point, often more than once. I write from the firmest conviction that the self-evident (including firm convictions) is ephemeral to the point of ghostliness, and that the shouted credo has no more importance than its echo.[282]

Dowell sent a copy of the novel to John Howard Griffin, who agreed to write a chapter for David Madden's forthcoming book, *Rediscoveries: Informal Essays in which Well-known Novelists Rediscover Neglected Works of Fiction by one of their Favorite Authors*. Griffin praised the novel, and after reading it he wrote in his personal journal, "The haunting pages of Coleman Dowell's novel remain with me this cold rainy day. Will it stay? Is it as good as it seems to me?"[283]About this same time A. S. Burack, editor of the Boston literary magazine *The Writer*, wrote to Dowell soliciting a piece about the process of writing. In the March 1968 edition Dowell discussed his approach to the craft, considering the differences between the short story writer and the novelist. He also voiced his recognition that the majority of authors find little financial reward. "But to write anything," Dowell indicated, "in the belief that livelihood will follow is delusional."[284] After receiving the piece Burack sent his thanks and enclosed a check for $10 in payment.

After years of struggling as a composer, playwright, and model, Coleman Dowell had reinvented himself as a novelist and he had finally found his métier. Though this first novel did not bring the financial rewards he desired, he had crafted a unique voice characterized by his use of shifting verb tense, psychological manipulation, and the southern setting of his youth. He had found a small but receptive audience. With this solid success behind him, Dowell returned to the other manuscripts he had drafted. For a short time he was able to put self-doubt behind him.

Summer vacations often meant spending time at the beach. Dowell and Slaff rented many seaside houses over the years; both men enjoyed boating and swimming, and found such trips an ideal way to dodge the heat and crowds of the city.

CHAPTER SEVEN

Shelter Island

The three years immediately following the publication of *One of the Children is Crying* were marked by extraordinary political activity and social unrest. Both the women's liberation movement and the Chicano liberation movement drew national attention. In 1967 the "Summer of Love" attracted swarms of young people to San Francisco. That same year, Martin Luther King, Jr. announced his opposition to war in Vietnam. In April 1968 King was assassinated in Memphis, Tennessee. The "Spring Mobilization to End the War in Vietnam" held rallies in New York City and San Francisco. The decade ended with the Woodstock festival and the Stonewall riots in New York City in 1969.

Coleman Dowell was as disappointed by those who claimed to speak for the new generation of revolutionaries as he was disillusioned by the novelists who were gaining favor in the literary world. He disliked Martin Luther King Jr. and he denounced counter-culture figures like Arlo Guthrie, whom he considered inarticulate and uninformed. Though he admired few of these activists Dowell was enthralled by the idea of revolution, and he began to work on a new novel that reflected the fate of artists in revolutionary terms. While observing the political situation surrounding him during the Nixon years he started to take notes for his new novel, *Mrs. October was Here*. The novel satirizes both the Nixon administration and contemporary American society, especially in the prevailing prejudice against blacks, Jews, and homosexuals. Although reluctant to join any mass movement, Dowell often wrote letters to political leaders to express his opinions. One letter, to President Gerald Ford, asked, "I wonder how it feels to pardon the man who almost brought democracy down?"[285]

* * *

In the summer of 1968 Coleman Dowell and Bertram Slaff rented a farmhouse on Smith Street, Shelter Island.[286] They had spent a good part of March looking for a summer home. Although the two men had rented many seaside houses over the years, the sprawling grounds of the farmhouse, which rented for $250 a month, suited Dowell's temperament and stimulated his imagination more than any of the others. In addition to its ocean access, the property had six acres that he could use for gardening. In spring the limbs of the pear and magnolia trees swayed with the weight of blackbirds, blue jays, and cardinals. The size of the house was perfect for entertaining overnight guests, and their neighbors on the island included the composer Jack Beeson and Dowell's literary agent, Lucy Kroll. "House is perfect dream," he wrote to Martha, "of barefoot R. C. Bobby Me."[287] The two men signed a lease to keep the house through the winter.

Dowell and Slaff took possession of the house in June 1968. The couple agreed that Dowell would spend most of his time on Shelter Island and Bertram Slaff would return on weekends from his work in the city. Early in the summer Dowell bought a set of oil paints and he and Slaff painted views of the surrounding landscape. In exchange for paying for winter storage, the couple borrowed a Boston Whaler motor boat from Joel and May Katz, friends of Slaff's who had first introduced them to Kim Hunter. In addition to the boat Dowell had a small automobile, a Fiat, which he used for outings with his dachshund Tammy to sun at Shell Beach, or for visits to the local library.

For the next eight years Coleman Dowell spent a large portion of his time on Shelter Island, gardening, entertaining visitors, and composing intricate fictional narratives. His time here would prove to be the most productive in his literary career, for he completed three novels: *Mrs. October was Here* (1974), *Island People* (1976), and *Too Much Flesh and Jabez* (1977).

Holidays, especially Thanksgiving and Christmas, were filled with activity and celebration. Slaff and Dowell held lavish parties for friends that included Maurice Sendak, Kim Hunter, and the Russian ballet dancer, Tamara Geva. Jack Beeson recalled these occasions:

> We went to dinner there quite often. Not . . . well . . . when they had parties. When we were included. In the fall, at least once, and I think two or three times . . . there was venison cooked, which took a couple of days. And *that* party was always very special, because lots of people came out from New York.[288]

The previous summer they had rented a house from Frances Adams on the north fork of Long Island. Like the other women close to him, (Ruth Landshoff York, Elizabeth Fey, and Yetta Arenstein), Adams had a strong, independent personality. She and her daughters Barbara and Jodi had a small cottage on the North Shore of Patomic Bay. Barbara, Jack Beeson recalled, was very exotic, occasionally visiting the farmhouse dressed in a sari. It was rumored that she was the Prince of Nepal's mistress and that she operated a travel agency paid for by the Prince as a cover until she was forcibly evicted from Katmandu. Frances Adams became Dowell's devoted friend and often consulted him for advice regarding her daughters.

Dowell was often alone during the week with Tammy. Living in developing isolation on the island, his active fantasy life led to jealousy of Slaff's life in the city and imagined affairs. Dowell's unbalanced state of mind mirrored the unbalance in his life: he would alternate between strict diets and binge eating, periods of sobriety interspersed with bouts of heavy drinking, and a strict routine of exercise and yoga frustrated by long periods of inactivity.

Slaff was now paying Dowell a salary of $7,000 a year for occasional secretarial work. When depression seized him, Dowell believed that Slaff loathed him and he viewed himself as a servant who kept house and cooked meals for someone who despised him. His uncertainty was aggravated by a comment Slaff made when he read portions of *Mrs. October*, "Nothing happens so far; all I can say is 'Get on with it.'" To make things worse, Tammy suffered muscle spasms and sometimes she could not move. Dowell nursed her back to health, administering ultra-sonic treatments and living in fear that his close companion might die.

As Dowell gained weight and his hairline receded, his self-perception, already at a low point, dropped considerably. This descent into self-loathing led to a need for validation and his infidelity and sexual activity grew more aggressive. In January 1969 he met Jim Hayward, a black, straight man, and invited him home for a dinner of ham and Hopping John. Hayward was often around the farmhouse and periodically agreed to have sex with Dowell in exchange for money that he used to buy marijuana. Hayward was one of a series of men, often unemployed and unskilled, that Dowell took as lovers during his years on Shelter Island. Some of these relationships provided source material for his novels.

Dowell did not hide these relationships from his Bertram Slaff, but he continued to express his commitment in their long-term relationship. Often he discussed his actions with his partner, analyzing his behavior in terms of his own self-perception. While Slaff was not happy with the arrangement, he nevertheless cared deeply for Coleman Dowell and struggled to make the relationship work.

The urge for suicide that had plagued Dowell in 1964 had also returned. Jack Beeson recalled one disturbing episode:

> I would occasionally stop by Smith Street to see Coleman in the late afternoon. One of these . . . unannounced visits was interesting to me because he was usually doing stuff around and I wasn't bothering him . . . and he was very good company. And so I would stop by and he came to the door and looked at me and then as soon as . . . he looked rather odd. And he said it almost with some relief, "Jack." I said . . . I probably said, "am I bothering you?" "No. You just saved my life."[289]

In December 1969 Dowell feigned a report of his own suicide as retribution to John Howard Griffin, who had not yet completed the promised essay on *One of the Children is Crying*. Dowell's penchant for revenge was strong, and carried with it a kind of irony that seemed to delight him. A letter from Griffin dated December 20, 1969, suggests that Dowell wrote to Griffin under the pseudonym "Mrs. Hackett," a character that would appear in his next novel, *Mrs. October was Here*. Griffin's reply to Mrs. Hackett expressed his sincere sorrow. "I am just desolated by this news," he wrote. "I have the awful feeling, judging from the fact that Coleman wanted these particular letters returned to me, that my inability to do the article on his book was a contributing factor to his depression."[290]

Two years later, in the fall of 1971 Dowell started a rumor among his friends that he was dying of leukemia. Such cruel hoaxes suggest that Dowell saw no boundaries between the fiction he created in art and the events of his daily existence. His friends, for all practical purposes, had become an audience, witnesses to the excesses of his creative imagination. Though his threats of suicide were surely real, they may have also provided the drama and tension he thought was necessary to hold their interest in his life.

Dowell kept control over these self-destructive urges through communication with other authors. Although Griffin had not completed the essay on *One of the Children is Crying* for *Rediscoveries*, he had written a letter in support of Dowell's application for a Guggenheim Fellowship.[291] About this time Dowell also started a correspondence with the Australian author, Sumner Locke Elliott, who was then living in New York. Dowell had been reading Elliott's novel, *The Man Who Got Away*, and wrote to express his admiration: "This is a book that honest people are going to find at least bits of themselves in. Parallel to the events in the book, I'm afraid that events of my own life ran . . ."[292] Elliott replied to Dowell in October, 1972, "I am delighted and thrilled at your lovely review and perception; though that may sound self congratulatory. George, oddly, didn't come out as I originally intended. I wanted him to be more attractive and picaresque."[293]

The first year in the farmhouse Dowell completed a draft of *Mrs. October was Here*, a political satire that compares the upheavals of the sixties with revolutions throughout history. Dowell considered this second novel his most original thinking, and stated that the book was "most completely" his.[294] It is a fantasy about writing, rich with black humor and philosophical speculation. Where *One of the Children is Crying* followed a fairly conventional narrative approach, *Mrs. October was Here*, composed of journal entries and "projections" written by the title character, exhibits Dowell's expanding exploration of form. The story unfolds against the backdrop of the Vietnam War, and

Dowell uses this setting to full effect. The novel's title comes from an amalgam of the October Revolution and "Kilroy was here."[295]

In some ways the book is a general indictment of war. The work contains references to the American Revolution, WWII, the October Revolution, and other historical conflicts. Dowell's struggles with anti-Semitism are also incorporated into the novel. Dowell was not reluctant to examine unpopular ideas such as those presented in a circular he purchased called "Holocaust Truth Missions" that questioned the "truth" of the Holocaust.

Finding a publisher for the book proved difficult. At the end of 1968 Dowell submitted a 116-page excerpt to his editor at Random House in hope of an advance, but the manuscript was rejected for being too mysterious. After Random House returned it he sent the manuscript to Fischer Verlag, Doubleday, Viking, and Little Brown, only to receive additional rejection letters. In all, Dowell received twenty-six rejections.[296]

Eventually *Mrs. October* was published by New Directions. The Beesons suggested that Dowell submit the manuscript to its founder James Laughlin, one of the most influential publishers of the time. In September, 1972, Dowell sent the manuscript along with a note that read in part, "The only other thing I can comment on is to say that the presence of a dachshund in everything I write—like my recurrant [sic] use of journals—is a signature, like Whistler's butterfly."[297] Laughlin took his time over the manuscript. He took care not to put Dowell off long, however, and wrote in November, "Just a line to reassure you that the intriguing Mrs. October has not disappeared into the deserts of the real Van Dieman's Land, but that I am reading her, slowly, as is my way with things that I really enjoy, and great pleasure. When something has real texture like this writing, I like to get every word, and absorb the overtones."[298]

In reply, Dowell sent Laughlin a copy of *One of the Children is Crying*. Laughlin wanted to make sure that Dowell did not have any further obligations to Random House, and when he questioned the author about Random House's potential interest in *Mrs. October*, Dowell responded,

> my editor there was impatient for it and I gave her the first 117 pages and she did not understand a word of it—an exact quote. She was wistful about what she called "narrative," and so we parted company—very gladly on my part, because Random House is too big for an unestablished writer who must be—is, by nature—experimental. I can write straight narrative like any other writer, but it does not hold my attention."[299]

Laughlin published many of Dowell's short stories in his anthology *New Directions in Prose and Poetry* (later collected in the book *The Houses of Children*), but at first he was reluctant to publish the novel, sending the manuscript instead to other publishers in Britain for consideration. Yet he assured Dowell that if those publishers turned it down, he would proceed with publication, comparing the novel to *Lolita* in its "special view of America and Americans."[300] Laughlin wanted to share composition costs with another publisher, to keep the price down for students. His marketing plan for the book took into consideration its complex nature, and he explained,

> there should be a special advance edition which would go out to a couple of hundred writers, literary opinion makers, etc, trying to solicit favorable statements about it, which would then go on the jacket of the real edition. It would be folly to emit a work of this singularity without a lot of careful buildup of this nature. The regular reviewers would either ignore it or massacre it unless intimidated by an impressive list of praise statements from good-names on the jacket. In other words, to do her justice I see Mrs. October as emerging from her egg about October of 1974 at the soonest."[301]

A series of events during the Christmas 1970 inspired Dowell to begin work on another piece that would become his most important novel, *Island People*. That holiday season Dowell invited a poet and his wife to visit for the holiday. Sections of his journal described their visit. Delighted with what he had written about the couple, he used the material from the journal to compose a short piece called "The Only Original Poet" (later renamed "The Keepsake"). A series of inter-related stories followed, and Dowell alternated work on them with

Mrs. October, occasionally submitting the shorter pieces to contests and literary magazines such as the *Virginia Quarterly*.

Work around the farm provided relief from the daily bouts of writing. In the summer Dowell planted roses, cannas, dahlias, and evergreens, and added a vegetable garden with zucchini, tomatoes, beans, melons, corn, radishes, Swiss chard and basil. He also worked on the house, hanging curtains, washing and repainting the walls. His ill feelings for the owners of the house preoccupied him. They had hired contractors to paint the house and in addition to the intrusion on his privacy, Dowell felt the men were dishonest. They would disappear for days at a time. Dowell took on much of the work himself, painting shutters and porch railings and the trim around the window screens.

After the first series of rejection letters he had received in response to *Mrs. October*, Dowell began to re-write the book. He believed that it had been turned down so frequently because it revealed his antagonistic perception of the "Jewish power structure" and parodied authors such as Norman Mailer, Philip Roth and Susan Sontag, who represented a world he longed to inhabit. During the first few months of 1972, while his friends were reading the manuscript, Dowell worked on several of the short stories that would later form the heart of *Island People*. In April of that year he included "The Keepsake," along with 25 pages of *Mrs. October* to New Directions. In August Dowell learned that New Directions would publish "The Keepsake." This encouraging news induced Dowell to continue work on *Mrs. October was Here*.

He had lofty ideas for the packaging of the novel. He wanted to include an index of the parts that an impatient reader could skip, and he wanted a song in the book, the "Tiger Song," to be included as a record with the book. The section called "Thoughts," he explained, had a variety of narrative voices, and needed to "have to look the way FLAIR magazine used to look, with paste-overs and pull-outs; some of it would look like a palimpsest (ideally) and other parts would have three layers of notes . . ." But he was realistic in his expectations, and continued, "I'm sure this is financially impossible, anyhow."[302] Instead Laughlin suggested as an alternative that they use four different typefaces to indicate whether Aurelie Angelique, Omerie, Roman, or Mrs. October is speaking.

In a letter to his editor at Random House, Lee Wright, Dowell clearly articulated his intentions for that novel. The major theme concerns the connections between revolution and the process of creativity. [303] Dowell noted that an artist must retain responsibility for those to whom he gives life. He called this novel his "atonement" for writing the deaths of his characters in *One of the Children is Crying*.[304]

Dowell struggled to capture the bigotry, boredom, and the insularity of small town America. His satirical approach included parodies of several contemporary novelists, and he willingly shared the names of those he imitated in a letter to Laughlin. "As you know, the book is full of parodies of other writers and I think the scene with Wanda and Marie Louise is still a reasonable parody of Purdy and Henry James, a good combination . . . I noticed on the copy that you originally read, in the margin beside a bit of parody writing (in the scene of Mrs. Hackett in the bookstore) that you had written 'Source'? That particular parody is of Philip Roth with a bit of Anthony Burgess thrown in (the use of parentheses—Betty)) Betty) Betty-Betty etc.)."[305] The depiction of the social fabric in the novel reflects the influence of the French philosopher, Henri Bergson, whose work examines the concept of free will. Prevalent in Bergson's philosophy is the idea that individuals must move from closed societies—which are static, mechanical and lack freedom or spontaneity—to open, progressive societies whose citizens embrace diversity and the mystic spirit. Although actions should be spontaneous rather than mechanical, Bergson believed that for most people free acts are the exception rather than the rule.[306] In Dowell's novel, *Mrs. October*, a mystical revolutionary who brings her ideas to Tasmania, had, in an earlier incarnation, been Bergson's close friend. Mrs. October attempts to test Bergson's philosophy by involving the citizens in her revolution.

Dowell was also influenced by Bergson's ideas regarding the direct, subjective experience of time versus the measured, objective mathematical time of science. Bergson sought to show that the subjective perception of time was not linear, nor infinitely divisible. In *Mrs. October was Here*, Dowell is careful not to fix the year of the story. The one fixed date is Christmas Eve, a day that holds significance in several of his novels. The prologue occurs much later than the chronological events narrated in the story. Incidents that should logically occur at a later time are sometimes foreseen at an earlier point in the tale. For example, when Bucky's bamboo cages are first mentioned in the novel, Marie Louise's daughter says that she has seen people in them. Her vision occurs before Mrs. October arrives in Tasmania, presumably before the revolutionaries have taken any prisoners (the logical occupants of the cages): the scene provides a projection of events to come.

Dowell explores notions of perceived time in a scene between Mrs. October and Aurelie Angelique:

> They could keep themselves fascinated for the length of a morning as they dueled on the following field: at what precise point, in what exact measure, does coffee with milk become the sublime café au lait?[307]

Mrs. October also pays homage to Van Vechten's 1920s novel *The Tattooed Countess*. In that book, Van Vechten examined the influence of social hierarchy on a small Midwestern American town. There are parallels between the two works that suggest *Mrs. October* was inspired by Dowell's work on the theater version of Van Vechten's novel. Dowell's novel is in many ways a modernist response to Van Vechten—reflecting on the same social themes and suggesting that the revolutions of the sixties were the direct result of the thinking that had pervaded small town America for most of the century. In *The Tattooed Countess* there is a bohemian colony much like the neighborhood in *Mrs. October* known as "The Wolf"; the Opera House plays a significant role in both novels (it is the scene of reception by the town for the two female protagonists); both novels are concerned with the effects of writing; each author describes the ramifications of prejudice; and both novels explore narrow-minded attitudes toward sexuality. *The Tattooed Countess* is written in a florid style that blankets its message. The action of the first novel takes place in 1897, near the turn of the century. Dowell's novel takes place more than a century later, "beyond the limits of the twentieth century."[308]

In Van Vechten's novel the Countess, Ella Nattatorrini, returns from Europe to her hometown of Maple Valley, Iowa, where she falls in love with a young boy named Gareth. She is received in a series of parties that culminate in a reception at the Opera House. To the citizens of the town, who are concerned with outward appearance and manners, the Countess, who wears make-up and smokes cigarettes, represents forbidden revolutionary ideas. She believes that the things one keeps hidden (like her tattoo), should be brought to light. But her modern ways have limits: her aesthetic lets her appreciate the opera, theater, and arts of the old European world. The Countess dismisses the Impressionists and praises an earlier French tradition. For Gareth, the Countess also represents the promise of spiritual escape; she helps him fulfill his yearning not to be bound by social conventions.

The Tattooed Countess is a novel of manners, but it also explores passion and sexuality. Her world is one propelled by passion, which sends "her staggering and spinning down the rough but exciting erotic highway."[309] Ultimately the Countess and Gareth seduce each other—his goal is freedom, and hers is the conquest of innocence.

In Dowell's novel Mrs. October appears in the fictional town of Tasmania, Ohio, after exchanging letters with a young boy named Bucky Jones. Bucky's first letter satirically sets the tone: he has revolutionary ideas about interior design and he mentions that the houses in Tasmania are from the Revolutionary period. Bucky represents the modern world, and his aesthetic is one of mixed metaphors and harsh realities exemplified by his interior designs.

From the beginning Dowell establishes the social barriers that exist in the town. Tasmania represents everything he disliked about small-town America. The citizens are narrow-minded, uneducated, and middle class. Bucky describes the citizens of the town to Mrs. October in his letters, and she determines from them that Tasmania is ready for a revolution. She uses the information in his letters to prepare "projections" (future predictions) about the key citizens of the town. Shortly after her arrival Mrs. October invites the citizens of Tasmania to the Opera House to discuss her plans.

In both novels, characters display their lack of education and refinement by mispronouncing or misusing French. To show that they are cosmopolitan, the ladies of Maple Valley use the expression *fin de siecle* to mean "fashionable," and Clara Barnes pronounces "Marguerite, ce n'est plus toi" phonetically as "Margareeta, see nest plus toy."[310] Dowell's characters argue about French pronunciation, and Aurelie Angelique, like Priscilla in *One of the Children is Crying*, finds that speaking in French provides a way to shield herself from others.

Both *The Tattooed Countess* and *Mrs. October was Here* are concerned with the process and uses of writing. In *The Tattooed Countess* the character Miss Jelliffe is the society columnist who reduces the events involving the countess to descriptions of costume and décor. Gareth, who aspires to become a writer, arranges and foresees his future, much as Mrs. October predicts her own future and the future of others. What Van Vechten's writer observes is the exterior appearance, the decorative dress and social manner. The Countess wears her notoriety like a pendant. Dowell's writers, on the other hand, try to puzzle out inner secrets. The theme of the writer inventing others would become a common one in Dowell's fiction.

It is worth noting that several themes from *One of the Children is Crying* appear in *Mrs. October*: social hierarchy, the notion of outer versus interior wounds, and crucifixion. In both novels Dowell creates characters who have scarred faces: Bucky has been burned by his mother, and this outer wound is similar to Luke's wounds in *One of the Children is Crying*. Homosexuality, represented in the first novel by Millicent, is more explicitly represented in the second novel by the character of Omerie Chad, who at first glance seems to fit a cliché, but is accepted readily by the community and seduces the police chief and other men of the town. When Omerie discovers Mrs. October's study he replaces the projection she has written for him with one of his own in which he finds success and restored youth.

Dowell talked extensively about the process of writing and he provided insight into his novels in interviews with editor John O'Brien and English professors John and Linda Kuehl. In his conversation with John O'Brien, Dowell noted, "I write about people writing. In *Mrs. October was Here* everybody is writing about everybody else."[311] When O'Brien asked how he began the novel, Dowell responded,

> I was thinking very much about the revolution that was trying to happen in America during the 1960s and I wondered whether there is any relation between revolution and creativity, where they come together and where revolution becomes the opposite of creative. And what art would be like in a country that had had a successful "revolution." What would be the latitude of creativity? I know that I wouldn't be allowed to write as I do, not for a second, in Russia.[312]

It was an interesting time to consider revolution and its relationship to artistic creation. In 1970 Susan Sontag (whom Dowell parodies in the novel) wrote an introduction to *The Art of Revolution* in which she discussed the relationship of printing and mass production to revolution. Her essay considers the effect revolution had on the production of poster art in Cuba and the role an artist has in a society changed by revolution. Revolutionary art, she says, must be "reduced (and experienced) collectively."[313] This becomes a significant theme in Dowell's novel when he has Mrs. October produce her art in the theater where all the citizens of Tasmania can experience it.

On the surface, the revolution in Tasmania is a non-violent one. Two characters, Mrs. October and Roman (a character based loosely on Norman Mailer) evoke change through language: Roman through his speeches and Mrs. October through her written projections. In addition, Mrs. October has all of the citizens act out their emotions on stage, and this role-play effects change. Mrs. October creates a series of theater pieces on the stage of the Opera House (what she refers to as 'the world stage'), and later at the scene of her crucifixion.

One is tempted to sympathize with her cause. But Dowell gives us glimpses into the unpleasant underside of the revolution. "Mrs. O's horrors are meant to be horrors," Dowell noted, "and I ask the reader to hate them with me."[314] There is a suggestion that bodies are taken from the nursing home to be used for sausage and shoe leather; the death of Omerie and his dog is written as a violent one, and Mrs. October's participation in the revolution leads to her crucifixion. The writer as revolutionary, by baring her soul, is exposing her beliefs to criticism, resulting in her crucifixion.

In the interview with John and Linda Kuehl, Dowell described *Mrs. October was Here* as the story of a revolution in which diary provides a second narrative. In the novel, he breaks down the creative personality into components: revolutionary, counter-revolutionary, and "spy and freak." Mrs. October's "characters embody various aspects of the creative personality."[315] Dowell emphasized his view of the characters in the novel, especially Aurelie Angelique, who is a black woman and a revolutionary who "at the end . . . is getting out of these roles."[316] When asked to identify the first person narrator, Dowell identified himself.

In his article "Pushy Jews and Aging Queens," poet and literary critic Thom Gunn sees social and psychological hate at the center of *Mrs. October was Here*. Gunn links *Mrs. October* with *Island People* in this exploration of hatred. He also links the two works thematically, and through Dowell's narrative strategies, based on an indirect storytelling method. He suggests that under rulers such as the Tudors and Joseph Stalin, historians have altered the past, and this then affects the future. By writing about the future Mrs. October causes it. Mrs. October's goal is to eliminate hatred: she wants the town to concentrate its hatred on one thing (in this case on her), then destroy that thing, thus destroying hatred. Gunn sees difficulties with the characterization of Mrs. October, who has participated in other revolutions, but has not learned the vital lesson that such insurrection teaches: revolutions ultimately fail.

Gunn writes extensively about Dowell's depiction of Jews in the novel. Wanda asks Darthy Redstone (described as "the pushy, vulgar, greedy Jew"), to help her get rid of her hate for "Hebrew persons." Dowell shows a contempt for anti-Semitism, yet exhibits it at the same time. Mrs. October tells Aurelie Angelique to present her as an anti-Semite, so her book will be a bestseller (a dig at contemporary novelists like Philip Roth and Norman Mailer), yet her pet project was to bring more Jews to Tasmania. For Gunn, this kind of contradiction demarcates Dowell's fiction. As Gunn notes, "Anti-Semitism is the perfect paradigm for social self-hatred."[317]

Mrs. October was Here was rejected more than twenty-six times. Carol Rinzler, an editor at Charterhouse Books, wrote in response to one submission:

> I'm certain that you do not need to be told that the quality of the writing is, to my mind at any rate, extraordinary. I suppose it is in the nature of an experimental novel such as this is, to be able to read on for several pages with a feeling of being lost, and yet read on because the prose is so remarkably compelling.[318]

Surprisingly, reviews for *Mrs. October was Here* were meager and from rather obscure sources. Nevertheless, this novel was Dowell's favorite. It attracted the attention of Peter Kaldheim, editor of the literary magazine *Edgeworks*, who wrote:

> I think we need to have more writing with the energy and imagination of MRS. OCTOBER WAS HERE. I would like very much to publish some of your fiction and feel confident that you will be pleased by our handling of any piece you might care to submit.[319]

Dowell also received praise from the critic Josef Dignan:

> I loved most of the characters in "Mrs. O," and even the unpleasant ones were so wittily & grippingly realized that they compelled interest whether one liked their personalities or not. I thought Bucky was one of the most slashingly cruel—yet ultimately compassionate "portraits" I've ever seen . . .[320]

In reply to the lack of reviews Laughlin wrote words of encouragement: "But don't lose heart, and don't be discouraged, 'Mrs. October' will be famous in the end, I am positive about it. She has what it takes, and so do you."[321] Dowell's response gives some indication of the anger he felt:

> That is quite a bonus of a letter from you. I'm awfully pleased to have it, and really moved to have you write as you do about OCTOBER, because there are some elements of nightmare about such total silence. A month after my first book appeared I had had fifteen provincial reviews, ten of them featured with headlines, and the Dublin Times and the Times Lit Sup. In Britain had both praised it, I

> thought, inordinately. Now, you know and I know that OCTOBER is so superior to the first book that there is simply no comparison, and it is almost degrading to know that that is WHY the new book is getting a cold shoulder.[322]

Dowell checked the local bookstores periodically to see whether or not the book was in stock. J B Lippincott Company distributed the books for New Directions, but there was a release problem at Lippincott and the clothbound copies weren't sent off to the stores and wholesalers on time. Furious, Dowell dashed off a nasty letter to Laughlin which read:

> I hate to have to bring this up, but there it is—the book itself is still not available in Louisville despite having been ordered by bookstores in early April. Nor is it available in New York at such as the Madison Avenue Bookshop, though friends of mine ordered it through them on April the 2nd. That is no jinx, but woeful mismanagement on the part of Lippincott. Finally books ordered in late March from the Greenport bookshop, just across the ferry from this Island, turned up last week.[323]

Happy at least that it had finally been published, Dowell was inspired to continue *Island People*. He had also begun a fourth novel, *Too Much Flesh and Jabez*, which would be his first full-length work dealing with homosexuality. Long before *Mrs. October* was published he had entered into a series of disastrous affairs. Though both he and Slaff had agreed that they would close the farmhouse at the end of every summer, by 1971 Dowell was spending late autumn and early winter there. In November of that year Dowell moved the boats into the barn just in time for the first snow. He got permission from the owners to order new storm doors and windows. Back in Manhattan, Bertram Slaff, whose recent stock investments had begun to soar, was looking for a new apartment.

CHAPTER EIGHT

Island People

In a journal entry dated March 17, 1968, Coleman Dowell briefly mentioned work on a piece that he referred to as "Webster." "Whenever thoughts of Webster and Victor come across my mind," he wrote, "I tremble in a kind of fear beyond fear: because of the work involved in evolving them." Webster's experiences with a Puerto Rican boy named Victor represent Dowell's first struggle with material that would form his most acclaimed novel, *Island People.* The story took a different direction from the traditional narrative form he used *in One of the Children is Crying.* With "Webster" Dowell began to explore more complex structures and to delight in more suggestive uses of language, focusing his attention on short stories that emphasized character development over plot.

As he polished these difficult pieces, Dowell shared them with his partner Bertram Slaff and friends like Maurice Sendak and Lore Segal, whose honest appraisals encouraged him to continue working in this new direction. Many of the stories from this period are autobiographical and reveal much about Dowell's life on Shelter Island. He culled material from the islanders and from his frequent visitors and used descriptions of them to create many of his characters. Other stories were based on older relationships such as his friendship with Carl Van Vechten, whom he spoofed in a section called "Up at Claudo's." Dowell readily acknowledged the models for a few characters (like his friends Jack and Nora Beeson), while the names of those he pictured in a less flattering light he shared only with close friends.

A few of the stories that Dowell crafted at this time evolved out of romantic liaisons. Although he and Bertram Slaff had an enduring commitment and an affectionate relationship, Dowell considered himself "amoral and promiscu-

From 1968 to 1976 Coleman Dowell spent the majority of his time on Shelter Island. He had a small Fiat, which he used for outings with his dachshund Tammy to sun at Shell Beach, or for visits to the local library.

ous"[324] and he frequently found the need to seek out short-lived affairs that he used for raw material in his works. But it would be inaccurate to suggest that his only motivation was inspiration. His need for admiration, companionship, and sex were strong catalysts for his conduct. These affairs also offered a sense of independence that Dowell could not find in any other way. Financially and emotionally dependent on his partner of eighteen years, Dowell needed to believe that he had some control over his own circumstances.

One early story, a haunting piece entitled "The Birthmark," narrates one of Dowell's most painful relationships. In July 1971 a friend introduced him to a young man named Bob, a bank auditor from Noyac, whose dark-hair and well-dressed appearance both impressed and attracted the older writer. Dowell described Bob as "ideally handsome, strong faced, even a trifle rugged, a perfect nose, wonderful eyes, madeira colored . . ."[325] He invited Bob to the farmhouse for a photography session that culminated in lovemaking. Dowell's lengthy journal entries about the affair suggest that this was one of the first times since he fell in love with Slaff that he willingly entered a relationship based, not just on pure sexual gratification, but also on a strong emotional attraction.

One of Bob's most interesting physical aspects was a large birthmark that "covered his back . . . and one leg from hip to knee with splotches on the other leg." Dowell described Bob as "a pied little pony, a dappled centaur . . ."[326] who spent most nights at the farmhouse. The younger man's admiration and attention boosted Dowell's ego, for the writer often fretted about his age, his weight, and his physical appearance. The couple planned trips to Vermont, New Hampshire, and Manhattan, yet the affair was tinged with tears and recriminations. Bob was jealous of Dowell's relationship with Slaff and of his celebrity. Dowell considered the younger man sentimental and destructive. They would argue and part, then Bob would return to make amends and spend the night again.

Although Bertram Slaff knew about the affair, he refrained from discussing it. On those occasions when he came to stay at the farmhouse, Dowell would see Bob in secret. Most of the time Slaff stayed in Manhattan where he was busy looking at apartments, and in November he found an enticing opportunity, an apartment on Fifth Avenue that was reasonably priced and had an affordable monthly maintenance fee. Financially, the timing was perfect. Slaff's initial $5,000 investment in Electronics, Missiles and Communications stock had grown to nearly $100,000, and he had recently received a check for $50,000 from a hedge fund investment, so Slaff decided to invest some of the money in real estate.

Dowell indicated that he would like to close the Shelter Island house for the winter and move back to New York once the real estate purchase was final. Though he often declared that his affair with Bob was over, it continued for almost a year and Dowell remained in the farmhouse for most of the winter. When he learned that Bob was seeing another man, Dowell, too, became jealous. His infatuation led him to visit Bob's lover Vincent in California, and they began a separate affair that lasted for almost two years.

"The Birthmark," based on his relationship with Bob, reveals much about the psychological dilemma Dowell faced as a writer and as a gay man. The character based on Bob is a 34-year old man named Low whose birthmark matches the description in Dowell's journal. Low begins a relationship with an older writer named Chris (modeled after Dowell), who lives on an unnamed island. The story turns on the Platonic idea that all objects are copies of an ideal, and all have imperfections. To most people, Low seems perfect until his birthmark is revealed. But Chris does not acknowledge the imperfection. Low takes this to mean that either Chris denies its existence, or is blind to it. In either case, it is a rejection of the symbol Low has come to see as his defining quality.

Dowell was still at work on *Mrs. October was Here* at this time and he incorporated several themes from that novel into "The Birthmark." Low is a victim, a theme that plays an important role in *Mrs. October*. Low compares his birthmark to the marks of a young fawn that cannot be hunted until it loses its youthful markings. Once the dappled spots are gone, it becomes potential prey. Dowell also uses the birthmark to introduce the anti-Semitic tone of *Mrs. October*, when he compares the birthmark to the star worn by Jews in Nazi Germany.

Ultimately, Low's physical scar is not the birthmark of the story's title. Chris indicates that everyone has a flaw, and the writer's is his need to render the events of his life in fiction in order to understand them. Dowell explained, "Chris's birthmark is much greater than Low's. Chris's is the one, the birthmark, of the title: that coldness and terrible, passionless curiosity."[327] In November, 1973, Laughlin gave a lecture at Colgate University. The second day was devoted to fiction that had appeared in *New Directions* 27, and he decided to introduce "The Birthmark" as part of his talk. Laughlin wrote to ask Dowell for "any particular points" the author might want him to make about it, to help stimulate student discussion. Dowell quickly replied,

> "In that story . . . I was equally fascinated with Chris' birthmark and rather think that it is the hidden one that the title refers to. Of course, this is my old theme of artist-as-user, rather more violently expressed in 'I Envy You Your Great Adventure.' But the story actually began because I wanted to know, or try to know, what such an affliction would feel like, for it was meant to be a step toward compassion in the development of 'Island People.'"[328]

After the class Laughlin was pleased to tell Dowell that the students "liked 'The Birthmark' by far the best of the five stories which we talked about, and their comments on it were extremely interesting. They were particularly interested and stirred up by what you had written about the concept of the artist as user, and the discussion really got centered on that, as well as on the implications of the two 'levels' of 'Birthmark.'"[329]

The affair with Bob was not the only relationship that made its way into Dowell's novel. Over the next few years he entered into a series of affairs that formed material for *Island People*; Dowell dedicated one section of the book to two of these men, Ephraim and Schlomo, whose relationship he fictionalized in "Midsummer Sextet." As he fictionalized these romantic entanglements, Dowell found that the focus of the novel was increasingly homosexual, and this caused him some consternation. In March, 1974 he wrote to Laughlin,

> One thing I am most emphatically not pleased with—which shows up more in the excerpts in the Anthologies than in the book itself—and that is what seems

> to be a overweighted "queer" tone. I dislike specialized writing, whether it's black, Jewish, or whatever—*limiting*, if that word has any meaning at all."[330]

Dowell's original intention may have been to publish *Island People* as an anthology of short stories. Josef Dignan, book critic for the Louisville *Courier-Journal*, wrote to Dowell to clarify his understanding of the work. "I had originally stated that 'Island People' is to be a novel," Dignan wrote, "but Joyce told me, no, it's to be short stories."[331]

Between 1973 and 1975 James Laughlin, who was still considering the best strategy for releasing *Mrs. October was Here*, published several sections of *Island People* in *New Directions in Prose and Poetry*. The publication dates provide some insight into the development of the novel. *New Directions #26* (1973) included "The Keepsake," the story that became the first chapter of the novel. *New Directions #27* (1973) contained "The Birthmark." "First Person Biography" appeared in 1974 (#29).

In that issue, dated October 1974, Laughlin also published a short piece by a British novelist, Martin Bax, editor of the English quarterly *Ambit*. Laughlin chose an excerpt from Bax's new novel *The Hospital Ship*. Dowell admired the excerpt and at the encouragement of Laughlin he wrote a letter to Bax, praising *The Hospital Ship* and requesting a subscription to *Ambit*. When Bax traveled to New York the two authors met and later Bax published an excerpt from *Island People*, "I am the Beast." Dowell became a frequent contributor to the quarterly in the following years.

The last section of *Island People* to be published separately by New Directions was "Victor," in 1975 (#30). As the novel progressed Dowell linked the shorter pieces by creating an unnamed character (the internal "author" of the stories) whose own narrative frames the others. As a work of postmodern fiction, *Island People* resonates with multiple literary sources and allusions. Dowell borrows or refers extensively to both American and European classics. Most important are his use of Gothic elements, his emphasis on the classical

Greek concept of *xenia* (hospitality) that echoes Homer's *Odyssey*, and his references to the novel by Icelandic writer Halldór Laxness entitled *Independent People*.

The idea of a haunted place sits at the heart of *Island People*, which is filled with elements of the New Gothic, a literary genre, according to Patrick McGrath, that explores "the way in which the past inhabits the present, the way in which the past condemns the present, haunts and tortures, the sense of a looming and often malignant influence that the past exerts on the present."[332] Seven untitled segments of *Island People* involve the ghost of a murderer who occupied the farmhouse in the 19th century.

Dowell's work is a complex, horrifying tale filled with puzzles, enigmas, and ambiguities. The novel is made up of stories, letters, journal entries and poetry. Like *Mrs. October*, the work itself comments on the novel form as characters become narrators who invent other characters. The narrators are unreliable and hard to identify. The names used in *Island People* provide no anchor, for the characters morph one into the other. There are, however, several devices Dowell relies on to delineate shifting characters and temporal perspectives. These are:

visual symbols that demarcate text (such as change in typeface)
descriptive terms ("my lady" versus "Ms. Gold" as names for the dachshund)
temporal headings to indicate a shift in narrative perspective (February, March)
association of structural elements with characters (prose/poem/diary/song)

Dowell was concerned with the psychological insight he could bring to his characters and *Island People* explores the anxiety and paranoia that might result when one suffers from isolation. The narrator, a middle-aged, gay playwright, moves to a farmhouse on an island where he spends time writing stories and keeping a diary. He has left New York to seek refuge from the violence of the city. His only companion is a dachshund he refers to as "my lady." From the beginning of his stay on the island, the narrator is taunted by the noise of hunters outside his window.

The novel begins with an account of a visit from friends, Jeremiah and Beatrix, but the reader soon learns this account is actually a short story. To quell his loneliness the narrator has invented Beatrix, his female alter ego. Unlike Dante's Beatrice, who brings Dante to a state of divine love through her compassion, Dowell's Beatrix drives the narrator to madness. There is the suggestion of androgyny, expressed in the cover illustration, which shows the superimposition of male and female—as Dowell explained, "trying to make them merge."[333] In his article "Exorcism and Grace: a Study of Androgyny in *Island People*," Stephen-Paul Martin compares Dowell's narrator to Tiresias, the blind seer from Greek mythology whose story is retold in *The Waste Land*. Martin provides a convincing argument for linking this balance between male and female to "a final state of Grace."[334]

Many critics consider *Island People* Dowell's finest achievement. Among those who praised the book was the playwright Tennessee Williams, who said the novel "attains a level of prose writing which is hardly distinguishable from a long, marvelously sustained narrative poem." Williams continued, "I suspect that it is a work in a genre of his own creation . . . moreover, it demonstrates how naturally a work of art can be both pure and sensual, both richly human and faultlessly tasteful."[335]

Critics have disagreed on some aspects of the novel's structure. Where the Kuehls see an "organizing voice" which provides authorial control, Christopher Sorrentino finds that voice lacking. He writes, "there is no point in the book at which there is any intrusion that might attest to the presence of the author."[336]

Island People has been compared to Italian author Italo Calvino's *If on a winter's night a traveler* (1979), a later novel which also uses embedded stories and comments on the act of writing. Like *If on a winter's night a traveler*, the reader has an expectation that the story will move forward, but this expectation is constantly thwarted by the beginning of a new story. The juxtaposition of first, second and third person voices enhances this sense of fragmentation. And yet the novel has an overarching unity, which only emerges toward the end of the novel. As Dowell indicated, "There are things in the first paragraph that set up the last sentence."[337]

The book is a novel rich in dual meanings, beginning with the title, which refers first to those who live on the island, but also echoes Dowell's major theme: the idea that certain people are themselves islands, separated from the mainland of human contact. Throughout the novel section titles illustrate this duality. *Island People* is organized into three major sections, "The Game," "Caught," and "The Sentence." The section heading "The Game" suggests the play between the narrator and his creation, Beatrix, who take turns writing the narrative, but "game" has a more significant meaning given the context and the events at the end of the novel: Dowell refers to the hunters, clearly intending to identify the characters of the novel as "hunted." (The game, started by Beatrix, is similar to a game of chess. However it is not an even match, for the moves do not alternate equally between the two players). "Caught" indicates 'trapped' as well as 'hooked'; "The Sentence" suggests both imprisonment and the act of writing; "May Day" implies a physical date as well as the term for "help."

"The Game" takes place on the island, between Christmas Eve and February 19th, beginning with the initial short story, "The Keepsake," which introduces Beatrix and lays out the game the two narrators play. Beatrix and the narrator take turns authoring journal entries, carrying on a dialogue, and their distinctive styles and address allow the reader to distinguish between them.

The reader's first challenge is to puzzle out the narrator or point of view for each of the many-layered sections. One might approach the novel as a series of stories presented by one unnamed narrator, or view it as a dialogue between two aspects of the narrator's psyche. Like other works of postmodern fiction, Dowell provides clues that suggest a strategy for reading the novel. First, he carefully describes the difference between the narrator's style and that of Beatrix, and gives a further clue in the fact that each writer uses a different name for the dachshund: Beatrix refers to the dog as "Miss Gold" or the "bitch" while the narrator uses the designation "my lady." The narrator refers to himself solely with the first person pronoun; however, Beatrix identifies him as "Chris." In the opening section, ISLAND PEOPLE, the author describes the book to come, which will take the form of a diurnal narrative written in third person, journal entries in the first person, a "translation of experience" written in all persons, and a nocturnal narrative. There are also typographic clues: an ornate Victorian symbol and a change in typeface indicate the ongoing ghost story; sections written in italics, or whose titles are in CAPS, are authored by Beatrix. Finally, the characters occasionally address messages to each other directly.

Dowell used the expression "Chinese boxes" to describe the interrelationship of Chris and Beatrix. This metaphor of nested objects reflects the idea that the two characters live inside each other's skulls. Beatrix and the narrator take turns writing, and what results is a series of stories interspersed with journal entries, letters, and poetry.

In the ensuing section, "Caught," the journal entries express the months passing: February, March, April and May. The narrator tries to hang on to reality by fixing the date, but Beatrix cleverly interrupts by moving the date ahead with one misplaced entry for June. The majority of "Caught" consists of stories written by Beatrix, interspersed with the ghost narrative. Her stories are: "Chris"; "Midsummer Sextet"; "The Birthmark"; "To The Dark Tower"; "Victor"; and "Up At Claudo's/A Remembrance." The interwoven ghost story is written by the narrator. The journal entries span the months of February through May and end on May Day.

Each of Beatrix' stories represents a series of couplings, examining the nature of sex and the control that one person holds over another. As the narrator's alter ego, Beatrix writes stories which emphasize his own isolation. Her main character is Chris, a poet whose life on the Island is characterized by solitude. "Nowhere in his new life," the reader learns, "was there a thought or wish for another person."[338] There is a bitter irony in this isolation, for each of the other narratives involving Chris center on his sexual relationships with others: Sabra and Efraim in "Midsummer Sextet"; Low in "The Birthmark"; Victor in the story of the same name; and Miriam in "Up At Claudo's." The unnamed narrator interrupts these erotic tales with brief sections of his ghost story, each of which is immediately followed by a dated journal entry.

Each of the seven untitled pieces that comprise the ghost story is preceded by a small woodcut symbol—a Victorian pattern of leaves on a vine that form an elegant square. The ghosts in this narrative form a second series of "Chinese boxes." The unnamed narrator is haunted, not only by his alter ego Beatrix, but also by the ghost of a farmer/sailor who himself is haunted by the ghost of his stepmother. The sailor's presence is evoked by the sight of a child's tin lamp, an object that "propels Chris back to the nineteenth century . . ." reminiscent, Dowell explained, of "Proust's madeleine."[339] This nineteenth century narrative relates the events of the sailor's boyhood, his mother's death, his father's remarriage, and the stepmother's murder at the hands of her stepson.

The final major section of the novel, "The Sentence," occurs over Memorial Day and the day after, and again the passing of time is indicated by the headings: "Morning," "Night," "Morning," "2 a.m.," and "p.m." The diurnal and nocturnal narratives are divided by short stories: "I Am The Beast"; First-Person Biography" parts I, II, and III, another section of the ghost story, "The Surgeon," "Spring!" and the final section of the ghost story, written by the narrator. These short stories explore the psychological hold one person can have over another and examine the manipulation that can result from such power.

"The Surgeon" narrates a mass murder in which the surgeon shoots every person on the Island, murders his own family, and commits suicide. The story is followed by "Spring!," another journal entry by the unnamed narrator that reveals the chilling result of his duality. Clues in "Spring!" suggest that the mass murder narrated in "The Surgeon" has in fact actually taken place: the unnamed narrator remarks that the post office is inexplicably closed and the usual noon sirens from the firehouse have not blared. The unnamed narrator and Beatrix have become one through the voice of Chris. Of this character Dowell said, "I don't like Chris but I like his search for himself and I like his cathartic act of writing that mass murder."[340]

New Directions announced the publication of *Island People* in April 1976, describing the work as "an allegorical fiction—largely in the form of private journal entries and short stories exchanged in a literary duel—that chronicles a bitter, defeated man's journey toward emotional tranquility."[341]

Most reviewers remarked on the fragmentary nature of the novel, and quoted the line, "All there is, is fragments, because a man, even the loneliest of the species, is divided among several persons, animals, worlds."[342] In his review of *Island People*, John Kuehl points out that it "seems fitting that Dowell's dominant storytellers are a 'failed playwright' (protagonist) and a 'New Novelist' (Beatrix) because the inaccuracies both purvey characterize 'the process of Art.'"[343] Kuehl examines the contradictions inherent in the novel, such as the delineation of "bad" and "good" represented respectively by Beatrix and Miss Gold and the tension between the book's comic and tragic aspects. He points out that in addition to the book's many literary references, there are frequent passages that remark on the process of creation.

Edmund White's review highlights the interplay between the book's structure and its content. White points out that the multiple documents allow the novelist to "assemble his own shadowy, insular feelings."[344] White sees the secondary characters like Else, Sabra, and Miriam Webster as guises of Beatrix, while the narrator is represented in the roles of Claudo and Chris. White captures the complexity created by these multiple personalities: "no single character stays put and assumes a definite existence except Miss Gold, the dachshund. Everyone is someone else."[345] Jim Marks further considers the ramifications of the authorial voice. "What bridges," Marks asks, "can a man, alone, writing, erect between himself and the world; to what extent, to use one of Dowell's images, can he turn an island into a peninsula?"[346]

In "Some Remarks on *Island People*" Gilbert Sorrentino sees the act of writing presented in the book as both an act of salvation and one of exorcism of "the ghost of self."[347] The artificial nature of fiction is nowhere more clearly conveyed than in the fact that *Island People* is a book within *Island People*. Sorrentino explains this as "Dowell's commentary on the novel as a closed system."[348] And in "Time Frames: Temporality and Narration in Coleman Dowell's Island People," Ursula K. Heise examines the narrative structure of the novel in relationship to its multiple frames. Heise concludes that the novel "takes the process of narrative framing to its limits, projecting, in a movement of inverted *mise en abyme*, its own frame into itself."[349]

Dowell had read Halldór Laxness' novel *Independent People* and praised it to his friend Isabella Fey in 1954. Although it would be incorrect to say that there is a direct correlation between *Island People* and *Independent People*, Dowell's title suggests a kind of homage to Laxness' work, and there are some interesting similarities.[350] First, there is the importance in both works of revealing the individual separated from society. "A man who lives on his own land," Laxness writes, "is an independent man."[351] "He later continues, "Independence is the most important thing of all in life. I say for my part that a man lives in vain until he is independent. People who aren't independent aren't people."[352] Dowell's narrator does not want this independence. As Dowell described it, he is "one man writing about every aspect of himself and trying to become a peninsula because he's so tired of being an Island."[353]

The narrators of both books refer to their dogs as "bitch," and these dogs serve as their most important companions. "The dog padded along beside him in blissful anticipation," Laxness writes, "And whenever she was a few yards ahead of her master, she would halt and look back at him with eyes full of an unwavering faith, then return to him on a big curve. Her reverence for her master was so great that she did not presume even to walk ahead of him . . ."[354] and, "as soon as he halted the dog came fawning upon him. She stuck her slim muzzle between his hard paws, resting it there and wagging her tail and all her body, and the man gazed at the animal philosophically for awhile, savouring, in the submissiveness of his dog, the consciousness of his own power, the rapture of command, and sharing, for a second, in human nature's loftiest dream, like a general who looks over his troops and knows that with a word he can send them into the charge."[355] In *Island People*, the narrator's only companion is his dachshund, who exhibits the same attention and faith in her master.

The section headings in *Island People* are similar to those Laxness used in *Independent People*. Some of Laxness' headings are "Winter Morning," "Day," and "Evening." Similarly in *Island People* Dowell uses section headings to indicate periods of time, hours of the day, and months of the year. Finally, both authors were interested in exploring the realm of haunted places. In Laxness' novel, the narrator's wife Rosa says, "Everybody with second sight says this place is haunted."[356] The story in *Island People* entitled "Chris" begins, "that first winter on the Island was haunted from its onset . . ."[357]

Island People also shares several important parallels with the Greek epic poem, *The Odyssey*. Though often discussed as an essential element of postmodern fiction, the framing device Dowell used was a standard feature of narrative fiction and poetry that can be traced to Homer, who emphasizes the art of the story teller in the *Odyssey*, sometimes letting Odysseus narrate his own adventures in the epic's story-within-a-story structure.

A more important parallel is Dowell's emphasis on the classical Greek concept of *xenia*. Elisabeth Vandiver has defined the term *xenia* in relationship to its root, as a reciprocal relationship between two *xenoi*—a word with a multitude of meanings that include *guest, host, stranger, friend,* and *foreigner*. According to Vandiver *xenia*, usually translated as a "guest-host relationship," is based not on friendship but rather on obligation. Ancient Greeks revered the sanctity of this relationship and this is of key importance for understanding the *Odyssey* and the characters of *Telemachos* and the suitors.[358] It also plays an essential role in *Island People*.

In Dowell's novel the narrator is both a stranger and a guest on the island. He also serves both as physical host to those who visit him and spiritual host to the ghosts that haunt him. His hospitality has stringent limits, shown in the opening section of the book, when his two guests violate the rules of *xenia* by littering the house, arguing with their host, and providing no reciprocal signs of gratitude. Almost every section of the novel involves an examination of this guest/host relationship, culminating in the most heinous violation—the final act of murder.

Two other connections to Homer's epic poem are briefly worth noting. Odysseus has an old scar that ultimately allows his old servant to recognize him and welcome him back into his household. Scars are significant in *Island People*, too, as a way to recognize an individual's true self. In addition, the fact that the narrator of *Island People* remains unnamed echoes the story of the Cyclops, tricked by Odysseus into thinking he has been blinded by *Outis*—or, *Nobody*.

In his interview with John O'Brien, Dowell provided one interpretation for the novel.

> The book is about a man putting himself through a great cross section of experience and finally committing that mass murder, which is all prepared from the very beginning.... The most essential thing to understand ... is that there are all those reflections; it's full of mirrors ... this man has been alone for two years in a house filled with telephones that never rang and where occasionally music blared out of the windows. But totally alone. He hadn't had any of the visitors or any of the lovers he wrote about.[359]

When the novel was published in 1976, *Island People* brought Dowell critical success, yet it did not generate extensive sales. Many contemporaries, including John Kuehl and Gilbert Sorrentino (who both taught the novel in postmodern literature classes), Ihab Hassan, and Walter Abish, praised the book. One acquaintance of long standing, James Purdy, wrote to Dowell about *Island People*:

> I borrowed *Island People* from Joyce as I couldn't bear waiting until next month to read it.... I'd like to tell you that you make more demands of me than any previous author.[360]

Critics compared the novel to T. S. Eliot's *The Wasteland* due to its complex, shifting points of view. Edmund White's review in the *New York Times* called it "a work of art" and said that Dowell had "evidenced courage and invention in creating a work of art so original and difficult as to be alive to baffling and baffled perceptions."[361]

These reviews brought Dowell national recognition, but his application for the Guggenheim award was rejected. Although he was deeply disappointed, he continued to work on other short pieces which were regularly published in *New Directions* and *Ambit*, including "I Envy You Your Adventure," "If Beggars were Horses," "Singing in the Clump," "The Moon, the Owl, my Sister," "I am the Beast," and "The Drought Ends."

Just prior to the publication of *Island People* Dowell and Slaff decided to give up the house on Shelter Island for good. Dowell felt that his descriptions of the islanders were particularly unflattering and the revelation of his homosexuality, which would be apparent in the similarities between his life and that of the narrator in the book, may have been a catalyst for his decision. "The Island has gotten too crowded for me," he complained.[362] Back in the city he had already established a wide social circle and his contacts in the literary world embraced his work. So in May 1976 he left Shelter Island for good. He looked forward to returning to New York, but with a kind of sad regret he described his final days at the farmhouse:

> This Island is a kind of paradise—when the summer people have gone and if you are able to ignore the Islanders—a big order, but one I am able to take and execute. Therefore, with only one day of the month left to go, I praise it for the return to health it has afforded me, for the modest work accomplished in its benevolent air; and I offer once again my thanks to this simple, sweet and lovely house for being the only real refuge I have on this earth; and yet that has for me no poignant overtones: how many people have even one refuge? I have more, actually: this house, and the inner spaces of myself, and the inner-outer spaces of myself with Tam and Bert.[363]

Bertram Slaff had redecorated the apartment on Fifth Avenue and Dowell had come to appreciate the fact that it was also his home. With the publication of three novels, he was now part of a wider literary circle and many of those who admired his books, including Edmund White and John Kuehl, offered friendship and fellowship in what Dowell must have seen as a formidable circle. Leaving Shelter Island was tinged with sadness, but he could now return to New York with a sense of accomplishment that he had never achieved in the theater.

CHAPTER NINE

Return to the City

Among his wide circle of friends Coleman Dowell was celebrated for his culinary skills as well as his literary talents. Maurice Sendak alluded to Dowell's passion for cooking in his children's book, *In the Night Kitchen*, which contains an illustration of a bottle, labeled "Cole's Orange Flower Water."[364] Sendak had been working on the book since 1969, when he had written to Dowell to ask:

> I have a favor to ask. Could you write to me—just words—about what goes into baking a bread & a cake—I don't need it like a cook book—just the words—the utensils—the ingredients. My book has something to do with a kid that gets baked & I want it to be right![365]

Dowell was particularly proud of the fact that Kim Hunter had included a section about him in her cookbook, *Loose in the Kitchen*. Hunter, who had asked Dowell for a recipe when she was completing the cookbook in 1975, admitted, "one chapter is mostly about you—and how intimidated I was to cook for you after having experienced your incredible spreads."[366] Hunter titled the chapter about Dowell "Good to Knows." "I have a writer friend," she wrote:

> who taught me a thing or two about dinner parties and such. He's a fantastic cook . . . turns out all sorts of gourmet marvels in his kitchen. I was getting along famously in mine these days, a far cry from my beginnings, but "gourmet" I wasn't. And Cole's magnificent spreads had me so intimidated I refused to invite him to our house for dinner. I told him so. Compete with his moussaka or pâté-in-shell? Not bloody likely . . .

Loose in the Kitchen contains two of Dowell's recipes and his advice for hosting a dinner party:

Bertram Slaff in his office, circa 1958. Slaff had moved his office to 1100 Madison Avenue, and he and Dowell shared a room there until they found an apartment at 58 East 83rd Street.

> [H]e complimented my derring-do by naming one after me! Mousse Kim Hunter! And at the risk of seeming unduly cocky, I've learned to do rather well by both of his creations. "Good-to-Knows": First . . . a dinner party is not to get all uptight trying to cook more than you're good at; and secondly . . . all elegant, delicious dishes are not necessarily culinary Mount Everests.[367]

By the time the book was published in 1975 Hunter was well established as a film and theater star. In 1951 she had won an Oscar for her role in the film version of *A Streetcar Named Desire* and, although she was blacklisted in the late '50s, she appeared regularly in television and off-Broadway productions. Dowell was extremely proud of their friendship since it validated his belief that he had moved beyond what he considered the uncultured climate of his Kentucky roots. When the cookbook came out Dowell wrote home to his sisters:

> I wanted you to know that I have a Christmas present for all three of you, and have had them for some time, but have been waiting until they could be signed by the author. This is my friend Kim Hunter's 'Autobiographical Cookbook', which has a couple of photos of me, and a couple of recipes, one for a mousse that I named for her and is really smashing.[368]

When Dowell returned to New York there were many opportunities to share these talents, for he was living a more active social life than the subdued existence he had cultivated on Shelter Island. He entertained celebrities such as Barbra Streisand, corresponded regularly with influential authors like Edmund White and George Whitmore, and even entertained John Kuehl's NYU graduate students, who had read *Island People* for a class in postmodern literature. Though he and Slaff hosted elegant, often extravagant dinner parties, Dowell's feelings about his reputation as a gourmet chef were complicated; he had written a poignant description of the narrator in *Island People* that must have echoed his own emotions on these evenings:

> when tribute was paid him at his own dinner table it was paid to the person who, silent, absent in the kitchen throughout the evening, had constructed such magical dishes; in short, the chef with whom one does not often actually sit down to dine. It was this sense of his duality that let his own guests turn their backs on

> him without feeling in the least rude. As far as one could tell by appearances, no more did he find such exclusion rude.[369]

This sense of duality often colored the gatherings for his guests could never be sure, after Dowell had had too much to drink, whether he would become abusive or remain a gracious host. He was prone to take offense easily, as illustrated by his rancor over a remark Edmund White made one Sunday evening in February 1978, when Dowell hosted a dinner party in White's honor. According to Dowell, at some point in the evening Edmund White called him "stupid,"[370] which was Dowell's interpretation of White's off-hand comment that he was not a cerebral writer but rather composed from the gut.[371]

White had recommended Dowell to a literary agent. "A woman," Dowell wrote, "who was actually excited about taking [him] on . . ."[372] With this incentive, he settled into his new office with the IBM Selectric typewriter Slaff had purchased for him and returned to work on two manuscripts that he had begun on Shelter Island. The first was a novel based on his early play *Eve of the Green Grass*, concerning his fictional McChesney family. The second work, a novella entitled *Too Much Flesh and Jabez*, involved a sexual relationship between a man and a young boy. In *Jabez* Dowell found a voice for his sexual frustration and feelings of insecurity, and he decided to put aside work on *Eve of the Green Grass* and concentrate on the shorter novella. He described the novella to Laughlin in a letter that stated,

> "I have had extremely good luck with writing out here and was racking up a score of 40 pages a week for a while. I've no notion whether the little book will interest you or not . . . it is intensely sexual, but I think that everything I write is. I call it a comedy of manners, and it is a comedy, in the sense of human comedy, and it concerns manners, too, though the people are farmers."[373]

His obsession with anonymous sex had grown more persistent. Dowell often enticed the gay street hustlers he picked up in Central Park to accompany him back to the apartment. He had also become infatuated again, this time with an ex-convict named Bruce. He wrote:

I would like to end it with Bruce, without violence, without much caring on either side. We have nothing but the illusion that we have something, and maybe the illusion has been entirely mine. LOVE.[374]

Coleman compared this new relationship to his earlier affair with Bob. Both men asked for money, and both often left him to spend time with other men. Of these lovers Dowell wrote, "All of them took me, but I asked for it, so I do not deserve compassion."[375]

Bruce was living in Providence and often phoned Dowell collect to offer promises that he would visit New York. When Bruce asked for money to purchase a bus ticket home, Dowell wrote in his journal, "I said to him, 'for once, let's level with each other. If you just need the money, say so and I'll send it.' "[376] The relationship inspired Dowell to write about his feelings for the Black ex-convict, and he began a story titled "The Snake's House," a chronicle of the convict's phone calls, visits, and pleas for financial support.

In January 1978 Bruce returned to New York. Shortly after his arrival he asked if he could live in the apartment on Fifth Avenue. At Dowell's insistence Slaff reluctantly agreed to the arrangement. Bruce stayed in the guest room but spent a significant amount of time with Dowell, going to gay bars and visiting Dowell's friends. The two drank frequently and often smoked marijuana. The relationship had little potential: Dowell was in contact with Bruce's mother and brother and soon learned that the ex-convict had a wife and children.

There was quite a bit of snow that January and when Bruce was away Dowell took advantage of the winter weather to hibernate in his office and work on *Too Much Flesh and Jabez*, a book about a farmer seduced by a young boy. Its narrator is Miss Ethel, a spinster school teacher. Dowell claimed that the book took ten years to write, and in it he took on the social concerns of child molestation and sexual repression. Of his character Miss Ethel, Dowell said she "fabricates an erotic 'confession' to fulfill her sexually repressed nature."[377] The novel concerns her unlived life and the conflict between her mind and body, a conflict that serves as the catalyst for her creative expression.

Jabez owes to Carl Van Vechten's *The Tattooed Countess* the plot of an older woman in love with a much younger man, and both novels have a character named Effie. However the similarities end there. The characters in the novel share traits with some of Dowell's earlier characters. Jim, like Robin in *One of the Children is Crying*, has a deferment from the war because there is no one to help him farm his land. Helen Taylor, like Birdie in *One of the Children is Crying*, spies on her neighbors, and Miss Ethel, like Mrs. Hackett in *Mrs. October was Here*, regresses to a childlike state and speaks foul language aloud.

Miss Ethel did not appear in the original manuscript, but when James Laughlin read the first draft he told Dowell that he found it hard to believe that Jim, a Kentucky farmer, would have been so educated. Laughlin wrote an extensive letter addressing his concerns to Dowell:

> . . . I am still beset by certain perplexities, which I hope will not cause you more concern than may warrant. Reading the book, and studying it, and thinking about it, have raised in my mind certain questions about the structure of fiction which have always plagued me, things I could not be sure about, and which now are recurrent. I am thinking particularly about "point of view" and the role of the "authorial voice." The new parts that you have written into the revision about Jim's background, and his connection with Miss Ethel, I think that is her name, the remarkable teacher who inspired him as a young man and made him much more intellectual than one would expect a farmer to be, are excellent, and I think they solve that problem. But it strikes me that in the process of rewriting you have also added greatly to the sophistication and intellectual level of Jabez, and also of Helen Taylor. You have written yourself, your own, high, intellectual and cultural level, into them in a way that I am not sure is logical. Is it likely that Jabez, given his background, would ever have gotten hold of a book by Oscar Wilde? Would such a book even be permitted in a library in the deep South? And how would he know about things in Greek mythology? As I see it, you have made Jabez an intellectual too, and I wonder if that is what you really intended. I had about him more, at first, the feeling that you thought of him as a very bright lad, but a kind of instinctual animal. But now you have put him up almost on the level of Jim himself, as far as the discrimination and sophistication of his thoughts are concerned.
>
> Similarly, I think you have imputed to Helen Taylor various subtleties of dis-

crimination and interpretation which simply don't fit with her background either.

In other words, I feel that you have written yourself into almost all of the characters except Ethie [sic], and is this good fiction construction? I wish you would get opinions from people who have a far better critical sense than I do.

What mechanism, what device of writing, of presentation, would make it possible for you to retain all of the subtleties and overtones and fine points of your own authorial point of view and comment, without embodying them in these people who would not normally have had, I feel, such subtle and penetrating thoughts, would not have been capable of imagining such involved and delicate "figures" as you, yourself, do?[378]

Dowell was at first offended by these remarks, for in many ways the character of Jim was based on his own education in Kentucky. But he took the comment to heart and later added a framing device, the story concerning Miss Ethel, who writes a novel about Jim and Jabez. Because she is a retired schoolteacher, Dowell's literary allusions are more plausible. Miss Ethel's intelligence is reflected by her references to Oscar Wilde, William Shakespeare, Joseph Conrad, and T. S. Eliot. Throughout the book there are allusions to Jack London's *The Call of the Wild* and Joseph Conrad's *The Heart of Darkness*, a quote from which ("the horror, the horror") Dowell incorporated as a reference to Miss Ethel's life.[379] The name she gives to Jim's companion, Jabez, serves as another literary allusion to support Miss Ethel's erudition: Jabez is the farmer in Stephen Vincent Benét's *The Devil and Daniel Webster*, and the name derives from the Hebrew for "he gives pain or sorrow."[380]

By adding the outer story suggested by Laughlin, Dowell incorporated another theme that had been significant in his earlier work: that of the writer and the effects a writer's words have on the world. Miss Ethel implores Jim to read the story she has written in order to help her complete it. Several passages explore the consequences of words, such as this one, after Jim has flattered his wife Effie and made her blush:

> he wondered if he could have made himself a pretty wife out of a steady application of such harmlessly flattering words. He saw the possibilities of such words as beeswax hand-rubbed into furniture.[381]

The style Dowell chose for *Jabez* is less complex than his earlier works, and the novel contains significantly more dialogue. The plot is perhaps the most linear in all Dowell's novels. An unnamed spinster schoolteacher retires at age seventy. It is the beginning of World War II, and in the first winter of her retirement she begins to write her memoirs. One figure recurs: Jim Cummins, who had been her most gifted student. During the First World War Miss Ethel had developed a fondness for Jim, recalling their relationship as "the only satisfactory association she had ever had with a pupil."[382] Even then she believed that his brain was "too large for his own good."[383] She had hoped to point out social ills and plant the seeds of knowledge in Jim, preparing him for a career in politics. Unfortunately, their frequent contact during private tutoring sessions provoked town gossip that forced the end of their relationship.

It is what Miss Ethel perceives to be Jim's desertion that leads to her revenge, the novel she composes that places the character Jim in a comprising situation with a young boy. The teacher visits the Cummins farm on two occasions before completing her manuscript. Each time she speaks to Jim's wife Effie, from whom she detects an unhappy marriage. On her second visit she finds the farmer Jim with a young, androgynous child, a child who recalls "the duality of her own youth."[384] The teacher decides to write a "perverse tale" about Jim, in which she fabricates characters who share her own peculiarities. She has done quite a bit of "secret reading"—buying books in plain brown wrappers—and the tale she writes takes on the erotic quality of those works. The novel she fashions from her memories begins at the close of winter, at the beginning of spring.

In her tale, Jim's mother has forced him to give up his true love, Ludie, in order to marry Effie. The teacher substitutes her student's large brain with an unnaturally large penis, creating a situation in which the character cannot have a satisfactory sexual relationship with his wife. The bulk of the story occurs several years after his marriage, during a time of drought, when Effie is summoned to her mother's house to assist in preparing her sister's wedding. The letter corresponds with the arrival of Jabez (Ludie's younger brother), who comes to stay with his aunt, Helen Taylor.

Helen rents a tenant house on the Cummins' property. She possesses knowledge of Jim's affair with Ludie, and in exchange for keeping that knowledge to herself, Jim has allowed her to rent the house for an insignificant sum. But Helen and Effie are close friends, and Effie tries to convince Jim to give Helen the house rent-free. All the characters pin their desires on Jabez, who enjoys wearing make-up and dressing in his aunt's clothing. To Helen Taylor he is her and Effie's son. Because Jabez resembles his sister Ludie, Jim is attracted to the boy, even though Jim has no homosexual desires and is rather repulsed by the idea. To Effie, Jabez is a secret companion.

Jim farms the land and Effie keeps a small garden. Jim has never had a satisfactory physical relationship and has had to rely on masturbation for sexual release. In order to couple with his wife, he must wear a device he calls "short pecker" that reduces his true size. Even when he wears the device Effie rejects his advances.

There is a drought symbolic of Jim's relationship with Effie: as soon as Effie decides to leave, a downpour begins. Jim's frustration, coupled with the fact that Jabez resembles Ludie, leads to his willingness to be seduced by the boy. Jabez seduces Jim and hopes that he has found a life-partner, but after their initial sexual encounter Jim turns violent. Helen Taylor suspects that Jim has raped the boy, and blackmails him into providing her house rent-free. At the end of the interior story, Jabez and Jim are on uncertain terms.

The final section of the book returns the reader to the outer frame. A closer look at this framing device reveals the complicated nature of the book's structure. On the teacher's first visit to see Jim Cummins, (the beginning of her 'search') she writes:

> I recall that I felt not young but ageless, and freed somehow, and I agreed with myself—beginning even then to divide, I see—that I would be the one to go native[385] if given the chance.[386]

and:

> I remember saying 'Don't expect too much,' meaning of him. After that I really did become 'in the third person.' Self victim? I still don't know.[387]

This paragraph introduces three important themes: the self-referential quality of characters as characters, the idea of 'too much' to express her expectations, and the idea of 'self-victim' which parallels other representations of victims throughout the book.

Dowell explores the first idea by making Miss Ethel both the narrator and a character in her own novel. Although Dowell described the book as a story with a framing device, the frame itself is more complicated than the author suggested. It is composed of two levels. One uses the first person and present tense and the second uses the third person and past tense. These two narratives frame the third person story, the novel Miss Ethel titles *Too Much Flesh and Jabez*. The work opens with a third person account that explains how an unnamed schoolteacher came to write the novel. This is the *second* level of the frame, a parenthetical story contained in a first person narrative (the teacher's present). The teacher writes:

> So the tale continues. I am setting this down, I tell myself, to 'frame' the story—an old device—but the search is dead earnest.[388]

This first person protagonist merges her 'present' with the narratives that precede and follow it, becoming an unreliable character in her novel as well as its frame. The frame ultimately returns to the third person since that is the only solution to the problem of continuing the story after Miss Ethel's death. But what is the reader to make of this first person narrator? First person interruptions occur periodically in the first section of the book: "I am writing this down . . ." "I nodded . . ." "I thought, without charity . . ." "I realize that I felt . . ." and "I remember saying . . ." [389] All serve as reminders to the reader that what follows is the schoolteacher's fictional memoir.

The second narrative refers to the nameless schoolteacher, "her" and "she" and "teacher." It is this third person "teacher" who writes the novel *Too Much Flesh and Jabez*. Like the narrator of *Island People*, she is given a name by the characters she creates. Of her visit to Jim the teacher writes, "She called his name and then hers."[390] But it is not until her second visit to the farm that her name is voiced. As she is leaving Jim calls after her, "Miss Ethel . . ."[391]

By having Miss Ethel describe her youth, Dowell also succeeds in framing the story between the two World Wars. The novel depicts rural life during the early years of World War I, when Miss Ethel and Jim began their acquaintance. Both the interior novel and the outer frame (the present) occur during World War II. Dowell based the drought and depictions of farm life on his own childhood experiences in Kentucky (and even mentions Prices's Mill, a community near his childhood home). Between the wars the country has changed little. The references to both wars also reinforce the isolation of the farm and Jim's separation from the world of men, and may represent Dowell's own feelings upon returning to Kentucky from the Philippines in 1946.

Miss Ethel's second theme involves the idea of "too much." Miss Ethel emphasizes the notion of excess throughout her tale. She implies that her virginity, having *no* sex, is equivalent to having had too much: "too much" is just as bad as having none at all. Too much of anything, she emphatically declares, makes a person sick, and this idea becomes an obsession. The first suggestion of this theme occurs when the teacher thinks of Jim, saying, "his brain is too large for his own good."[392] Too much knowledge may represent what Miss Ethel believes she has given Jim, and at the end of the novel she sees that she herself remembers too much.

Excess is also represented in terms of gluttony. We learn that as a young boy Jim would go to the orchard and gorge on green apples, and later he would be sick in the hot sun. Early in the war Jim bought candy for a starving child and force-fed him until the boy became sick.

The reader learns that Jabez was "too manly" and he has "too much and not enough company." And Effie says, "too goddammed much of anything's a source of *nothing*."[393] This echoes Miss Ethel's comments about her own life of thought, "'And of that,' she said, 'too goddamned much.'"[394]

The third theme examines the nature of victims. The characters of her novel are all 'victims,' a word Dowell emphasized in describing the novel: "*Jabez*" he said, "is about natural victims."[395] The book's epigram, from Jakob Wasserman's *The World's Illusion*, reads: "Those who are by nature the victims must bear a punishment in addition." The novel concerns three types:

natural victims, victims of circumstance or accident, and victims of manipulation.

By drawing attention to the extreme size of Jim's penis, Miss Ethel creates a man who is victimized by nature. As a farmer, Jim is a victim of the elements. Most of the characters are victims of manipulation. Helen is willing to sacrifice Jabez to Jim in order to win control of her house. Both Jim and Jabez are victimized by their fathers. Jabez explains, "They were doing it to me. Billy and Amos and all the rest."[396] And later, "It was a lesson he had learned at the hands of Billy Taylor. . ." Jabez later explains that Billy Taylor is his father. Like Jabez, Jim also felt he was his father's victim, but later discovers he was the victim "of his own lust."[397]

Jim provides the ultimate definition of a victim: ". . .not somebody who paid . . . but rather . . . somebody from whom something was extracted and nothing given in return."[398] Jabez presents a different viewpoint when he says "the hog tier was just as involved as the one tied up"[399]—ultimately it is both the victim and the victimizer who suffer from the imbalance of power. Ultimately, both definitions describe Miss Ethel's own life as a teacher.

Miss Ethel incorporates the victims of the Holocaust into her tale by including a story about Jim's brother Will, who has gone to Germany to enlist. Jim remembers a torn piece of paper found in Will's pocket that reads "Lebensborn."[400] Jim is never quite certain why his brother participated in the German war effort, but he perceives a correlation between the horrors of the war and Will's understanding about sex, for he also finds among Will's possessions a semen-stained photograph of a young German girl.

There are several other significant and recurring ideas addressed in the novel. Dowell was fascinated by that moment between sleep and waking and may have been referring again to Haldór Laxness, to whom he had alluded in *Island People*. Consider this passage from Laxness' *Independent People*: "Long, long she lay trembling in terror before she sank into a dazed confusion, a tense stupor that was neither sleep nor waking rest, but a difficult, reluctant journey through a world landless and without time, where she lived over again the most incredible events of the past and met people she had once known, in visions most unnatural in their clarity, most horrible in the minuteness of their detail."[401] And, "It was bright day when she woke again. What had she been dreaming of? She passed a hand over her eyes and forehead to break the threads between sleeping and waking, to separate dream from reality."[402]

In *Jabez*, Dowell's characters cannot distinguish between dream states and reality. These two states of consciousness coexist in the novel, and the characters are not always quite sure which state they are in: "When he fell asleep," Dowell wrote, "it was as though he entered it from a dream reluctantly abandoned."[403] The idea is repeated frequently, but a few examples will be sufficient. "He fell asleep, or out of his dream";[404] "You're walking in your sleep";[405] and "The icy water shocked him out of the nightmare he had been in"[406] all serve to reinforce the idea that Jim cannot distinguish reality from dream. His sexual awakening corresponds to his liberation from a dream back to the real world.

Miss Ethel embodies her characters with qualities she herself possesses. Jabez is a writer and keeps a secret journal, which he hopes to reveal to his aunt. Helen Taylor, who on one occasion served as a substitute teacher, fashions herself to be a schoolmarm. Jim's relationship with a boy parallels Miss Ethel's relationship with him. *Jabez* explores alternative states of being and examines concepts that contain inherent contradictions. Jabez represents both male and female. Contradictions appear in Miss Ethel, who has no sexual identify, seeing herself as androgynous: "she was androgynous when she was a girl."[407] Miss Ethel finds a way to rationalize this state: "But such a state is equivalent to a state of grace. Angels were androgynous . . ."[408]

The sexual focus of the novel is a projection of Miss Ethel's preoccupation with something she does not understand. Miss Ethel comes to realize that she has been denied a sexual life, and sexuality becomes an obsession. She represents "somebody getting old and feeling sterile."[409] Yet she cannot fully address female sexuality. Ludie, the one sexual woman in the story, goes crazy when she learns of Jim's pending marriage to Effie. Miss Ethel cannot imagine what sex would be like for a woman for she has remained a virgin, so in her narrative she does not let any of the female characters get penetrated. By creating a boy as the recipient of Jim's love, she does not have to imagine herself in the act of sexual intercourse. She invents Jabez "out of revenge" for what she perceives as Jim's desertion.[410]

She sees the loss of virginity as the same things as death,[411] therefore sex makes the participants victims. She alludes to sexuality in a variety of contexts, including black sexual prowess,[412] and peppers her text with references to Oscar Wilde.[413] She uses this ruse as a way to reveal things about herself at times so personal she cannot face them any other way, such as her first person account of the only time she had been penetrated, by her brother.[414] Miss Ethel gives her memory to Helen Taylor but the reader can see the connection with her own past by the description of the "rainy day" which links together her girlhood experience with the present day description. Her incestuous experience also links Miss Ethel's "reality" to the past she creates for Jabez.

The final section of the novel returns to the outer frame, in which Jim pays a visit to his former schoolteacher and she asks him to read the tale she has invented. As he reads the novel, he comes to understand the meaning of their relationship in new terms. "It was plain for him to see, plain enough, that the book was *their* story . . . As though she dictated even his current responses, at the thought of taking her before it was too late he stirred in his manhood . . ."[415] His realization comes to late, for sometime during the course of the night she dies, her eyes fixated on him as he reads.

After submitting the manuscript for *Too Much Flesh and Jabez* to New Directions, Dowell found himself frustrated by what he perceived as their reluctance to move forward with its publication. He wanted Ralph Steadman, an English cartoonist whose work had appeared in *Rolling Stone*, to illustrate the jacket, but the designer had other ideas. Although the staff expressed concern over the homosexual aspect of the novel, New Directions moved ahead with the project. Dowell received the galleys in May, 1977, with notification that it would be printed as a paperback. Edmund White agreed to send a copy of the galleys along with a letter to *The Advocate*, recommending the novel for their book club. New Directions also suggested the book to the Lambda Book Club.

New Directions published *Too Much Flesh and Jabez* in November 1977. Two months later, on January 1, 1978, Dowell's sister Ruth called to tell him that their mother had died. Beulah Dowell had lived for 28 years after the death of her husband. Her passing made the writer think about a discussion he had often had with Bertram Slaff concerning the reunion of loved ones at death. Would she, he wondered, be greeted by Morda? "Bert would say she would not catch up, but I have hopes that he has not been running, but has been waiting."[416]

Dowell had some good news on that New Year's Day. Gilbert Sorrentino reviewed *Too Much Flesh and Jabez*, referring to the novel as "a tour de force of the imagination."[417] The review appeared in the *New York Times Book Review* on the very first page of reviews. Several of Dowell's friends called to congratulate him. Terence Winch, reviewing the book for the *Washington Post*, said, "the narrative itself is often captivating."[418] His friend George Whitmore reviewed the book in that month's issue of *Christopher Street*, the first time Dowell was mentioned in the gay press. These reviews meant a great deal to Dowell, and he remarked in his journal:

> Yesterday another good review, this one in Best Sellers, a publication in Washington; the best part was that it was written by a retired schoolteacher in Schenectady. Her approval is somehow sweeter than the others for she does not criticize my handling of Miss Ethel."[419]

Miss Ethel had been modeled and named after one of Dowell's own elementary school teachers. When she learned of the novel, Miss Ethel wrote several letters to Dowell, fondly recalling him as a student.

Dowell's depression had returned and he was taking Librium and Valium. He had applied for a CAPS grant for $4000, but was turned down. And he continued to obsess over Bruce. "I feel him (my lighter in his pocket) practicing some kind of witchcraft on me. . . I am, I repeat, quite close to a mental breakdown."[420] His interest in astrology had also resurfaced, and those who plotted his chart promised great things. One horoscope reading that occurred on March 23rd, 1978 lifted his spirits temporarily. "In October 1980 occurs the event," the horoscope predicted, "that, by fall of 1981, will have [Dowell] a very rich man—quote 'richer than anybody has a right to be.'"[421]

Such advice only lead to more disillusions. Dowell had not heard from James Laughlin in several months and the silence affected his enthusiasm for New Directions. His books did not generate the income he longed for, and he believed this was the result of a lack of publicity. He wrote: "ND will let that book die if I don't fight hard, and I don't know how just now."[422]

Dowell also published several other works that year. *New Directions: An Anthology of Prose and Poetry* published "My Father was a River" (#36, 1978), and *Ambit* published "A Lifetime Proposition" (#73, 1978) and the poem "Partridge House" (#76, 1978). Dowell was also considering a new work for the stage. "I am discussing seriously with George Whitmore," he wrote, "a musical to be set mainly in a disco, concerned with ménage à trios—two men and a woman."[423]

In May 1978 Gilbert Sorrentino called Dowell to say that a young literary critic, John O'Brien, wanted to interview him for a new book about contemporary writers that would feature Sorrentino, Wallace Markfield, and others. O'Brien flew from Chicago to interview Coleman Dowell on tape. The two men spent seven hours together, and the interview was eventually published in the "Review of Contemporary Fiction," Fall 1982.

During this period Dowell's sexual activity with strangers had taken a disturbing direction. He began to correspond with a prisoner called Sugar who had placed an ad in *SCREW* magazine. Dowell also began a telephone communication with a prisoner named Stewart and started to visit another inmate, Frankie Jay, who was scheduled for release that spring. Dowell was obsessed by the fact that he was aging, but he was encouraged by Frankie Jay's remark that appearance did not matter.[424] Dowell invited the inmate to visit him at the apartment, but soon after leaving prison Frankie Jay called to say that he had decided to stay with a girl he knew from school, and that he would be living with her in Hempstead, Long Island.

Such behavior had unforeseen consequences. In April 1978 Dowell complained of high fevers, chills, and rectal nodes. When he described the symptoms his doctor expressed concern that he might have contracted syphilis. The doctor put him on penicillin. "Today, as though to point out the shame in my life," Dowell wrote, "I went back to the doctor for syphilis blood tests, this shame to continue over the months until next April."[425]

Dowell's health problems were mirrored by Tammy's. His beloved dachshund was growing more ill every day. She had been losing weight for some time, she was now blind, and had difficulty breathing. Although Dowell considered having her put to sleep, he could not. Instead he fed her Valium, hoping that would help her sleep. In frustration he would often yell at the dachshund, and occasionally he would pick her up and throw her against the pillows.

This behavior tormented Dowell. He found himself acting more and more cruel toward Tammy, throwing her out of bed at night, kicking her, or locking her out on the patio in the cold. He began to believe that he had an inner demon, a "distinct and separate and alien personality, the road not taken, which is trying to BE taken and to take me and my life and the lives of those I love." He recognized that this was a kind of monster, "one that also hates Jews, that informs my anti-semitism, my intolerances, that keeps me from achieving what I set out to achieve."[426]

On July 31, 1978, just three days short of her 16th birthday, Dowell and Slaff took Tammy to the animal clinic, where she received an electrocardiogram. Although they decided to take her home the couple could tell that she was in agony, struggling for life, and the two men returned to the clinic to have her put to sleep. Afterwards they brought her home, wrapped in a blanket, and slept with her between them.

Coleman Dowell, circa 1968. When he began work on White on Black on White *in 1983, Dowell was clinically depressed and talked about suicide frequently. Though friends encouraged him to press on with his work, he was more preoccupied with growing old, and he was tormented by memories of his youthful good-looks.*

CHAPTER TEN

White on Black on White

By 1977 Coleman Dowell's obsession with African American men had reached a critical stage that bordered on clinical obsession. According to his journal, he sometimes had sex with three or four different men a day. After the first encounter he would find himself prowling Central Park in search of another partner, and he was both excited and shamed by occasional rape fantasies in which he imagined himself a willing victim. His continued correspondence with black prisoners added to these fantasies, since their letters often described the violent acts of penetration they would submit him to when they met.

Dowell's sexual activities were occasionally tinged with danger. He would visit his correspondents in prison and invite them to stay with him when they were released. Sometimes he engaged in anonymous sex with strangers in the bushes of Central Park—in an area known as "The Ramble"—rather than return with them to his apartment. Yet he could not equate his own illicit behavior in the park with other clandestine activities that went on there. In June 1977 he wrote a letter to *The New York Times* questioning the priorities of the police who patrolled the area:

> Last Sunday I walked through Central Park to Bethesda Fountain, where I was harassed by two dope dealers who offered me heroin, cocaine, pot, acid. They clung like mosquitoes; they insinuated and disparaged and subtly threatened. There was not a bloody cop in sight.[427]

In long discussions with Bertram Slaff, Dowell tried to examine and understand his behavior. Slaff could offer a balanced psychiatric perspective informed by years of practice, but his advice must have been influenced by their emotional relationship. Because these conversations did not result in the same catharsis Dowell achieved through writing, he incorporated his experiences into fictional narratives with characters that exhibited his own sexual interests in African American men. He regarded his obsession as an acknowledgment of eroticism in black culture missing from the Anglo-Protestant world of his childhood.

Most of the black men Dowell took as lovers were already involved in other relationships. The secondary role he assumed in their lives led him to believe that they were attempting to make him jealous. Dowell equated eroticism with promiscuity—this aroused jealousy, which in turn provoked callous behavior. "One is chased amorously," he wrote in his journal, "as long as one is cool, 'white,' uncommitted, but once one has made the vow of love . . . then there is a corresponding cooling . . ."[428]

His conviction that Slaff considered him a servant in the apartment had also resurfaced. Although they had a housekeeper, Dowell shopped, cooked, cleaned, and organized, letting these tasks divert his attention from writing. He detected an unintended maliciousness in Slaff's comments about the difficulties of living with a writer. In his journal he described his partner as "icy" and "silent." He also believed that Slaff was unwilling to accept his erotic nature. Their usually calm relationship was now fraught with bouts of screaming. Dowell suffered fits of crying. His fantasies of suicide took the shape of throwing himself under a subway train or off the apartment terrace. "My cleanest impulse," he wrote in March 1977, "is to finish this and jump out the window. . ."[429]

This mental anguish accompanied a series of physical infirmities. Dowell had several teeth extracted, he was tested for venereal disease, and for a short time he experienced deafness in his left ear. He contracted a skin ailment, impetigo, on his face. As a result, he had to take antibiotics and bathe with iodine soap. He was also taking Ornade, Darvon, and Valium in varying doses, to ease his toothaches and to help him sleep.

Income from his publications was slim, but Dowell's fiction continued to garner critical praise. In March 1977 his sister Ruth called to read him a review of *New Directions Anthology #33* that had appeared in the Louisville *Courier-*

Journal. The anthology contained his short story "The Moon, The Owl, My Sister" and the reviewer complimented the story highly.[430] Acclaim for the story also appeared in a review in the *Lehigh Valley Labor Herald.*

The *New Directions Anthology* continued to publish his work on a regular basis. Nevertheless, Dowell believed the staff was deliberately rude to him and he began to imagine that James Laughlin was ignoring him. He longed for another publisher and a wider audience, and he sent new stories to a series of national publications, including *Playgirl, Esquire, Playboy,* and *The Atlantic Monthly.*

Two important stories preoccupied him at this time. The first, about two characters he called Ivy and Eager, examined the nature of interracial eroticism. The second was a work he called "The Snake's House." Both had at their root Dowell's particular relationships with black men. The two stories ultimately formed the basis for his final novel, *White on Black on White.*

The Ivy and Eager story had been on his mind for many years. His interest in writing about interracial relationships and tensions between white and black culture went back to 1962, when he had been in correspondence with John Howard Griffin, the author of *Black Like Me.* The two writers exchanged letters discussing race relations, and Griffin's comments may have influenced Dowell's work on *White on Black on White.* In a letter to Dowell dated April 2, 1962 Griffin had written:

> I have not been able to prove or disprove it yet, but I have a feeling that deeply involved and on an unconscious level there remain the poisons of an enormously flattering sexual domination which white-skinned people cannot ferret out and give up. I felt this as a Negro. It exists in puritans who would never consciously admit to such desires.[431]

Dowell wanted to explore subtleties of this sexual domination in his story. Ivy, a white woman, moves to Harlem where she has nightly encounters with black men who dominate her until she reaches a point of total humiliation. In plotting the story Dowell recognized Ivy's need for redemption. This redemption, like his own, could come only in the form of unadulterated love.

While working on this piece, Dowell was romantically involved with a significantly younger man, a 19-year-old African American named Mervin. As in other relationships Dowell established a romantic bond countered by equivalent feelings of jealousy and suspicion. Dowell could be cruel. He would refuse to speak to Mervin, taunted him with stories about other lovers, and tore up his phone number with the hope that—after there was no communication from him—Mervin would beg to come back. Dowell confessed that he enjoyed making Mervin cry and wrote after the affair ended, "I believed I owned him."[432]

This behavior was also a kind of self-torment. His anticipation of sex with the young man was often overpowered by images of Mervin with other men. "My jealousy—and Ivy's must be—is rooted in a belief that what my lover has with some one else is better than what they have with me, a self-defeating belief that leads to violent promiscuity . . . in spite of vows to be faithful."[433]

Dowell's related story, "The Snake's House," was a piece about his relationship with Bruce, the affair he had started in June 1977, while completing *Too Much Flesh and Jabez*. Bruce was a 36 year-old, African American who admitted that he had recently been in prison for dealing drugs. Bruce satisfied Dowell's "need for a real man."[434] Dowell invited Bruce to move into the apartment on Fifth Avenue in the summer of 1977, but the arrangement proved too uncomfortable for Bertram Slaff. In October Dowell arranged to take a house in Southold, Long Island, where he could spend time alone with his new lover. Though Dowell rented the house for six weeks, he began to fear Bruce might physically harm him and after only eleven days they returned to the city.

Dowell recorded the events of the vacation in a 13-page, single-spaced journal entry written upon their return from Southold. When he reread the entry later he wrote that it "curdles my blood: how can I possibly wish to see such a person again?" The entry continued:

> I've decided, at any rate, to present the journal entries as they are, only names changed, as a story for my White on Black on White, and abandon the novella I meant to write about Bruce and me exchanging personalities, which never did

happen and seems too much of a task to take on. Also, with him away, I cannot get the cadences of his speech, black speech, or the prison jargon.[435]

As the first half of 1978 passed Dowell continued to explore his obsession with Bruce in writing. The idea for the story first took the shape of a poem he dedicated to Martin Bax, the editor of *Ambit*, titled "Partridge House:"

Thank you for the book
of poems.
I was away, or meant to be,
Six weeks;
A famous house, the old
North Sea—
Dreadful, dreadful—
Tension, and some real
psychopathy. [436]

As he fleshed out the story he wrote less about the real events and more about a nameless narrator with a small dog, Xan, and a character named Calvin Hartshorne. Writing the story was a way to exorcise his demons. "I had, by writing about him as Calvin Hartshorne," Dowell decided, "and thinking about him as he was the last night here, cleared him out of my mind for long periods of the day and night; suffering was gone, is nearly gone."[437]

Bruce was living in a Muslim community in Providence. Although Dowell told Bruce he no longer wanted a relationship, the two men continued to communicate by phone. After rejecting numerous collect phone calls, Dowell agreed they should talk once a week. Dowell bought Bruce clothing and other gifts. He wanted desperately to be part of Bruce's daily life, to the extent that he often talked to Bruce's ex-wife on the telephone. Dowell made a birthday dinner for Bruce's daughter on her 14th birthday and invited her friends over for the party. He even tried to help his lover get a job.

By May Dowell decided to see an analyst. After the first session he started to link his feelings for these black men with repressed feelings for his father. "I won't, in this illiterate account," he wrote after the first session, "bring out the connection . . . between my feeling for Bruce and my feeling for my father."[438]

Part of Dowell's depression resulted from his continued mourning for Tammy. Slaff suggested a European vacation, but Dowell was adamant to get another dog. Both men realized that such a commitment would restrict their ability to travel. In August 1978, after long discussion, they adopted a Jack Russell terrier named Daisy. The day Dowell brought the puppy home from the ASPCA Slaff greeted them both with a large banner that read "Welcome."

Dowell began to supplement his creative writing with work as a literary critic. Between 1978 and 1985 he wrote book reviews for the *Courier-Journal* of Louisville, Kentucky. The reviews indicate a wide-ranging interest and demonstrate his extensive familiarity with literature. The first piece, titled "Four Failures and One Success," included reviews of books by Paddy Chayefsky, Abby Vann, Richard Shickel, and William Javonovitch.

Often the authors he reviewed wrote to express their gratitude for his critical opinion. When he praised David Madden's novel, *The Suicide's Wife* in October 1978, Madden wrote,

> Your review speaks from inside the novel itself. The quality is very rare in a review and I'm grateful to you. You made me experience my own novel from slightly different, but very appropriate, perspectives.[439]

Dowell continued his friendship with Martin Bax by mail. In April 1979 Bax wrote to request a piece for the next issue of *Ambit*, with a promise that it would be illustrated by Dowell's favorite artist, Ralph Steadman. Dowell mailed off the just-completed manuscript for "The Snake's House," which *Ambit* published in the Fall 1979 issue. In September of that year Dowell received a request from Judy Talcott, the project director for Kirkwood Community College, in Cedar Rapids, Iowa. The Community College was planning a tribute to Cedar Rapids' native son, Carl Van Vechten, in honor of Van Vechten's 100th birthday, and wanted to perform *The Tattooed Countess*.[440] Talcott wrote to ask Dowell for permission and to request a copy of the script. Dowell sent the lyrics and first act, and in October Talcott wrote to say:

> I have received Act I. of THE TATTOOED COUNTESS along with the music and lyrics for the first act. Thank you very much for the time you have spent putting this all-together! If we have any questions regarding the material we will be in touch with you. I will let you know as soon as I have a firm commitment from our production people about going ahead with THE TATTOOED COUNTESS.
>
> I have just briefly looked through the lyrics, and find them most fascinating! I hope we can pull it off.[441]

Bruce Kellner, who later wrote *Carl Van Vechten: the Irreverent Decades*, had suggested that the college produce a concert version of Dowell's score, but the planning committee decided instead to produce a readers' theater production. The script was completed by James V. Hatch, a member of the planning committee, and directed by Bob Aldridge, head of Kirkwood's theater department. According to Kellner, the show "was under-rehearsed and badly cast and not very good."[442]

To Dowell the matter was unimportant. His active sex life, his absorbing social circle, and what he regarded as his duties around the apartment kept him from focusing on plans for the production. But he also began to realize that such activities were taking priority over writing.

In March 1980 Dowell and Slaff took another seaside cottage, High House, overlooking Little Peconic Bay on Long Island. Here Dowell could concentrate on his novel, away from the frantic pace of Manhattan. He was fascinated with the history of the house. It had been erected on the cliff sometime during the Civil War period and the architecture—gables, a trap door, a peaked roof, and cellar—aroused his curiosity. From the attic Dowell could see the south shore, Nassau Point and Robin's Island. But it was not the view that captured his imagination: Dowell was certain after spending the first week in the house that it was haunted. "In another century," he noted in his journal, "when it was first bought it was called haunted. I have felt the presences, respected them as I respected the ghosts of The Farm House."[443]

Five weeks after he and Daisy moved into the house, Dowell and his terrier were walking on the beach when he noticed several large silver swans floating on the creek. He recorded the observation in his journal: "It was another century, several centuries ago; nothing broke the illusion. The sailor was the silver swanne herself."[444] For Dowell the image of the swan combined with his notion that the house was inhabited by ghosts. For a short time he was obsessed with what he considered "ghostly occurrences" and he began to draft a story titled "The Silver Swanne," a title he borrowed from a 16th century madrigal by the composer Orlando Gibbons.[445] The succinct lyrics captured the anguish he suffered each time he considered suicide or pondered his failure as an artist:

> The silver Swan who living had no note,
> When death approached unlocked her silent throat:
> Leaning her breast against the reedy shore
> Thus sung her first and last, and sung no more:
> 'Farewell all joys, O death come close mine eyes,
> More geese than swans now live, more fools than wise.'

Dowell remained at High House until the end of June, and returned again in September for two months. During this time he finished "The Silver Swanne," and sent it to Martin Bax for possible inclusion in *Ambit*.

Dowell described this work as "Gothick." He told his friend Jack Collins:

> I have a story, my only Gothick tale, published in England, a mass of typos, misspellings, and outright substitutions for my own words, so scarcely, except for the superb illustrations, a matter of untinged pride for me.[446]

The narrative may have included material discarded from the ghost story in *Island People*. It alternates between November 1770, 1840 and 1980, and narrators from each of the three different centuries interweave their tales. In 1770, Robert Vilet is haunted by a doe. His ghost story is composed by the 1840 narrator, who seeks distraction from writing a planned book on John Cabot. The outermost frame of this story is provided by the 1980 narrator—another writer who sees a swan on his balcony—who, seeking refuge, begins to write the tale that takes place in the nineteenth century.

Throughout the story concerns itself with language and its literary context. Dowell's own explication of "The Silver Swanne" included among his papers illustrates the author's use of verbal puzzles and hidden meanings, his love of etymology, and his erudition. It indicates a wide range of historical and literary allusions contained in the story's text. These allusions include the "retreating sea over the shingle," referring to the loss of faith in *Dover Beach*; a quote from *Piers Plowman*, Life of Do-well[447] (Dowell's "signature"); and a mention of "seventy fountains" taken from Agathocles. Personal allusions to friends and family are contained directly in the text, such as the name Vilet, which was Dowell's mother's maiden name. Historical figures mentioned in the text include John Cabot and Leonardo Da Vinci, alluded to through flight and machinery, and the phrase a "sound of pebbles dropping to mark the Roman mile," which refers to the first odometer, invented by Da Vinci. Dowell also culled vocabulary from his readings in science, and he identified Thomson's *Science of Life* (1899) as his source for terms including "littoral," "abyssal," and "pelagial."[448]

A second manuscript in the Dowell archive, "The Writing of the Silver Swanne," documents the circumstances surrounding the composition of the work. Concentrating all summer on *White on Black on White*, he had started "The Silver Swanne" as a diversion. One room in High House sparked his imagination and Dowell found himself writing automatically. He describes a kind of trance-state in which he found himself using language according to the century of the context in which it occurred, His mood swung from ecstasy to despair, and within a week he had completed the 34 page manuscript. He explained:

> On two narrative levels of the story, the little dog (called Daisikins in 1840 and Marguerite in 1770) is abandoned by her owners while they pursue fantoms. To recover her, the 1840 man and the 1770 man will have to kill, the latter killing the doe and the former killing a child.[449]

The narrator in the story abandons his manuscript about Cabot, just as Dowell had abandoned *White on Black on White*. Dowell documents his "fear that when [he] strayed too far from autobiography, however vague to begin with, [he] was no longer a persuasive writer."[450] But he also saw the story as an attempt to write something other than personal biography: the 1840 narrator's illness represents Dowell's belief that creativity itself is an illness.

Bax published "The Silver Swanne" in *Ambit* in 1980. That same year Dowell made his break with New Directions. Frustrated with the lack of promotion of his books, Dowell notified James Laughlin that he wished to find a new publisher. Laughlin replied:

> A sad turn of events for us, but since we never managed to sell your books very well, I think you are doing the right thing. I hope that we will remain good friends, and that you will have a real success with the new book.[451]

In December 1980, Dowell wrote in his journal that "[m]y fifth novel, WHITE ON BLACK ON WHITE, was xeroxed on Friday, Edmund (White) picked it up to read, for he is to be my agent on the book, and last night he called to say that he had read the first 70 pages and his praise was high and heady."[452] The novel became a synthesis of the ideas he had explored in earlier books. A reference to the novel among his personal papers describes its roots in Shakespeare's *Othello*.[453] He created a scheme for the book that took the form of a three-part layout, beginning with a historical perspective of how blacks and whites viewed each other, an examination of the white world devoid of blacks, and finally the integration of the two cultures.

Edmund White and Christopher Cox helped Dowell solicit publishers, sending the manuscript to Farrar, Straus and Giroux, Knopf, Putnam and Sons, Dial Press, Dutton and others. Dowell was convinced that Susan Sontag, then an editor at Farrar, Straus and Giroux, deliberately rejected his book because he had satirized her in *Mrs. October was Here*. He read similar motivations into other rejections. But John and Linda Kuehl had also submitted his manuscript to Lou Kannenstine at Countryman Press, and in January 1982 Dowell, learned that the press, which produced only nine titles a year, wanted his book. He signed the contracts in February, and received an advance of five hundred dollars.

While polishing *White on Black on White,* Dowell also composed a series of literary reviews. When John O'Brien, the literary critic who had earlier interviewed Dowell, founded the *Review of Contemporary Fiction* in 1980, he solicited several critical pieces from Dowell, which included "Gilbert Sorrentino's *Aberration of Starlight,*" published in Spring 1981,[454] and "Literary Balcomb Greene," published in Spring 1982.[455]

In March 1980 Bradford Morrow wrote to Dowell to solicit a work for his new literary journal, *Conjunctions.* Gilbert Sorrentino had recommended Dowell to Morrow, who wanted to publish a section from *White on Black on White.* At first Dowell was reluctant, for he had learned that Morrow's first issue had been a Festschrift in honor of James Laughlin that contained contributions by many of his contemporaries. "I had not been asked," he wrote in his journal. "The more I thought about it the more livid I became."[456] Nevertheless, Dowell invited Bradford Morrow and his friend Leslie Miller to dinner. The three were soon close companions.

Dowell also renewed his correspondence with James Laughlin during this period. When he wrote in February, 1982 to say he had heard about the Festschrift, Laughlin replied,

> Thank you so much for writing me about that crazy Festschrift. It was all done behind my back, as a 'surprise,' and all sorts of people who should have been invited, such as yourself, weren't, and a whole lot of others were who shouldn't have been, and I think they just looked in their manuscript boxes and picked out something they hadn't been able to sell anywhere else.[457]

There had been enough critical response to Dowell's work by this time to warrant serious attention, and John O'Brien paid tribute to Dowell in the Fall 1982 issue of the *Review of Contemporary Fiction.* This issue, the Paul Bowles-Coleman Dowell number, included the majority of critical essays about Dowell's work. The author was especially pleased that his friends John and Linda Kuehl had contributed an essay on Miss Ethel and *Too Much Flesh and Jabez.* The special issue was followed by more good news. In October Leslie Miller, who had recently established Grenfell Press, asked Dowell for a piece she might publish in a special limited edition. They decided on a reprint of "The Silver Swanne."

Dowell continued to work on *White on Black on White*, and finished a series of short stories that included "Wool Tea" and "The Great Godalmighty Bird." He was interrupted frequently by lovers who showed up at the building demanding his attention, so he left instructions for the doormen to turn them away. He changed his telephone number and for a time he pretended to be out of the country, going so far as to forward a packet of letters addressed to these men to a friend in Switzerland, with instructions that she periodically mail them back to the States.

Leslie Miller showed Dowell the proof for "The Silver Swanne" in January, 1983. He was thrilled with the end papers, the leather spine, and the colors of the book design. In addition to the $450 advance, Miller also promised him a copy of the book, which would sell for $150. Bradford Morrow had accepted several stories for publication in *Conjunctions*, and in May Dowell received the first copy of *White on Black on White*.

Finally published by Countryman Press in 1983, *White on Black on White* was billed as an exploration of the mutual fascination between blacks and whites. The title comes from a passage in the novel, ". . . it's America fucking, twos and threes and mores, white on black on white. . ."[458] a line which is echoed later in the text as ". . . the bittersweetness of the fucking of America . . . it's America fucking, twos and threes and mores."[459] The title may have also been inspired by the 1963 book *White on Black*, a collection of essays by white Americans that included "Some of My Best Friends are Negro," by Eleanor Roosevelt and "A Southerner Looks at Prejudice," by Tallulah Bankhead.[460]

The sexual obsession of the novel's characters, unlike that of Miss Ethel in *Too Much Flesh and Jabez* or the narrator of *Island People*, takes on a more symbolic quality. Dowell uses sexual desire to explore issues of racial tension in American culture, a theme he had first examined in *One of the Children is Crying*.[461]

Shortly after its publication James Laughlin wrote to Dowell to express his appreciation for the work:

> The book is at moments almost unbearable in its i[n]tensities, but your wonderful style carried me along at points where I almost felt I couldn't take anymore.[462]

Some of the critical reception of this novel took a negative tone. One review called the book "flawed" and another, by Lawrence Howard that appeared in *Best Sellers*, began, "There is no doubt that this book is the worst that I have been given to review."[463] Not all critics were unreceptive to its message. In a review for the the *New York Times*, David Evanier called the novel "a bold examination of black pain and anger and white guilt that crackles with insights." In the novel, according to Evanier, "all interracial sex is seen as aggression and political anger, masochism and revenge."[464]

In an interview with John O'Brien, Dowell described *White on Black on White* as "direct and brutal." "[T]here are almost no adjectives or adverbs," he noted, and described the characters as, " psychotic people with singular motives and a nostalgia for death."[465] He called it a "hermetically sealed" book about violence, murder and hatred, told by "a white. . .writing about black and white relations."[466]

In her article "Uncivil Rights and the Sins of the Fathers," Shena Mackay provides a succinct summary of the novel and examines these issues of race:

> Dowell tackles the enormous theme of the corrupt interdependence and collective fear and hatred of blacks and whites in America. Dowell's characters, living in the 1980s, and still under the long shadow of the Vietnam war, are saying that nothing has changed very much in the past 30 years; "Miss Anne" and "Mr. Charlie" (contemptuous names for whites, whose predilection for young, black flesh has always been an open secret in the South) still hold all the aces, and the sins of the fathers are visited on even the best-intentioned of the children.[467]

Dowell incorporated the story "The Snake's House," into the first section of the book. It recounts events between December and January, a period that represents in Dowell's works a time of change, a period in which the characters experience a reawakening that corresponds to the new year. The text includes journal entries similar to those in *Island People*, dated December 15, December 16, December 18, December 19, and December 24.

Dowell described "The Snake's House" as "a straight-forward narrative of sustained horror."[468] What he had hoped to achieve in this first chapter was an "unrelenting psychological bombardment"[469] in which two characters, a white man and his black lover, Calvin, come closer and closer to physical intimacy as they are psychologically drawn further apart. Calvin, like Jabez, is desired by many, and his flirtation with others drives the narrator mad with jealousy. Dowell recognized that "The Snake's House" was ultimately about "the horror that sexual things can be in the imagination."[470]

The narrator's lover Berthold, (based on Bertram Slaff), chauffeurs the interracial couple to Partridge House on Cutchogue, Long Island, where he leaves them to enjoy an extended vacation. Xan, the narrator's blind, dying dachshund provides the one bond between the narrator and Calvin, who claims to care for the dog's well being. But the dog's illness progresses in tandem with the violent nature of their relationship. Calvin's power over the narrator stems initially from sexual attraction, but the dynamic shifts to one based on fear and suspicion. The narrator discovers that Calvin is a hired killer, and suspects that the black man has seduced a local white woman. The narrator uses Xan's illness as an excuse to escape the house and visit a local veterinarian, where the dog must remain for several hours. While waiting to reclaim the dachshund, the two men visit a nearby village, where they notice a white woman with red hair escorted by a black policeman; though not stated, the evidence implies that they are Ivy and Cayce, a couple who play an important role later in the novel. This scene provides one link between the narrator and Ivy, and helps set the correlation in time between their stories.

Calvin comes to realize that he represents nothing more than an object of sexual desire. He threatens to kill the narrator, but cannot. His shame and their mutual lack of respect culminate in a brief sexual encounter. After they part the narrator returns to New York City, where his obsession with Calvin manifests itself in his preoccupation with the things Calvin has left behind at the apartment, objects he regards as talismans.

Shortly after his return he receives a bill for the rented house, accompanied by an exorbitant phone bill with the details of all the calls Calvin made during their brief stay there. The narrator traces Calvin's relationships by calling the numbers on the phone bill, and speaks to Calvin's mother, daughter, mistress, and another gay man who also desires Calvin.

Part Two incorporates the Ivy and Eager story, beginning with a first-person narrative that explains how the narrator came to meet Ivy Temple, a white woman who shares his obsession with black men. The narrator reveals details of Ivy's early life, details he learns through a series of extensive conversations. Ivy's story begins with events that occurred prior to their meeting, as a student in a school for gifted children. As an adult she becomes a civil rights campaigner in Selma, Alabama, and begins an affair with Eager, a black Civil rights work. Her affair with Eager is examined in relationship to the actions of those whites that used blacks for sexual gratification throughout the history of the south. When Ivy returns to New York she continues a brief correspondence with Eager, but also begins a correspondence with Roger, a black prisoner. She visits black men in jail and corresponds with them, and soon begins exploring Harlem to find black lovers, each of whom treats her with less and less respect.[471]

Ivy's self-degradation leads to a gang rape, and she ends up in prison after killing the doctor who examines her. Out of prison she returns to the island and meets Cayce, a friend from her youth and the only black pupil who had attended her school. Presumably this is a restatement of the scene in Part One when Calvin and the narrator see her with Cayce.

Ivy's contemporary narrative, "Ivy's Story" follows a third-person narrative interspersed with first-person references and letters. Much of this section, told from Ivy's point of view, traces her experiences from late October through the months of November and December, and a third-person section described as "a reconstruction"[472] takes her through December to January. This section reveals Ivy's relationship with Cayce. There is a suggestion that what happens to Ivy and Cayce in November and December parallels the events of the narrator's affair with Calvin.

Her narrative is interwoven with stories pertaining to Cayce and to Coreen, another focal character representing racial discord in ways that have little to do with sexuality. Coreen's and Cayce's histories explore black perceptions of whites from sociological, political, and emotional points of view.

Authorial perspective shifts in these stories erratically. Coreen's story switches between third-person, Ivy's point of view, and the point of view of the first person narrator. Coreen's story switches rapidly between Coreen's point of view and Ivy's, and between third person accounts of Coreen and Ivy and first-person narratives. Coreen's home life contrasts significantly with Ivy's, but it is Coreen who has retained her dignity in the face of adversity.

Cayce's story, which begins in the first-person, then takes the form of a third-person narrative that offers the reader an explanation of the narrator's own interpretation of Cayce's story. Cayce's story culminates in a section called "The Dinner Party," an event involving Cayce, Meredith, and Cat. Meredith "passes" as a white woman; her role in the story suggests that there may be a compromise between the radical extremes represented by the racially "pure" white and black characters. During the dinner party, Cayce imagines that the two women are seducing him. His role in this event is much the same as Calvin's initial role with the narrator.

Part Three, the final section of the novel, is a transcript of a tape-recorded message by Cayce Scott, a straight black policeman, remarking on the manuscript of his story. Scott reveals that the entire explication of his association with Ivy and his attendance at the dinner party have been fabricated by the narrator, and he is given his own voice to respond to the white narrative of his life. He says "whites have always written the lives of blacks and filled them with enough exaggeration of one kind or another."[473] Scott regards his account as an attempt to get at the truth of what keeps the races apart.

The novel further explores integration of the races and sexual relationships between blacks and whites from a historical perspective—there are references to "Dan Coon" (a black man pleasing white women) and "Miss Anne" (his counterpart)—but it also examines how one culture appropriates traits of the other. "I am a white man," the narrator thinks, "and my ass is hanging out of my clothes and it is as black as it is in real life."[474] Dowell creates a tension between the white superior attitude associated with the expression "nostalgie de la boue"[475] (a longing for the mud)—used at a party the narrator attends and repeated later in the novel in reference to the cleanliness of "hogs in the mud"[476]—and the idea that those who can pass as either black or white, such as Meredith, are best suited to happiness.

"Black and white" reverberates in other ways in the novel. Dowell uses the imagery of shadows and light to develop a theme of discovery. And, while the major theme of the book involves racial tension and relationships, the expression "black on white" might also indicate type on paper, reinforcing the suggestion that the book's theme is writing. This is a recurring leitmotif in Dowell's books, which are frequently about one's reactions to manuscripts: Jim's reaction to Miss Ethel's book (*Too Much Flesh and Jabez*), Omerie's response to Mrs. October's manuscript (*Mrs. October was Here*), Cayce's response to the narrator's manuscript (*White on Black on White*).

Throughout the novel the nameless narrator struggles with definition and meaning. This compulsion is represented most clearly in the importance given to name and identity. Dowell exaggerates the symbolism of names. Ivy Temple represents "the classical building hung with vines."[477] The black men have names suggestive of their functions in the novel. When Ivy first meets "Eager" her response is: "Are you?"[478] Calvin's surname is "Hartshorne," a word originating from the use of hart's horns as the chief source of ammonia used in smelling salts. The image suggests Calvin's ability to awaken the narrator's desires. But the name also implies the idea of "heart *shorn*"—to deprive of something as if by cutting. The narrator is deprived of Calvin, and depression and madness result. Dowell also uses a variant of the name to describe the relationship between blacks and whites:

> Is it possible for a black man and a white woman to provide mutual warmth, or does first one and then the other leave his/her deposits of venom in the receptive and unsuspecting warm flesh? Can we be both bite and antidote, venom and hartshorn?[479]

Edgar Cayce Scott is named after the real-life psychic healer, Edgar Cayce, who spent a large portion of his adult life in Selma, Alabama, where Ivy begins her work for the Civil Rights movement.[480] Scott is the one man who can cure Ivy of her illness. Other names are more suggestive of physical attributes or personal characteristics, like Cat, who is described by Cayce: "He watched Cat lick at the cream . . .";[481] and Berthold, who ultimately "holds" onto the narrator and keeps him from going mad.

The novel displays many similarities to earlier works. In all of the novels human interactions are portrayed as games. The narrator says of Calvin, "I would play the game by his rules or not at all."[482] Ivy's relationship with Eager is similar, and she thinks, "He was teasing her in a different way, playing another game with her." Like Miss Ethel in *Too Much Flesh and Jabez,* the characters in *White on Black on White* define themselves by other literary characters. Among those mentioned in *White on Black on White* are Bigger Thomas, Jay Gatsby, Jake Barnes, and David Copperfield. In addition, Dowell alludes to Orwell and Horace.

The disunity between the brain and the body, an essential concept in *Too Much Flesh and Jabez,* returns in this story. Ivy puzzles out theories of life, hoping to discover her purpose in the world. She asks, "And the brain? you may well ask. And I may well reply, I haven't got a single clue."[483] Like Jabez, the characters in *White on Black on White* are never quite sure whether they exist in the concrete world or in a dream state. Consider the line "he dreamed that he woke to a morning"[484] which echoes the line in Jabez, "He fell asleep, or out of his dream . . ."[485]

Structurally, Dowell explores a variety of techniques that fragment the narrative. The tenses change constantly. Dowell creates uncertainty with the first sentence: "Today is a month from when I would have returned to town." *Would have* suggests a future construction, in contrast to the *from when,* which implies past action. Throughout the novel, time shifts unexpectedly between past and present action. Often Dowell switches to present tense to address the reader, showing that the preceding section is simply speculation.

An interesting aspect of the novel is its reliance on threes. The novel has three parts, and generally Dowell groups his characters in threes: Berthold, the narrator, and Calvin; Ivy, Eager, and Parker; the whore, Ivy, and Chester

Field[486] and Cayce, Meredith, and Cat. These groups consist of all possible combinations of white and black, but never involve solely one race.

The tension of the plot is echoed in the tension of the form. In his article "Thoughts on *White on Black on White*," Edmund White describes this aspect of the book, which, he says, "exemplifies Chekhov's remark that good fiction must be half fairy tale and half newspaper story." White explains that the newspaper aspect of the novel involves its meditation on race riots, Civil Rights, and the Vietnam War. In juxtaposition, White asserts, "the fairy tale aspect of the book is frightening and progressive, in the sense that an illness progresses."[487] White also notes that Dowell pairs the idea of white obsession with blacks to gay men who obsess over straight men, but does not find fault with this comparison. "The politics of *White on Black on White* are irreproachable," White concludes, "because they are documentary not propagandistic, because the book renders rather than recommends."[488]

Ultimately, *White on Black on White* represents the actual love story between Dowell and Slaff, revealing the painful journey Dowell traveled in order to leave Bruce and return home. Like Ivy, he was at least temporarily "cured" of his illness—the sexual obsession for the "taboo" or "other." In the novel, Cayce must point out to the narrator that he "had somebody back home . . . Berthold is his name." And Cayce adds, "To lose that person after all the hate and the love and the games and the obsession would feel like the end."[489]

Stemming as it had from the facts of Dowell's dangerous affair with Bruce, the conclusion of the book suggests that for a brief time the author was able to embrace his life with Bertram Slaff. He had found some measure of peace after a string of unsuccessful affairs. But he could not give up his sexual proclivities. Seeing the book in print triggered a desire to see Bruce again, and after a silence of almost five years, he tracked down the ex-prisoner and resumed the affair.

Many friends had acknowledged and supported Dowell's talent during the years he composed *White on Black on White*. Editors John O'Brien, Bradford Morrow, and Martin Bax, publisher Leslie Miller, authors Edmund White and Chris Cox, literary scholars John and Linda Kuehl, all had gone out of their way to aid Dowell and to encourage an audience for his prose. Though there had been few reviews for the novel, the critics had offered laudatory comments. While waiting for these reviews to generate sales Dowell worked on his manuscript, *Eve of the Green Grass*. Bradford Morrow also suggested that Dowell compile his short stories into a book, and Dowell decided on the title *Houses of Children*. Though these projects helped stave off depression, failing health and a growing unhappiness with life was leading Dowell to withdraw from his friends more frequently, and his references to suicide took on a much more serious aspect.

CHAPTER ELEVEN

The Balcony Beckons

On Monday night March 21, 1983, Coleman Dowell and Bertram Slaff threw a birthday party for their terrier Daisy. They invited Bradford Morrow, Leslie Miller, Edmund White, and John Purcell. Miller brought proofs for *The Silver Swanne*, along with Dowell's advance for the book. The advance, including the cost of one copy of the book ($150), came to $450—just fifty dollars less than his advance for *White on Black on White*. *The Silver Swanne* launched the Grenfell Press series, which later included works by other authors such as John Hawkes (*Innocence in Extremis*), Guy Davenport (*The Bowmen of Shu*), and William Gass (*Culp*).

Prospects for publishing his work that year were good. Bradford Morrow was interested in reprinting *The Silver Swanne* in his literary journal *Conjunctions*. *Ambit* accepted "Wool Tea," and an excerpt from *White on Black on White*. Yet none of these accomplishments seemed to improve Dowell's faltering self-perception. He was clinically depressed, talking about suicide frequently. Though friends encouraged him to press on with his work, he was more preoccupied with growing old. For a short time he struggled with the manuscript of a novel, *Eve of the Green Grass*, but he put it aside to begin work on a memoir about the theater.[490] He wanted to call it A *Dark Book*, and explained this title in a letter to James Laughlin: "[I] once said to Carson McCullers that I envied her the title REFLECTIONS IN A GOLDEN EYE and she said 'It's a dark book.' . . . So indirectly I claim Reflections etc. as my title." [491]

Letters to friends often focused on his failing health. He was taking Penicillin, weight loss pills, and Donnatal (an anticholinergic drug used to treat ulcers and to control nausea). For a short time Dowell thought he had cancer. In October he wrote to Jack Collins:

Coleman Dowell and Bertram Slaff with their Jack Russell terrier, Daisy, on the balcony of their Fifth Avenue apartment overlooking Central Park. The day Dowell brought the puppy home from the ASPCA Slaff greeted them both with a large banner that read "Welcome."

> My body has attempted to do what I predicated for it—to kill me: last month the word was 'perhaps leukemia'; last week it was (after the second bone marrow—hellish procedure—operation)—'probably immunologic'—anything from AIDS to lupus and all in between.[492]

One friend suggested that he consider taking anti-depressants. Once before he had tried Elavil, prescribed by his internist, but the drug did not seem to ease his depression. Slaff offered him Desaryl, but that made him drowsy. "I have tried everything else," he wrote, "and must have some relief from self-hatred."[493]

Dowell had completed his story "The Great Godalmighty Bird" in 1982 and submitted it to *The New Yorker*. Charles McGrath, the managing editor for fiction, replied to Dowell's submission:

> I'm afraid that THE GREAT GODALMIGHTY BIRD didn't quite make it here, and so I am regretfully and apologetically sending it back. The problem—problem for us, that is—is that for most of the way this piece assumes a fictional form that we have been trying hard to get away from lately.[494]

The manuscript was rejected several more times before Bradford Morrow accepted the story for *Conjunctions*. Lois Morrow, Bradford's mother, praised it in her letter of September 17, 1983:

> I've enjoyed following the progress of my son's literary journal, Conjunctions, but can't remember ever having read something that moved me so much as "The Great Godalmighty Bird." It's a story of such poignant, inherent sensitivity, I wept![495]

Morrow published many of Dowell's short stories in the following years, including a reprint of *The Silver Swanne*, an except from *Eve of the Green Grass*, and "Writings on a Cave Wall." He convinced Dowell to select a series of other short stories for a collection, *The Houses of Children*—a title Dowell took from a tribute for his dachshund Tammy after her death. Dowell was briefly excited by the idea and wrote in his journal, "I am at work on a collection of stories, many of them previously published, to be called 'The Houses of Children'—those 'houses' also applying to the adults they become."[496]

Dowell continued to review for the Louisville *Courier-Journal* and completed several short stories, including "Wool Tea"[497] and "Kitty,"[498] an autobiographical piece based on his early years in New York. He also wrote a piece for the Kentucky Education Association that talked about his early education in Logan County. The *Russellville News-Democrat* picked up on the piece and wrote a follow up story on Dowell's early teachers. When she saw the piece Dowell's first and second grade teacher responded to the paper. The Russellville paper tracked down two other teachers, and wrote an article about their memories of the author.

Dowell received a letter from the principal of the old Simpson County High (now renamed Franklin-Simpson High), asking if students could interview him by mail for the paper. Dowell offered a set of his books if they would be allowed in the school, but he secretly believed that the library would not accept them. These connections with the past provided some comfort and let him believe for a short time that his work had not gone unnoticed in his hometown. Yet he could not turn down the chance to impress upon them his success, even to the extent of exaggeration. "Miss Ethel Hancock has begun writing to me," he wrote in his journal:

> she whose namesake Miss Ethel in JABEZ is; she's now 82 and a bore, let us face it, long-windedly Christian; and I have written to her twice, and yesterday, in the writing, decided to pull out all the stops and lie my head off for the record, and told her I was going to my house in France in two weeks—my house that is 350 years old, with 37 rooms and gardens with fountains, and also on the Ocean. Why not? Spoke of my two servants who live in and take care of the place when I am not there, and lots more. Last night decided that was so much fun that I showed Brad and Leslie pictures of my "family," my "sisters," and those pictures were: Dorothy Carliss (Miki), Tamara Geva (Ruth) and some pretty girl whose name I have long forgotten but whose glossy screen test photo I still have. I gave them one authentic photo—myself as rendered by Van Vechten; and they proclaimed us the most beautiful family in the world.[499]

Dowell was eager for reviews and news of his book *White on Black on White*. He held out hope that the book would bring him wealth and daydreamed over how he might spend the money, fixing up the apartment, or buying a car and a house on the water.

> First rumor of a review, said to be good, came yesterday: Sallie Bingham (!) Called Kannenstine and said a "very good" review would appear in this coming Sunday's paper, and wanted biographical material ... continued TOTAL good response to WOBOW except my oldest sister, who told my youngest sister that it was "filthy." There goes you-know-who. I have no family now accept Eleanor (through compassion) and Gayle, Jim and their sons.[500]

Dowell recorded information about these reviews in his journal dutifully. "Good review in *Publisher's Weekly*!"[501] he wrote in April 1983, and "I got a lousy review in the Virginia *Kirkus* paper,"[502] in May. "Review of WOBOW in yesterday's *Times Book Review* ... I took eight careful years and nearly went broke to rent the house in which to do the final writing ..."[503] The *New York Times* review, by David Evanier, mentioned Dowell's "superb dialogue, psychological acuity, and political insight. . ."[504] and Dowell believed this review would mark a turning point in his career.

The book seemed to be selling well. Dowell got reports from Edmund White and Bradford Morrow, who would pass along news from mutual friends. Dowell also made frequent visits to the local bookstores to see the book on display. He had discovered a trick to assure the books did not get sent back to the publishers:

> I went down on impulse on Saturday to the Three Lives Bookstore on Sheridan Square, wanted to see my novel in the window display. Then went into the shop and bought a book, one of mine, naturally, after which I introduced myself very tentatively to the nice-faced woman behind the register. I was most gratified at the reaction. She introduced me to her two colleagues . . . and they told me how I had a following and how well the book was doing. I bought the next-to-last copy and autographed the remaining one, and when they get their re-order in I am to go down and sign those — always a good policy for signed books can't be returned. Kannenstine wrote to me that Giovanni's Room, in Philadelphia, had re-ordered — fifty copies, which seems a lot to me.[505]

Dowell's list of lovers continued to grow—Felix, Darryl, Cornelius, Damian—and Bruce had returned, asking for money. "If the only comfort I can find is between a Black man's legs," he decided, "then let me enter that world wholeheartedly and go after what I want."[506] In July 1983 Dowell considered the possible consequences of his sexual activity. "I haven't been buggered in months," he wrote in his journal, "and am reluctant, I suppose because of AIDS."[507]

In May Edmund White threw a birthday party for Dowell's 58th birthday, inviting Bradford Morrow, Leslie Miller, John Purcell, Bertram Slaff, and Daisy. He served Vodka, caviar, and champagne. Miller gave Dowell stationery that she had designed and imprinted on her press. Dowell thought the evening was perfect: "the planning and execution were like Edmund's writing," he wrote, "beyond reproach and filled with delicate surprises which turn out to be surprisingly sturdy."[508]

In July Bev Smith, a black radio talk show host at WGBS in Miami, interviewed Dowell by telephone—a live on-air interview—to discuss *White on Black on White*. Later that month Leslie Miller brought the unbound but otherwise completed *Silver Swanne* for Dowell to autograph. He signed his name on more than 150 copies. Describing the experience, he wrote "though I have dreaded it with a mysterious fear, it did not go slowly, I did not get tired, and I did not spoil one precious copy."[509]

The book went to the bindery in early August 1983 for a September release. Miller asked Dowell to compile a cookbook containing his recipes, which she planned to print on handmade paper. Dowell wanted the title to be *The Liars Cookbook*, "which will have many meanings beyond the first one; it will also be a book whose recipes the cook can claim to have made up; some recipes will claim, 'no calories in this delicious dish.'"[510]

The reviews of *White on Black on White* continued to be positive. In July Dowell's friend Christopher Cox sent him a copy of a review from the *Washington Post* by Bob Halliday.[511] Later that month he picked up a copy of the *Courier-Journal*, which carried a review of the novel by Gregg Swem. Both reviews praised the book. Stephen-Paul Martin contacted Dowell to discuss his

PhD dissertation, which compared *Island People* to *Orlando, The Waste Land, A Dream Play, Patterson*, and *Nightwood*. Edmund White had completed a piece on the book for *Christopher Street*, and Dowell hoped Margot Jefferson might write a review for *The Village Voice*.[512]

Although Dowell was happy to have White's piece appear in *Christopher Street*, he did not have a high opinion of the publication. His feelings about the growing gay movement were complex, and he wrote of the magazine: "It is what it is and that's why I discontinued my subscription years ago. I am one of the conservative queers who regrets just about everything that militant gay people glory in."[513]

His personal opinions regarding gay fiction often conflicted with those of his friends. Several of the writers he knew at the time were members of the Violet Quill,[514] the literary group comprised of Christopher Cox, Robert Ferro, Michael Grumley, Andrew Holleran, Felice Picano, Edmund White, and George Whitmore, who met for a very short period in the early 1980s to share and discuss their works-in-progress. Although these writers were at varying points in their careers, their work reflected a common interest in exploring what it meant to be a gay man in a society whose attitudes still reflected the events of World War II and the McCarthy era. Their work shares several common features, among them a co-mingling of the sacred and profane, exploration of the erotic in Gay culture, use of autobiographical elements, and the representation of central characters who are often unlikable. The writers were highly influenced by a European tradition of literature that included authors such as Jean Genet and Christopher Isherwood, and rejected the gay literary history prevalent in the U.S. in the forties and fifties. In addition, they were interested in the social expectations of the gay novel, rejecting the medical view of homosexuality as a sickness and exploring homosexuality instead in terms of religion and morality. Though he shared certain sensibilities with the group, Dowell could not align himself with their political beliefs.

With construction scheduled in the Fifth Avenue apartment building between May and August 1983, Dowell found that he could not concentrate on writing. Leslie Miller invited him to visit. When Dowell asked if he could stay for a week, arrangements were made for him and Daisy to stay at Still Pond Cottage, Miller's grandmother's house. Miller picked up Coleman and Daisy on the 10th of August and took them to the house in New Jersey. Miller and Bradford Morrow vacationed in the house next door. For Dowell, it was a short visit. "Except for a welcoming lunch," he wrote, "I have cooked all the meals for which they (and guest(s)) arrive at cocktail time, dinner is eaten at seven, and they depart as soon as coffee has been drunk."[515] The hostility Dowell felt for his hosts resulted in his early departure.

The trip had other consequences. It was during this time that Dowell discovered a series of bruises that worried him considerably.

> Daisy and I returned from the disastrous New Jersey visit a week early, and I was so full of venom it may have poisoned me. Of course the calls FROM there began immediately but I pretended the telephone was on the blink and I could not hear, even when they got the operator to assist . . . while I was there I found immense bruises on me, caused by the Jacuzzi and by diving into the pool; I mentioned this to Bert who said I must go immediately to the dr. and I did and blood was taken, and for about three days it was believed that I had leukemia. I went to a hemotologist who took bone marrow, a pint of blood, and other materials from me, including $450. For services performed in two hours.[516]

Dowell complained of bladder and kidney pains. To help ease his suffering, Slaff gave him shots of B-12. Both men suspected that the bruises and pain were the result of a lack of B-12 and uric acid.

During the fall, Dowell distracted himself from his illness by redecorating the apartment. The interior design consisted of new carpeting, marble tile, a new mirror, a new kitchen floor, and fresh paint. He also purchased furniture, including an old Taiwanese double cabinet in teak and brass. Although his depression continued, he planned additional decoration for the coming year. He found himself again in debt for medical expenses, and in October he returned to the doctor for a CAT scan, bone scan, and more platelet counting.

Dowell suffered from night sweats and high temperatures and talked of severe pain. To sleep, he took Valium. Both the bone scan and CAT scan results appeared normal. "I have spent $3000 on laboratory tests on the two doctors, Brown and Wolf, and they know no more about me now than they did. John is determined to give me AIDS; Wolf says AIDS is unlikely."[517]

Morrow recommended Dowell for two Pushcart prizes, for "The Great Godalmighty Bird" and *The Silver Swanne*, and Edmund White put him up for a Guggenheim award. Dowell was counting on this money. He believed that receiving a Guggenheim would provide him with funds to find another country home and leave the city. Nostalgic for his life on Shelter Island, he returned for a brief visit to the farmhouse, bringing with him a signed copy of *Island People* to present to the current owner.

John Kuehl wrote Dowell that Stephen-Paul Martin had written an excellent review of *White on Black on White* for the *Review of Contemporary Fiction*. Dowell's publisher indicated that orders were still coming for the book. Edmund White, now living in Paris, mentioned to Dowell that the French press Mazarine might consider publishing a translation of *White on Black on White*. A translator that White knew was reading the novel. Dowell also got some good news concerning his health:

> Passed AIDS test with flying colors and on the same day received the first royalty check of my life, for $308.00, which makes my earnings on WOBOW, from June to November, $808!![518]

Although Dowell and Slaff were both dating other people, they continued to spend a significant amount of time together and in December they exchanged Christmas presents. Dowell's pleasure with Slaff's gifts and his decision to continue writing indicate that he ended 1983 with high hopes. "I plan to begin writing soon in the New Year. Don't know exactly what, whether EVE or HOUSES. But something."[519]

1984 was the last year Dowell kept a journal. He wrote about his health and life with Bertram Slaff and Daisy. He drank quite a bit and wrote of "a conscious effort to split my mind apart and leave only the optimistic half."[520] He was especially upset that Countryman Press invited him to a party to celebrate their ten years in publishing, but did not mention his book in the promotional brochure. The relationship seemed to mirror his earlier relationship with New Directions: Dowell had hoped that the good reviews he garnered might be used by Countrymen Press to advertise the book. His publisher, however, did little to promote it.

Leslie Miller sold the first copy of *The Silver Swanne* for $145. The deluxe edition sold nine copies the first week of February, 1984. One Texas dealer ordered five copies.

In March Dowell finished the piece on Van Vechten ("began my memoirs!" he wrote in his journal[521]). *Vanity Fair* sent him a letter indicating they might be interested in publishing it. He was still at work on *Eve of the Green Grass*, and Bradford Morrow planned to publish the first 41 pages of that work in *Conjunctions*. Morrow suggested that Dowell find an agent for the new book. Dowell gave Morrow permission to offer the excerpt to Rosalind Targ, but she rejected it, noting "there are too many loose ends . . ."[522]

Dowell continued to draft his memoirs. He longed to be in the country "where the tracks are light and elegant, deer tracks and bird tracks, and where the blanketing silence is deep and enriching . . ."[523] He was turned down for the Guggenheim. In March he wrote in the journal that he had contacted Kannenstine at Countryman Press, breaking off relations.

Dowell did not write in his journal for another seven months. In October he indicated that during the year he had encountered several deaths—his sister Eleanor, his brother-in-law (Ruth's husband), and Truman Capote. Dowell was furious at his family, for Eleanor had left $22,000 to his sister Martha and he had received nothing. In order to pay off debts he cashed in stocks totaling $10,000. He noted that he "desperately need[ed] medical attention" for his nausea attacks and prolonged headaches.[524] He still worried about his weight, which fluctuated between 187 and 190, and he suffered from an inner ear infection. "Platelets down to (up to) 80,000," he wrote, "have been at 69,000 but on the rise."[525]

* * *

In the fall of 1984 *BOMB* magazine published an excerpt from his memoir under the title "At Home with Drosselmeier." The short piece discusses Dowell's adventures in New York City and his relationship with Carl Van Vechten, as well as his early theatrical career.[526] *Conjunctions* came out with the first part of *Eve of the Green Grass*. Morrow's plans for the collection of short stories had stalled. When he approached New Directions, James Laughlin asked his assistant Griselda Ohannessian to review the manuscript, and she fired off a malevolent memo, riddled with typos, that said in part:

> I have now read six stories. I honestly can't say that I have a better feel about them that [sic] I have about Coleman's overall writing. I really did, believe it or not, approach each with as nearly an open mind as possible. I do not think ND should publish a collection of his short stories—some are okay but there is a lot of poison in most, flowering writing that does bear close scrutiny (especially in light of the gists and wisps and the "me") and bottom line [sic] is there are quite a few short story writers to which his do not hold a candle.[527]

He had written nothing new in several months. In November of 1984 Bruce returned and asked for more financial help, this time for transportation to his new job. Though Dowell gave him money freely, the pressures of debt seemed overwhelming and he took it out on Bruce, who did not stay long enough to suffer from Dowell's insults. That same week Dowell was interviewed by Belgian radio and television stations. He was filmed at his apartment. The documentary, a fifty-minute program which was to air in Belgium in April of 1985, was also to include Jerzy Kozinski and William Gaddis.

Still seeking ways to gain financial freedom from Bertram Slaff, Dowell approached New Directions about obtaining the rights to his work or the possibility of reprints. Peter Glassgold, his previous editor, replied:

> Following our recent telephone conversation, I spoke with Griselda, and you will find enclosed a letter reverting to you all rights to *Too Much Flesh and Jabez*, the one book of yours published by New Directions that is now out of print.
>
> *Mrs. October was Here* has ample stock, both in cloth and paperbound editions. We would consider a mass-market lease, but no other reprint offer at this time.

Island People, which we brought out in cloth only, is still in stock. We would gladly consider leasing a paperbook edition, mass-market or trade.[528]

Slaff went to Africa and the couple grew increasingly more distant. Dowell suffered feelings of abandonment—Slaff had been his safety net but was now seriously involved with someone else. "His calm and kindly surface," Dowell wrote about his partner, "conceals all the monsters of mythology."[529] He was so depressed that he told his niece Gayle he regretted his life, having never done anything important for humanity. When she asked about his writing he said he thought that it was not important. He believed that he had failed as a writer and he felt insignificant.

Dowell did not live long enough to see either his collection of short stories or his memoir in print. In the early morning hours of Saturday August 3, 1985, after scribbling out an explanation for Slaff, Dowell jumped from the balcony of his fifteenth-floor apartment. Officials at the scene found two scrawled notes. The first read:

Dear Bert,

I just can't bear the pressure anymore. I am so very sorry. Coleman.

A second sheet simply said:

Last Will & Testament

Everything I own and all my writings I leave without equivocation to my dear friend Bertram Slaff. Coleman Dowell.[530]

When Dowell's childhood friend Dorothy Donnell Steers read the announcement of his suicide, she tried to obtain copies of his books. On August 6, 1985 she wrote a letter to the New Directions Publishing Corporation in New York, which read in part, "To say that I, and all his friends here, are very upset about his death, is putting it mildly. I had hoped there would be some planned memorial service for him here but after finally locating the family of his sister in Hendersonville, Tennessee, this morning, I find out differently. It just doesn't seem possible that Coleman could have taken his own life, but the reference to his having left a note makes it obvious that he did." Her letter to the publishing company was returned, "Moved, Not forwardable."[531]

At 3:00 in the afternoon, on Sunday, November 3, 1985, a small gathering of Dowell's friends met to celebrate his life and work in the apartment he had shared with Bertram Slaff for more than fifteen years. Seated at the grand piano where Dowell had composed so many of his early songs, Elizabeth Rich set the tone for the afternoon gathering by performing Mozart's exuberant yet melancholy *Sonata in A Minor*. James Laughlin was the first to speak. The poet Ann Lauterbach read a statement from Gilbert Sorretino (who was not able to attend), followed by a poem she had composed for the occasion titled "Uneasy Requital to Coleman Dowell."[532] Slaff's nephew Stephen Schneider read the final letter he had written to Dowell. John Kuehl shared thoughts about his friend and Bradford Morrow read Dowell's "Dedication and Elegy," a touching piece Dowell had written for Tammy when she died. The program ended with a performance of Bach's *Jesu, Joy of Man's Desiring*.

Sorrentino's memorial began, "I suspect that Coleman ended his life because the death that was present in all his work finally refused to be held at bay by the language behind which he had for so long successfully concealed his self."[533]

Several months passed before Slaff scattered Coleman Dowell's ashes out to sea off the shore of Shelter Island.

Many of Dowell's short stories were published posthumously. These include "The Surgeon," in *New Directions in Prose and Poetry* 50, 1986; "In the Mood," in the *Review of Contemporary Fiction*, 1986; and "City Sundays," in *Harper's Magazine*, April, 1987.[534] In 1987 Weidenfeld & Nicolson first published *The Houses of Children: Collected Stories*, which assembled thirteen short stories published prior to Coleman Dowell's death. These stories appeared in *New Directions in Prose and Poetry*, *Ambit*, the *Review of Contemporary Fiction*, and *Conjunctions*.

Comprehensive analyses of the stories in *The Houses of Children* by Rena S. Kleiman, Lorrie Moore, and John and Linda Kuehl, and Miriam Fuchs offer insight and critical interpretation. These critics tend to focus on the dreamlike or surrealistic aspect of the stories, which are marked by Dowell's rich, poetic language, his reordering of temporal events, and his juxtaposition of varying points of view. The stories in the first half of the book are told from a child's point of view (with the exception of "Mrs. Hackett," an elderly woman who is reliving her childhood). The protagonists of these stories, human and animal, generally experience a metamorphosis of some kind. Kleiman points out that "Dowell set his eyes on the violent and the lurid in modern life: the insane, the senile, the cannibal, the hunchback, the loner, the freaks."[535] She compares the stories to those of Hemingway's protagonist Nick Adams in *In Our Time*, for "Dowell's boy narrators see and record, but do not yet have the power to understand what they see."[536] Fuchs concentrates on two stories: "My Father was a River" and "If Beggars Were Horses." Although Fuchs acknowledges the surreal aspect of the stories, she is quick to point out the narrators generally provide a "strong and compassionate presence."[537]

The six stories that make up the second half of the book, "The Consequences of Breath," concern adult life; as John and Linda Kuehl explain, "their protagonists tend to be paired adults at odds with each other. Cities and small towns replace farms, and symbiotic relationships replace erotic desires."[538]

Most of the stories are fantasies. The themes are familiar: importance of place, the link between hatred and violence, the conflict between mind and body, and obsession with death. In his story "Writings on a Cave Wall" the theme of the writer's life returns. The majority of the stories are about houses or homes, and Dowell explores the importance of home—whether it is a Toll House, a cave, or a river—as Lorrie Moore says, "houses as embodiments of all personal construction and endeavor."[539] The places in these stories were home to Coleman Dowell—the seaside cottages, the farmhouse, the New York apartment—each provided a place where he could let his imagination roam freely.

* * *

Articles, translations and reprints of Coleman Dowell's work are leading to a revival of interest in his career. Several of his novels have been translated into French and Spanish, and in 1987 Weidenfeld & Nicholson reissued *One of the Children is Crying*. Dalkey Archive Press has reissued *Too Much Flesh and Jabez* (1987), *Island People* (1996), and *The Houses of Children* (2000). Yet many of Dowell's stories remain uncollected and several manuscripts unpublished. At the bequest of John Kuehl, professor of English at New York University, Bertram Slaff, Dowell's literary executor, donated Coleman Dowell's papers to the Bobst Library in December 1986. Among the papers are the manuscript for his final novel, *Eve of the Green Grass*; Dowell's private journal (1968–1984), a running diary of his life, writings, attitude towards people, and observations for stories; and Dowell's autobiography entitled *A Dark Book*. The book recounts Dowell's early adventures in New York and his relationship with Carl Van Vechten, as well as his early theatrical career. The memoir was published in 1993 as *A Star-Bright Lie*.

NOTES

1. Bertram Slaff, interview by Eugene Hayworth, February, 2001.

2. John Kuehl, "An Interview with Coleman Dowell," *Contemporary Literature*, 22.3, 1981, 272–91.

3. Slaff, interview, 2001.

4. Coleman Dowell, interview by Bev Smith, WGBS Radio, August 8, 1983.

5. Best known as the author of *Nigger Heaven*, Van Vechten was a photographer and friend of many Harlem writers and singers, and was Gertrude Stein's literary executor.

6. Carl Van Vechten to Edward Leuders, Bruce Kellner, *Carl Van Vechten*, 280.

7. Coleman Dowell, *White on Black on White*, 161.

8. Kuehl, "Interview," 283.

9. Edmund White, interview by Eugene Hayworth, "Edmund White on Coleman Dowell," *Context* no. 8 (2002), 3. White also uses this term to describe *White on Black on White*, in Edmund White, "Thoughts on *White on Black on White*," *The Burning Library*, 135.

10. Edmund White, *Burning*, 116.

11. Stephen-Paul Martin, "Exorcism and Grace: A Study of Androgyny in *Island People*," *Review of Contemporary Fiction*, 2.3, 1982, 124–28.

12. Slaff, interview.

13. Dowell's sister Martha attempted to verify the rumor. She contacted the Posey County Clerk's Office, and a researcher there replied:

> I can find no record of Coleman Dowell's disappearance among the court records nor in the newspaper accounts at this time. However, an old man told me the same story. He disappeared in the area of the Lanston Saloon which was close to the river in Mt. Vernon. This man said as a small child this was quite a rough area and several people disappeared from it and he was afraid to go by the area by himself. Usually such bodies were buried in what was called the "Potters" section of the local graveyard. If you desire further research, I do have a fee of $2 an hour. [to Martha Cline. private collection of Gayle Wohlken].

14. Ruth Willis to the author, October 15, 2000.

15. Martha recalled to her daughter Gayle that when her father Morda came home, he had a strong feeling something was wrong. He was grateful to see his family together standing outside the burning house. Such superstitions and insights helped shape Coleman Dowell's later reliance on the occult and premonitions.

16. John O'Brien, "An Interview with Coleman Dowell," *Review of Contemporary Fiction*, 2.3, 1982, 85–99.

17. Coleman Dowell to Martha Cline, undated, private collection of Gayle Wohlken.

18. Ibid.

19. Kuehl,"Interview," 275.

20. Coleman Dowell, *Island People*, 268.

21. Coleman Dowell, A *Star-Bright Lie*, 151.

22. Gayle Wohlken, e-mail to the author, March 17, 2002.

23. Ibid.

24. Excerpt from Coleman Dowell letter, no year, but dated April 13:

> "I asked mother on the weekend about various family names, but she was not even sure what her mother's maiden name was, only that she had been adopted."

25. Like her brother, Martha was an avid reader and she kept an account of the books she read, which gives some indication of the types of books Coleman would have had available from the local library. Her list included such titles as *Ranch Romances*, *No Honor Lost*, Zane Grey's *Code of the West*, *Laddie* by Gene Stratton Porter, *Kidnapped* by Robert Louis Stevenson, *Ramona* by Helen Hunt Jackson, *Keeper of the Bees* by G. S. Porter, *When Beggars Choose* by K. N. Burt, and *Second Violin* by Grace S. Richmond.

26. Kuehl, "Interview," 280.

27. Gayle Wohlken, e-mail to the author, April 30, 2002.

28. Virginia Page, "Author Praises his Former Logan Teachers," *The News-Democrat*, Thursday, February 17, 1985.

29. In a letter to James Laughlin dated November 16, 1975 Dowell wrote, "My next to oldest sister rode horseback every day, a sixteen mile round trip, to study Latin and Greek, which was offered in a one-room schoolhouse in the backwoods. She read Virgil as others read bestsellers nowadays. I went to a country school, a five-room job, through the eighth grade, and my eighth grade book report was on Oedipus." (Houghton Library, Harvard. bMS Am 207 (477) Coleman Dowell, Correspondence, 1972–1985.)

30. Coleman's sister Martha kept a diary during her early years, from January 1, 1937

until December 20, 1939, which provides intimate details of daily life and insight into family relationships. Martha was 14 when she started her diary on New Year's Day, and Coleman was 12. Martha talked about her cousins Marie and Lucille, daughters of her father's brother, and often mentions Coleman, whom she called "R.C."

31. Coleman Dowell, personal journal, November 12, 1976, a photocopy from the private collection of Bertram Slaff. The original journal is held at the Fales Library, New York University, which is closed until 2010.

32. Martha Dowell, private journal, March 28, 1937, private collection of Gayle Wohlken.

33. Coleman Dowell, personal journal, February 2, 1978.

34. Ibid.

35. Copies of Dowell's high school newsletters, *The Middleton Monitor* and *Hi-Lights*, were provided courtesy of Dorothy Donnell Steers.

36. Kuehl, "Interview," 275.

37. For a discussion of Dowell's early reading habits see: O'Brien, "Interview," 96 and Kuehl, "Interview," 284.

38. *Hi-Lights*, December 1941, private collection of the author.

39. *Hi-Lights*, May 1943, private collection of the author.

40. Coleman Dowell, to his mother, undated, private collection of Gayle Wohlken.

41. Darnall General Hospital. Hospital Regulations H.R. No. 5-5, February 5, 1942.

42. Coleman Dowell, personal journal, January 17, 1975.

43. Coleman Dowell to Martha Cline, undated, private collection of Gayle Wohlken.

44. Coleman Dowell to his mother, undated, private collection of Gayle Wohlken.

45. Coleman Dowell to his parents, undated, ca. 1942, private collection of Gayle Wohlken.

46. Coleman Dowell, "Awakening of a Bombed City," Fales Collection, Series II, Subseries A, Box 13, Folder 7.

47. Ibid.

48. Ibid.

49. Coleman Dowell to Beulah Dowell, undated, ca. 1946, private collection of Gayle Wohlken.

50. Coleman Dowell, *A Star-Bright Lie*, 53.

51. Coleman Dowell to Martha Cline, undated, private collection of Gayle Wohlken.

52. Coleman Dowell to Martha Cline, October, 13, 1947, private collection of Gayle Wohlken.

53. Coleman Dowell to Martha Cline, undated, [Valentine's day], private collection of Gayle Wohlken.

54. Ibid.

55. Coleman Dowell to Martha Cline, May 6, 1948, private collection of Gayle Wohlken.

56. Coleman Dowell to Martha Cline, undated, private collection of Gayle Wohlken.

57. Ibid.

58. Here are his lyrics:

No nights left just to spend in lovin',
No days left just for dreamin',
Till you're home again, but 'till then
I'll keep you in my heart,

No time left just to count my worries,
No time left just for schemin',
Till you're home again, but 'till then
I'll keep you in my heart.

Kisses remembered always make me blue,
And now there's work to be done,
But soon we'll be together, the moon,
Myself and you,
When there's no evil under the sun.

Stars all gone from the sky above me,
Lights all gone off of Broadway,
But they'll come on again, and 'till
then I'll keep you in my heart.

59. Coleman Dowell, *A Star-Bright Lie*, 15. It is interesting to note that in an undated letter to his mother, Coleman referred to Walter Dowell as "a distant relation."

60. Ibid, 25.

61. Coleman Dowell, "Haymarket," Fales Collection, Series II, Subseries B Box 2, Folder 10, 1–1–1.

62. Ibid, 1–1–2.

63. Ibid,

64. Ibid, 1–2–16.

65. Ibid, 1–2–23.

66. Coleman Dowell, "A Lady Who's Shady," Fales Collection, Series III, Subseries A, Box 1, Folder 2.

67. Coleman Dowell, *Haymarket*, Fales Collection, Series III, Musical Works and Lyrics (1950–1961).

68. For further information about Audrey Wood and the playwrights she represented, see her memoir entitled *Represented by Audrey Wood*.

69. In his letter to his sister, Dowell called the poet "Isabella Motts," however later letters to his sister Martha suggest that this was Isabella Fey, who had a home in Crestwood, New York, and who visited Alec Nyary frequently. Nyary was Godfather to her son, Esdras, who explains the possible confusion of her name: "Isabella Motts *has* to be my mother. "motts", altho i never heard that, must have been a play on her appellation for my father, Maurice, whom she intimately called "Muttsy." why or how she came to do this i can't imagine. but if Cole met them as a couple, it seems a reasonable thing." [e-mail to author, 10/19/03].

70. Coleman Dowell, to his parents, undated, private collection of Gayle Wohlken.

71. Ibid.

72. Isabella Fey, "The Tale of Annie Christmas," private collection of the author.

73. Coleman Dowell, to his parents, undated, ca. December, 1950, private collection of Gayle Wohlken.

74. "A Good Song is Hard to Find," *Look Magazine*, February 13, 1951, 100–103.

75. Coleman Dowell, "Once Upon a Tune Theme Song." Fales Collection, Series III, Box 2, Folder 4. Dowell later used the same melody for another song he titled "On and On."

76. "1925 Scopes Trial Haunts Tv Forum," *New York Times*, December 29, 1952.

77. Willard Swire, "Closed-Circuit Fiasco," *New York Times*, April 10, 1955.

78. Sam Zolotow, "Adelphi to Offer Legitimate Fare," *New York Times*, February 19, 1957. The playhouse was demolished in 1970.

79. Coleman Dowell, to his parents, undated, ca. December 1950], private collection of Gayle Wohlken.

80. *Performers Television Credits Volume* 3, 2723.

81. *Performers Television Credits Volume* 1, 104.

82. Coleman Dowell, *A Star-Bright Lie*, 41.

83. Edmund Leamy, "Unpretentious Experiment in TV: Aiming High at Low Cost," *New York World-Telegram and Sun*, April 21, 1951.

84. Ibid.

85. Bob Rothstein, "Behind the Scenes: Loewi Sings an Original Tune," *Tele-Talent*. April 23, 1951.

86. Bob Rothstein, "Noted in Passing," *Television Week*, April 28–May 4, 1951.

87. Bill Leslie to Coleman Dowell, September 30, 1950, Fales Collection, Series I, Box 3, Folder 10.

88. Coleman Dowell to his parents, undated, ca. December 1950, private collection of Gayle Wohlken.

89. Jack Gould, "'Once Upon a Tune' DuMont Musical Program Demonstrates the Problems of Experimentation," *New York Times*, May 6, 1951.

90. Coleman Dowell to Martha Cline, undated, ca. 1951, private collection of Gayle Wohlken.

91. Ria A. Niccoli, "Writer Hits Tin Pan Alley Through Medium of TV," *Down Beat*, October 5, 1951.

92. Seventh Heaven opened at the ATNA Theater in 1955, starring Ricardo Montalban and Gloria DeHaven.

93. Lesser did acquire the rights in 1952 and hoped to persuade Cole Porter to write the songs and Roland Petit to provide the choreography. See Sam Zolotow, "Seventh Heaven' Bought By Lesser," *New York Times*, Feb 18, 1952. In March 1953, the rights passed to Stella Unger. Sam Zolotow, "Lyrics Shaping Up For '7th Heaven,'" *New York Times*, June 26, 1953.

94. Coleman Dowell to Martha Cline, undated, private collection of Gayle Wohlken.

95. Coleman Dowell to Martha Cline, undated, private collection of Gayle Wohlken.

96. Coleman Dowell to his parents, undated, private collection of Gayle Wohlken.

97. Coleman Dowell to Martha Cline, undated, private collection of Gayle Wohlken.

98. Ibid.

99. Ibid.

100. In Dowell's memoir he places these events after his collaboration with John Latouche, however one early mention of Cole Porter's work on this show occurred in Louis Funke, "News and Gossip of the Rialto," *New York Times*, November 29, 1953, two years before Dowell's collaboration with Latouche.

101. Coleman Dowell to Martha Cline undated, private collection of Gayle Wohlken.

102. Ibid.

103. Coleman Dowell to Martha Cline, undated, but probably June, 1953, private collection of Gayle Wohlken.

104. Ibid.

105. Coleman Dowell to his parents, private collection of Gayle Wohlken.

106. Secrest, *Leonard Bernstein*, 154.

107. Megan Rosenfeld, "David Merrick, The Imperious Light of Broadway." *Washington Post*, April 28, 2000.

108. Ibid.

109. Coleman Dowell to Martha Cline, undated, ca. February/March, 1954, private collection of Gayle Wohlken.

110. Isabella Fey to Coleman Dowell, August, 1954, Fales Collection, Series I, Box 1, Folder 23.

111. Coleman Dowell to Martha Cline, undated, circa January, 1955, from the private collection of Gayle Wohlken.

112. Ibid.

113. Sam Zolotow, "Miss Holm May Do Play For Miller," *New York Times*, April 8, 1955.

114. Lewis Funke, "Abe Burrows Takes A New Assignment—Theatre Guild Plans—Other Items," *New York Times*, April 17, 1955.

115. Coleman Dowell to Beulah and Morda Dowell, undated, private collection of Gayle Wohlken.

116. Coleman Dowell to Beulah and Morda Dowell, undated, circa April, 1955, private collection of Gayle Wohlken.

117. In 1939 York co-authored *The Man who Killed Hitler* with Dean Southern Jennings and David Malcolmson, and her plays, produced off-Broadway, included *Love Song For Mrs. Boas* and *Lullaby For A Dying Man*. York also translated another of Dowell's stories, "Der junge Knecht" ("The Young Servant"), but it was not published until much later, under the title "Ham's Gift."

118. Ruth Landshoff York, "For Coleman Dowell to fit one of his spare tunes to," Ruth York Collection, The Howard Gotlieb Archival Research Center at Boston University.

119. William C. Bamberger. *Kenward Elmslie: a biliographical profile*. Bamberger Books, 1993 (p. 2).

120. Coleman Dowell to Bertram Slaff, April 18, 1955, from the personal collection of Bertram Slaff.

121. Coleman Dowell to Bertram Slaff, April 19, 1955, from the personal collection of Bertram Slaff.

122. Coleman Dowell to Bertram Slaff, April 21, 1955, from the personal collection of Bertram Slaff.

123. Coleman Dowell to Bertram Slaff, April 23, 1955, from the personal collection of Bertram Slaff.

124. Coleman Dowell to Bertram Slaff, April 25, 1955, from the personal collection of Bertram Slaff.

125. Latouche actually died on August 7, 1956.

126. Coleman Dowell to Martha Cline, undated, ca. 1956, from the private collection of Gayle Wohlken.

127. Produced by David Merrick, the show opened October 22, 1959 at the Shubert Theatre (New York) and ran for 448 performances.

128. Bertram Slaff, interview by Eugene Hayworth, November, 2004.

129. Coleman Dowell to Martha Cline, undated, private collection of Gayle Wohlken.

130. Ibid.

131. Bruce Kellner, *Carl Van Vechten*, 304–5.

132. Robert Downing to Carl Van Vechten, May 3, 1957, Carl Van Vechten Collection, Box I, Folder 24.

133. Bruce Kellner, *Carl Van Vechten*, 273.

134. Slaff, interview, 2001.

135. Ibid.

136. Carl Van Vechten, *The Tattooed Countess*, 160.

137. Coleman Dowell to Carl Van Vechten, February 1957, Carl Van Vechten Collection, Box II, Folder 5.

138. Coleman Dowell to Carl Van Vechten, February 21, 1957, Carl Van Vechten Collection, Box II, Folder 5.

139. Ibid.

140. Ibid.

141. Coleman Dowell to Carl Van Vechten, April 29, 1957, Carl Van Vechten Collection, Box II, Folder 5.

142. Ibid.

143. Eileen Herlie to Coleman Dowell, November 30, 1959, Fales Library, Series I, Box 1, Folder 31.

144. Coleman Dowell to Carl Van Vechten, July 2, 1957, Carl Van Vechten Collection, Box II, Folder 6.

145. Coleman Dowell, "A Fable for Carlo's Amusement," June 17, 1957, Carl Van Vechten Collection, Box II, Folder 5.

146. Coleman Dowell to Martha Cline, undated, private collection of Gayle Wohlken.

147. Slaff, interview, 2001.

148. Coleman Dowell to Beulah Dowell, undated, private collection of Gayle Wohlken.

149. Coleman Dowell to Carl Van Vechten, July 11, 1957, Carl Van Vechten Collection, Box II, Folder 6.

150. Coleman Dowell to Carl Van Vechten, undated, ca. August, 1957, Carl Van Vechten Collection, Box II, Folder 6.

151. Dowell gives the date as October 28, however they returned to the states on September 8. Perhaps he intended August 28, but it is possible the meeting did not occur. Slaff could not recall that Coleman had any music or show in the works in London, and suggested that Dowell may have exaggerated to impress his family.

152. Coleman Dowell to Beulah Dowell, undated, private collection of Gayle Wohlken.

153. Oct. 15, 1957.

154. Coleman Dowell to Carl Van Vechten, November 7, 1957, Carl Van Vechten Collection, Box II, Folder 6.

155. Vocal coach for Gertrude Lawrence and Julie Harris, also responsible for the arrangements for *Annie Get Your Gun* and *Kiss Me Kate*.

156 Coleman Dowell to Carl Van Vechten, November 7, 1957, Carl Van Vechten Collection, Box II, Folder 6.

157. Ibid.

158. Carl Van Vechten to Coleman Dowell, November 6, 1957, Fales Collection, Series I, Box 3, Folder 12.

159. Coleman Dowell to Carl Van Vechten, November 7, 1957, Carl Van Vechten Collection, Box II, Folder 6.

160. Coleman Dowell to Carl Van Vechten, January 10, 1958, Carl Van Vechten Collection, Box II, Folder 8.

161. Carl Van Vechten to Coleman Dowell, June 24, 1959, Carl Van Vechten Collection, Box II, Folder 9.

162. Louis Calta, "English Comedy Coming in March," *New York Times*, February 6, 1958.

163. Coleman Dowell to Beulah Dowell, undated, ca. January 1958, private collection of Gayle Wohlken.

164. Coleman Dowell to Beulah Dowell, undated, ca. January 1958, private collection of Gayle Wohlken.

165. Coleman Dowell to Beulah Dowell, undated, private collection of Gayle Wohlken.

166. Coleman Dowell to Beulah Dowell and Martha Cline, undated, Easter Eve, private collection of Gayle Wohlken.

167. Coleman Dowell to Carl Van Vechten, March 23, 1958, Carl Van Vechten Collection, Box II, Folder 7.

168. Slaff, interview, 2001.

169. Sam Zolotow, "Theatres to keep cut in ticket tax," *New York Times*, January 2, 1959.

170. Sam Zolotow, "2 May produce London hit here," *New York Times*, November 27, 1959.

171. "Theatre tonight," *New York Times*, March 3, 1959.

172. "Theatre tonight," *New York Times*, June 24, 1959.

173. "Barr plans 3 plays," *New York Times*, September 26, 1960.

174. Coleman Dowell to Carol Cline, January, 1960, private collection of Gayle Wohlken.

175. "Beautiful Dreamer rift," *New York Times*, November 4, 1960.

176. Irene Manning to Coleman Dowell, March 26, 1961, Fales Collection, Series I, Box 2, Folder 11.

177. Kenward Elmslie to Coleman Dowell, January 9, 1961, Fales Collection, Series III, Box 5, Folder 5.

178. Carl Van Vechten telegram to Coleman Dowell, May 3, 1961, Fales Collection, Series III, Box 5, Folder 5.

179. David Hollister telegram to Coleman Dowell, May 5, 1961, Fales Collection, Series III, Box 5, Folder 5.

180. Howard Taubman, "Theatre: Corn in Ioway." *New York Times*, May 4, 1961.

181. Jack Gaver, "Music's Good, Libretto Bad: Countess' just dull in off-broadway bow," UPI, May 4, 1961.

182. Judith Crist, "First night report: 'The Tattooed Countess,'" *Herald Tribune*, May 4, 1961.

183. Carl Van Vechten to Coleman Dowell, May 4, 1961, Fales Collection, Series I, Box III, Folder 13.

184. Ruth Landshoff York to Coleman Dowell, May 5, 1961, Fales Collection, Series III, Box 5, Folder 5.

185. Virginia Payne to Coleman Dowell, Saturday, May 12, 1961, Fales Collection, Series III, Box 5, Folder 5.

186. Kellner, *Letters*. 280.

187. Kellner. *Letters*. 280.

188. Carl Van Vechten to Coleman Dowell, January 4, 1964, Fales Collection, Series I, Box III, Folder 13.

189. Coleman Dowell to Martha Cline, undated, private collection of Gayle Wohlken.

190. Coleman Dowell to Martha Cline, April 9, 1962, private collection of Gayle Wohlken.

191. Coleman Dowell to Carol Cline, April 15, 1962, private collection of Gayle Wohlken.

192. Coleman Dowell to Carol Cline, December 11, 1961, private collection of Gayle Wohlken.

193. Coleman Dowell to Beulah Dowell, April 9, 1962, private collection of Gayle Wohlken.

194. *Frankfurter Hefte*, 17 Jahrang, Heft 4, April 1962.

195. Coleman Dowell to Martha Cline, May 21, 1962, private collection of Gayle Wohlken.

196. Coleman Dowell to Martha Cline, November, 1962, private collection of Gayle Wohlken.

197. John Howard Griffin, personal journal, Thursday, 1 A.M., ca. May, 1962). Box 33, Folder 831, 1204.

198. Coleman Dowell to Martha Cline, May 21, 1962, private collection of Gayle Wohlken.

199. Coleman Dowell to Carol Cline, May 15 [1962], private collection of Gayle Wohlken.

200. Slaff, interview, 2001.

201. Stefani Hunzinger to Coleman Dowell, July 17, 1962, Fales Collection, Series I, Box 1, Folder 25.

202. Fisher Verlag to Coleman Dowell, August 20, 1965, Fales Collection, Series I, Box 1, Folder 25.

203. Coleman Dowell to Martha Cline, November, 1962, private collection of Gayle Wohlken. Dowell's letters to Van Vechten are actually part of the Van Vechten collection at New York Public Library.

204. Ibid.

205. Ibid.

206. Coleman Dowell to Gayle Cline, May 2, 1963, private collection of Gayle Wohlken.

207. Coleman Dowell to Gayle Cline, undated, ca. December, 1963, private collection of Gayle Wohlken.

208. Coleman Dowell, personal journal, January 9, 1964, Fales Collection.

209. Ibid.

210. Coleman Dowell to Martha Cline, February 15, 1965, private collection of Gayle Wohlken.

211. Yetta Arenstein "Magazine Editor Contributor to the *Saturday Review* Was Also Lecturer," *New York Times*, February 1, 1965.

212. Coleman Dowell, personal journal, January 13, 1964. Fales Collection.

213. Ibid.

214. Coleman Dowell, personal journal, January 27, 1964. Fales Collection.

215. Coleman Dowell to Gayle Cline, undated, ca. February, 1964, private collection of Gayle Wohlken.

216. Coleman Dowell to Carol Cline, November 14, 1964, private collection of Gayle Wohlken.

217. Coleman Dowell to Cline Family, November, 1964, private collection of Gayle Wohlken.

218. Jeannette Gilbert to Coleman Dowell, undated, Fales Collection, Series I, Box 1, Folder 25.

219. Coleman Dowell to Martha Cline, December 10, 1964, private collection of Gayle Wohlken.

220. Bill Inge to Coleman Dowell, February 19, 1959. Fales Collection. Series I, Box 1, Folder 33.

221. Undated [ca. February, 1965], private collection of Gayle Wohlken.

222. Coleman Dowell to Martha Cline, undated, private collection of Gayle Wohlken.

223. Coleman Dowell to Ted Brooks, March 12, 1965, Fales Collection, Series III, Box 2, Folder 5.

224. Barbra Streisand to Coleman Dowell and Bertram Slaff, May 24, 1965, Fales Collection. Series III, Box 2, Folder 5.

225. Coleman Dowell to Martha Cline, August 19, 1965, private collection of Gayle Wohlken.

226. Liz (probably Lady Elizabeth Eliot) to Coleman Dowell, October 8, 1965, Fales Collection, Series I, Box I, Folder 17.

227. Bertram Slaff. Interview with the author. 2001.

228. Coleman Dowell to Martha Cline. October 11, 1965, private collection of Gayle Wohlken.

229. Coleman Dowell, *The Eve of the Green Grass*, unpublished manuscript, 2. Fales Collection, Series II, Subseries A, Box 11, Folder 2.

230. Slaff, interview, 2004.

231. Lady Elizabeth Kinnaird wrote under the nom de plume Elizabeth Eliot.

232. Dowell may have started this novel as early as 1962. There is a reference to a novel in a letter Dowell wrote to Madeleine Aman, dated December 16, 1962, in which he mentions that his novel "went to the publisher on Monday."

233. Those she represented included Carl Sandburg, Helen Hayes, Jonas Salk, Jane Alexander, Alex Haley, Norman Mailer, Lillian Gish, Pat Carroll, Ossie Davis, and Elizabeth Kubler-Ross.

234. Desmond Flower to Coleman Dowell, June 20th, 1966, Fales Collection, Series II, Subseries A, Folder 2, Box 4.

235. Coleman Dowell to Martha Cline, April 5, 1966, private collection of Gayle Wohlken.

236. Coleman Dowell to Madeleine Aman, April 20, 1966, private collection of Bertram Slaff.

237. Letter dated October 5th, 1966, Fales Collection, Series II, Subseries A, Folder 2, Box 4.

238. Nicholas Flower to Coleman Dowell, January 18, 1967, Fales Collection, Series II, Subseries A, Folder 2, Box 5.

239. Lucy Kroll to Nicholas Flower, January 24, 1967, Fales Collection. Series II, Subseries A, Folder 2, Box 4.

240. Ibid.

241. Coleman Dowell to Martha Cline, undated, ca. 1967, private collection of Gayle Wohlken.

242. Laura Ford to Coleman Dowell, June 8, 1967, Fales Collection, Series II, Subseries A, Box 2, Folder 5.

243. Coleman Dowell to Martha Cline, October 5, 1967, private collection of Gayle Wohlken.

244. Coleman Dowell to Lady Elizabeth Kinnaird, February 21, 1967, private collection of Bertram Slaff.

245. Differences in the text include American versus British spelling and the use of the word "fuck" which was omitted from the English edition.

246. Don Robertson, "Review of *One of the Children is Crying*, by Coleman Dowell," *Cleveland Plain Dealer*, March 3, 1968.

247. Dorothy Donnell Steers, e-mail to the author, December 13, 2001.

248. Kuehl, "Interview," 276.

249. The year is never given in the novel, however at the start of the novel Erin reveals that Robin has been away from home for three years. Later in the novel Robin re-

members the night in 1959 (194) when he leaves town will the intention he will never return.

250. Kuehl, "Interview," 276.

251. Coleman Dowell, *One of the Children is Crying*, 132.

252. Maria Vittoria D'Amico, *Postmodern Fiction*, 342.

253. Coleman Dowell, *One of the Children is Crying*, 3.

254. Ibid, 53.

255. Kuehl, "Interview," 276.

256. Coleman Dowell, *One of the Children is Crying*, 4.

257. Ibid, 47.

258. Ibid, 308.

259. Ibid, 53

260. Ibid, 79.

261. Ibid, 111.

262. Ibid, 127.

263. Ibid, 196.

264. Ibid, 130.

265. Ibid, 119.

266. Ibid, 126.

267. Ibid, 47.

268. Ibid, 73.

269. Ibid, 175.

270. Ibid, 183.

271. Ibid, 240.

272. Ibid, 240.

273. Kuehl, "Interview," 276.

274. Coleman Dowell, *One of the Children is Crying*, 243.

275. Ibid, 248.

276. Ibid, 253.

277. Ibid, 294.

278. Ibid, 307

279. Ibid, 304.

280. Ibid, 310.

281. James Ethridge to Coleman Dowell, June 25, 1968, Fales Collection, Series I, Box 1, Folder 17.

282. Coleman Dowell to James Ethridge, undated, personal collection of Bertram Slaff.

283. John Howard Griffin, personal journal, January 6, 1968, Box 34, Folder 838, 1906.

284. "Coleman Dowell," *The Writer*, 81:3, March 1968.

285. Coleman Dowell to Gerald Ford, Sept. 9, 1974, private collection of Bertram Slaff.

286. I have indicated in other sources that Coleman Dowell and Bertram Slaff rented the house on Shelter Island in 1967. This was based on a comment Dowell made indicating he spent his first year there finishing his first novel. Letters discovered recently, however, indicate that the couple did not take the farmhouse until the summer of 1968.

287. Coleman Dowell to Martha Cline, June, 1968, private Collection of Gayle Wohlken.

288. Jack Beeson, interview with Eugene Hayworth, May 30, 2002.

289. Ibid.

290. John Howard Griffin to "Mrs. Hackett," December 20, 1969, Fales Collection, Series I, Box 1, Folder 28.

291. Griffin had, in fact, done some work on the essay, but was overwhelmed with assignments. He wrote in his journal, "[I] ... have been working on the book, THE CHURCH AND THE BLACK MAN, working on the Continuum Merton issue, accepted the commission to write the official Merton biography ... also have done work for the Hallmark Books edition of Merton and worked on the chapter for Rediscoveries (my chapter dealing with Coleman Dowell's book)." [Personal journal, May 12, 1969, Box 34, Folder 839, 2091.] When *Rediscoveries* was finally published in 1971, it did not include a chapter on Dowell, but Madden included the title, *One of the Children is Crying*, in an appendix called "A Partial List Worthy of Rediscovery."

292. Coleman Dowell to Sumner Locke Elliott, October 2, 1974. Sumner Locke Elliott Collection, Howard Gotlieb Archival Research Center, Boston University.

293. Sumner Locke Elliott to Coleman Dowell, October 4, 1972, Fales Collection, Series I, Box 1, Folder 17.

294. Kuehl, "Interview." 285.

295. Ibid, 285. An expression American soldiers scribbled on walls during their tour of duty in World War II.

296. O'Brien, "Interview," 95.

297. Coleman Dowell to James Laughlin, September 13, 1972, Houghton Library, Harvard, bMS Am 207 (477), New Directions Papers. Coleman Dowell, Correspondence, 1972–1985.

298. James Laughlin to Coleman Dowell, November 16, 1972, Houghton Library, Harvard, bMS Am 207 (477), Coleman Dowell, Correspondence, 1972–1985.

299. Coleman Dowell, to James Laughlin. November 29, 1972, Houghton Library, Harvard, bMS Am 207 (477), Coleman Dowell, Correspondence, 1972–1985.

300. Coleman Dowell, personal journal, July 26, 1973.

301. James Laughlin to Coleman Dowell, Dec 12, 1972, Houghton Library, Harvard, bMS Am 207 (477), Coleman Dowell, Correspondence, 1972–1985.

302. Coleman Dowell, to James Laughlin, July 30, 1973, Houghton Library, Harvard, bMS Am 207 (477), Coleman Dowell, Correspondence, 1972–1985.

303. Dowell kept a copy of this letter, which is among his personal papers, dated 9/23/70.

304. Kuehl, "Interview," 286.

305. Coleman Dowell to James Laughlin. March 20, 1973, Houghton Library, Harvard, bMS Am 207 (477), Coleman Dowell, Correspondence, 1972–1985.

306. Bergson, *Time*, 167.

307. Coleman Dowell, *Mrs. October was Here*, 42.

308. Carl Van Vechten, *The Tattooed Countess*, 1.

309. Ibid, 160.

310. Ibid, 146.

311. O'Brien. "Interview," 87

312. Ibid, 94.

313. Stermer, *The Art of Revolution*, xix.

314. Coleman Dowell, personal journal, September 29, 1970.

315. Kuehl, "Interview," 273.

316. Ibid, 286.

317. Thom Gunn, "Pushy Jews and Aging Queens: Imaginary People in Two Novels by Coleman Dowell," *Review of Contemporary Fiction*, 2.3, 1982.

318. Carol E. Rinzler to Coleman Dowell, undated, Fales Collection, Series II, Subseries A, Box 3, Folder 9.

319. Peter Kaldheim to Coleman Dowell, December 27, 1974, Fales Collection, Series II, Subseries A, Box 3, Folder 9.

320. Josef Dignan to Coleman Dowell, undated, Fales Collection, Series I, Box 1, Folder 13.

321. James Laughlin to Coleman Dowell, May 21, 1974, Houghton Library, Harvard, bMS Am 207 (477), Coleman Dowell, Correspondence, 1972–1985.

322. Coleman Dowell to James Laughlin, May 22, 1974, Houghton Library, Harvard, bMS Am 207 (477), Coleman Dowell, Correspondence, 1972–1985.

323. Coleman Dowell to James Laughlin, May 22, 1974, Houghton Library, Harvard, bMS Am 207 (477), Coleman Dowell, Correspondence, 1972–1985.

324. Coleman Dowell, personal journal, October 26. 1971.

325. Ibid, July 30, 1971.

326. Ibid, July 20, 1971..

327. O'Brien. "Interview," 90.

328. Coleman Dowell to James Laughlin, November 4, 1973, Houghton Library, Harvard, bMS Am 207 (477), Coleman Dowell, Correspondence, 1972–1985.

329. James Laughlin to Coleman Dowell, November 27, 1973, Houghton Library, Harvard, bMS Am 207 (477), Coleman Dowell, Correspondence, 1972–1985.

330. Coleman Dowell to James Laughlin. March 7 [1974]. Houghton Library, Harvard. bMS Am 207 (477) Coleman Dowell, Correspondence, 1972–1985.

331. Josef Dignan to Coleman Dowell, undated, Fales Collection, Series I, Box 1, Folder 13.

332. Patrick McGrath, "Interview with Bradford Morrow," *Review of Contemporary Fiction*, 20.1, 2000, 17–32.

333. Kuehl, "Interview," 282.

334. Martin, "Exorcism," 124.

335. Dust jacket blurb.

336. Gilbert Sorrentino, "Reading Coleman Dowell's *Island People*," *Review of Contemporary Fiction*, 2.3, 1982, 122–23.

337. Kuehl, "Interview," 280.

338. Coleman Dowell, *Island People*, 42.

339. O'Brien, "Interview," 96. In Proust' *Remembrance of Things Past*, the taste of the madeleine is the catalyst for recalling all that follows.

340. Ibid, 90.

341. "News From New Directions," ca. 1976.

342. Coleman Dowell, *Island People*, 287.

343. John Kuehl, "Review of *Island People* by Coleman Dowell," *Commonweal*, 103.19, 1976, 602–3.

344. White, "*Island People*." p. 40.

345. Ibid.

346. Jim Marks, "Ménage à Trois: *Island People* by Coleman Dowell," *Lambda Book Report*, 5.4, 1996, 8–9.

347. Sorrentino, "Some Remarks," 122.

348. Ibid, 123.

349. Ursula K. Heise, "Time Frames: Temporality and Narration in Coleman Dowell's *Island People*," *The Journal of Narrative Technique*, 21.3, 1991, 274–288.

350. Dowell may have included a reference to the Icelandic author in the line, "Did

I mean that in summer the self, camouflaged in permissiveness . . . recognized laxness as part of earned leisure?" (13).

351. Laxness, *Independent People*, 13

352. Ibid, 31–32.

353. O'Brien, "Interview," 87.

354. Laxness, *Independent People*, 132.

355. Ibid, 11.

356. Ibid, 33.

357. Dowell, *Island People*, p. 37.

358. Vandiver, "The *Odyssey* of Homer," Lecture 2.

359. O'Brien. "Interview," 92.

360. James Purdy to Coleman Dowell, July 29, 1976, Fales Collection, Series I, Box 2, Folder 15.

361. Edmund White, "Review of *Island People*, by Coleman Dowell," *New York Times Book Review*, September 19, 1976.

362. Coleman Dowell to Hella Sessoms. April 17, 1975. Fales Collection. Series I Box 1 Folder 15.

363. Coleman Dowell, personal journal, October 30, 1975.

364. Sendak, *In the Night Kitchen*, p. 7.

365. Maurice Sendak to Coleman Dowell, April 7, 1969, Fales Collection, Series I, Box 3, Folder 3.

366. Kim Hunter to Coleman Dowell, April 25, 1975, Fales Collection, Series I, Box 3, Folder 32.

367. Hunter, *Loose in the Kitchen*, 63–64.

368. Coleman Dowell to Martha Cline and Ruth Willis, December 24, 1975, private collection of Gayle Wohlken.

369. Dowell, *Island People*, 34

370. Coleman Dowell, personal journal, February 28, 1978.

371. Recalling the evening, Edmund White said, "As for my calling cole 'stupid,' I THINK I said that he wrote from the gut and was not a cerebral writer—which he interpreted as my calling him stupid. he had a large, mythic imagination and a faulkner-ian intensity—he wasn't 'an intellectual.' I think it was Camus who said that American writers were the only ones in the world who didn't think they had to be intellectuals. . . . Cole read a lot but in the usual american writer magpie fashion to find things he could use . . ." Edmund White, e-mail to the author, September 27, 2004.

372. Coleman Dowell, personal journal, February 2, 1978.

373. Coleman Dowell to James Laughlin, May 29, 1975, Houghton Library, Harvard, bMS Am 207 (477), Coleman Dowell, Correspondence, 1972–1985.

374. Ibid, January 5, 1978.

375. Ibid, January 23, 1978.

376. Ibid, January 18, 1978.

377. Kuehl, "Interview," 272.

378. James Laughlin to Coleman Dowell, March 3, 1976, Houghton Library, Harvard, bMS Am 207 (477), Coleman Dowell, Correspondence, 1972–1985.

379. O'Brien, "Interview," 87.

380. Buttrick, *Interpreter's Dictionary*, 779. In the Old Testament Jabez was one of the descendants of Judah from I Chronicles 4:9–10.

381. Dowell, *Too Much Flesh and Jabez*, 8.

382. Ibid, 3.

383. Ibid, 3.

384. Ibid, 10.

385. This is Miss Ethel's first reference to *The Heart of Darkness*, in which the character Mr. Kuntz takes on the characteristics of the African natives.

386. Dowell, *Too Much Flesh and Jabez*, 7.

387. Ibid, 8.

388. Ibid, 1.

389. Ibid, 6–7.

390. Ibid, 8.

391. Ibid, 11.

392. Ibid, 3.

393. Ibid, 84. These references ironically echo Queen Gertrude's line from *Hamlet*, considering a character in the play who resembles her: "The lady doth protest too much, methinks." Miss Ethel's story within a story also cleverly echoes Shakespeare's play within the play. She refers to Hamlet again later, "undreamed in her philosophy" (132), an allusion to Hamlet's speech.

394. Dowell, *Too Much Flesh and Jabez*, 12.

395. Kuehl, "Interview," 281.

396. Coleman Dowell, *Too Much Flesh and Jabez*, 99.

397. Ibid, 97.

398. Ibid, 97–98.

399. Ibid, 141.

400. Lebensborn is a compound German word that means "fountain of life." Hein-

rich Himmler created the Lebensborn Eingetragener Verein ("Registered Society Lebensborn") in 1935. The goal of this society was to care for pregnant women who were referred to them by party agencies. After the children were born the organization often adopted them. Some people believe that the SS transformed these nurseries into brothels where SS officers could meet German women and produce "racially pure" children. The Lebensborn also kidnapped Germanic children from the occupied territories. Often the children were taken from orphanages but some were also kidnapped from members of the resistance. Thousands of children were transferred to the Lebensborn nurseries in order to be "Germanized." Most of the children were finally transferred to concentration camps and exterminated.

401. Laxness, *Independent People*, 70–71.

402. Ibid, 73–74.

403. Dowell, *Too Much Flesh and Jabez*, 91.

404. Ibid, 102.

405. Ibid, 106.

406. Ibid, 115.

407. O'Brien, "Interview," 88.

408. Coleman Dowell, *Too Much Flesh and Jabez*, 10.

409. O'Brien, "Interview," 86.

410. Kuehl, "Interview," 289.

411. Dowell, *Too Much Flesh and Jabez*, 151.

412. Ibid, 73.

413. Ibid, 110.

414. Ibid, 105.

415. Ibid, 150.

416. Coleman Dowell, personal journal, January 1, 1978.

417. Gilbert Sorrentino, "Perverse Story *Too Much Flesh and Jabez*," *New York Times*, January 1, 1978.

418. Terence Winch, "Too Big for His Britches," *Washington Post*, January 29, 1978.

419. Ibid, February 28, 1978.

420. Ibid, January 16, 1978.

421. Ibid, March 23, 1978.

422. Ibid, January 5, 1978.

423. Ibid, July 4, 1978.

424. Ibid, March 6, 1978.

425. Ibid, April 3, 1978.

426. Ibid, February 3, 1977.

427. Coleman Dowell, "Letter to the Editor," *New York Times*, June 3, 1977.

428. Coleman Dowell, personal journal, February 2, 1977.

429. Ibid, March 30, 1977.

430. *Courier-Journal*, Sunday, March 6, 1977.

431. John Howard Griffin to Coleman Dowell, April 2, 1962.

432. Ibid, August 16, 1977.

433. Ibid.

434. Ibid, June 17, 1977.

435. Ibid, January 8, 1978.

436. Bax printed the poem in *Ambit* 76 in 1978.

437. Coleman Dowell, personal journal. February 6, 1978.

438. Ibid, May 16, 1978.

439. David Madden to Coleman Dowell, November 17, 1978, Fales Collection, Series I, Box 2, Folder 11.

440. Judy Talcott to Coleman Dowell. September 14, 1979, Fales Collection, Series III, Box 5, Folder 5.

441. Judy Talcott to Coleman Dowell. October 8, 1979, Fales Collection, Series III, Box 5, Folder 5.

442. Bruce Kellner. Letter to the author, May 5, 2006.

443. Coleman Dowell, personal journal, March 27, 1980.

444. Ibid. May 7, 1980.

445. Ned Rorem had used Gibbons' lyrics from the song in his own piece, *The silver swan: for voice and piano* in 1950.

446. Coleman Dowell to Jack Collins, February 5, 1983, Fales Collection, Series I, Box 1, Folder 14.

447. Langland's "Vita de Dowel" is in the second part of *Piers Plowman*.

448. Coleman Dowell, "Explication of THE SILVER SWANNE," undated, Fales Collection, Series II, Subseries A, Box 1, Folder 12.

449. Coleman Dowell, "The Writing of the Silver Swanne," undated, Fales Collection, Series II, Subseries A, Box 1, Folder 12.

450. Ibid.

451. James Laughlin to Coleman Dowell, August 8, 1980, Fales Collection, Series I, Box 2, Folder 6.

452. Coleman Dowell, personal journal, December 1, 1980.

453. Ibid, undated.

454. *Review of Contemporary Fiction*. (Spring, 1981), 143–152.

455. *Review of Contemporary Fiction*. (Spring 1982), 99–100.

456. Coleman Dowell, personal journal, March 23, 1982.

457. James Laughlin to Coleman Dowell, March 11, 1982, Houghton Library, Harvard, bMS Am 207 (477), Coleman Dowell, Correspondence, 1972–1985.

458. Dowell, *White on Black on White*, 161.

459. Ibid, 194.

460. Era Bell Thompson and Herbert Nipson, eds. *White on Black*, Johnson Publishing Company, Inc., Chicago, 1963. There is no evidence that Dowell was familiar with this book.

461. Dowell had explored this theme in an earlier, unpublished work, the musical *Haymarket*, which concerns a love affair between a white woman and a black man—one of the key aspects of *White on Black on White*.

462. James Laughlin to Coleman Dowell, December 31, 1983, Fales Collection, Series I, Box 2, Folder 6.

463. Lawrence Howard, "Review of *White on Black on White*," Best Sellers, volume 43, August 1983, 161.

464. David Evanier, "Review of *White on Black on White*," *New York Times*, November 13, 1983.

465. O'Brien, "Interview," 97.

466. Kuehl, "Interview," 279

467. Shena Mackay, "Uncivil Rights and the Sins of the Fathers," *London Times*, January 28, 1990.

468. Kuehl, "Interview," 282.

469. O'Brien, "Interview," 95.

470. O'Brien, "Interview," 88.

471. Dowell describes his own visits to Harlem in *A Star-Bright Lie*, 11.

472. Dowell, *White on Black on White*, 129.

473. Ibid, 233.

474. Ibid, 250.

475. A quote from D. H. Lawrence's *Lady Chatterley's Lover*, loosely translated as "a longing for the mud."

476. Dowell, *White on Black on White*, 184.

477. Ibid, 62.

478. Ibid, 65

479. Ibid, 112.

480. Edgar Cayce, one of America's most famous psychics, was born near Hopkinsville, Kentucky, just 47 miles northwest of Dowell's birthplace in Adairville. Dowell shared Cayce's interest in dreams and the unconscious mind.

481. Dowell, *White on Black on White*, 219.

482. Ibid, 11.

483. Ibid, 114.

484. Ibid, 184.

485. Dowell, *Too Much Flesh and Jabez*, 102.

486. Dowell, *White on Black on White*, 109.

487. White, "Thoughts," 113.

488. Ibid.

489. Dowell, *White on Black on White*, 251.

490. Published after his death as *A Star-Bright Lie*.

491. Coleman Dowell to James Laughlin, June 6, 1984, Houghton Library, Harvard, bMS Am 207 (477), Coleman Dowell, Correspondence, 1972–1985.

492. Coleman Dowell to Jack Collins. October 6, 1983, Fales Collection, Series I, Box 1, Folder 14.

493. Coleman Dowell, personal journal, May 4, 1983.

494. Charles McGrath to Coleman Dowell, July 8, 1982, Fales Collection, Series I, Box 1, Folder 11.

495. Lois Morrow to Coleman Dowell, September 17, 1983, Fales Collection, Series I, Box 1, Folder 11.

496. Coleman Dowell, personal journal, July 19, 1983.

497. *Ambit* 94, 1983, 58–66.

498. *Ambit* 100, 1985, 59–68.

499. Coleman Dowell, personal journal, July 20, 1983.

500. Ibid, July 19, 1983.

501. Ibid, May 10, 1983.

502. Ibid, April 21, 1983.

503. Ibid, November 14, 1983.

504. Evanier, "Review."

505. Coleman Dowell, personal journal, June 14, 1983.

506. Ibid, April 27 1983.

507. Ibid, July 20, 1983.

508. Ibid, May 31, 1983.

509. Ibid, July 27 1983.

510. Ibid, July 20, 1983.

511. Bob Halliday, "Triple Fugue: Race, Sex, and Obsession," *Washington Post Book World*, July 17, 1983.

512. Ibid, August 1, 1983.

513. Ibid, August 5, 1983.

514. For an excellent study of the group see David Bergman's work, *The Violet Hour: the Velvet Quill and the Making of Gay Culture*, Columbia University Press, 2004.

515. Coleman Dowell, personal journal, August 14, 1983.

516. Ibid, August 29, 1983.

517. Ibid, November 2, 1983.

518. Ibid, December 27, 1983.

519. Ibid.

520. Ibid, January 10, 1984

521. Ibid, March 30, 1984.

522. Ibid, January 19, 1983.

523. Ibid, January 19, 1984.

524. Ibid, October 2, 1984.

525. Ibid, March 30, 1984.

526. *BOMB* published two excerpts from the memoir, "At Home with Drosselmeier" (Number 10, Fall 1984) and "A Handful of Anomalies" (Number 13, Fall 1985).

527. Griselda Ohannessian and Peter Glassgold to James Laughlin, January 25, 1985, Houghton Library, Harvard, bMS Am 207 (477), Coleman Dowell, Correspondence, 1972–1985.

528. Peter Glassgold to Coleman Dowell, August 1, 1985, Houghton Library, Harvard, bMS Am 207 (477), Coleman Dowell, Correspondence, 1972–1985.

529. Coleman Dowell, personal journal, October 2, 1984.

530. Suicide note copy sent by the New York City Department of Health Office of Chief Medical Examiner September 14, 1985, 520 First Avenue, New York, NY 10016. Chief Medical Examiner, Case 91185-6071.

531. Dorothy Dowell Steers, e-mail to the author, December 13, 2001.

532. Ann Lauterbach, "Uneasy Requital for Coleman Dowell," *The Paris Review*, 27:98, Winter, 1985).

533. Tribute to Coleman Dowell, Gilbert Sorrentino Papers, Department of Special Collections and University Archives, Stanford University Libraries.

534. *Harper's Magazine*, #274, April, 1987.

535. Rena S. Kleiman, "Review of *The Houses of Children* by Coleman Dowell," *Los Angeles Times*, May 24, 1987.

536. Ibid.

537. Miriam Fuchs, "Coleman Dowell's Short Stories," *Review of Contemporary Fiction*, 2.3, 118–21.

538. John Kuehl, "Review of *The Houses of Children* and *One of the Children is Crying* by Coleman Dowell," *Review of Contemporary Fiction*, 7.3, 258–59.

539. Lorrie Moore, "Down the Throat of Night," *New York Times Book Review*, May 24, 1987.

BIBLIOGRAPHY

MANUSCRIPT COLLECTIONS

Dowell, Coleman. Papers, 1950–1985. Fales Library, New York University.

——. Correspondence. Grenfell Press archive collection. Library of Congress.

Elliott, Sumner Locke. Sumner Locke Elliott Collection. The Howard Gotlieb Archival Research Center at Boston University.

Griffin, John Howard. John Howard Griffin Papers. The Rare Book and Manuscript Library, Columbia University.

Laughlin, James and Coleman Dowell. The James Laughlin Papers. Houghton Library, Harvard University.

Lebherz, Richard. The Richard Lebherz Papers 1968–1976. Fales Library, New York University.

Sorrentino, Gilbert. The Gilbert Sorrentino Papers. Department of Special Collections, Green Library. Stanford University Libraries.

Van Vechten, Carl and Coleman Dowell. The Carl Van Vechten Papers, 1833–1965. Manuscripts Division, New York Public Library.

York, Ruth Landshoff. "For Coleman Dowell to fit one of his spare tunes to." Ruth York Collection. The Howard Gotlieb Archival Research Center at Boston University.

BOOKS

Bergson, Henri. *Time and Free Will: An Essay on the Immediate Data of Consciousness*. New York: Harper, 1960.

Buttrick, George Arthur, ed. *The Interpreter's Dictionary of the Bible*. New York: Abingdon Press, 1962.

D'Amico, Maria Vittoria. "Coleman Dowell," in *Postmodern Fiction: A Bio-bibliographical Guide*. Ed. Larry McCaffery. Westport, CT: Greenwood Press, 1986.

Darnall General Hospital. "Hospital Regulations H.R. No. 5-5," February 5, 1942.

Hayworth, Eugene. *Swan on the Balcony*. New York: New York University, 2003.

Hunter, Kim. *Loose in the Kitchen*. North Hollywood, CA: Domina Books, 1975.

Kellner, Bruce. *Carl Van Vechten and the Irreverent Decades*. Norman, OK: University of Oklahoma Press, 1968.

——. *Letters of Carl Van Vechten*. New Haven, CT: Yale University Press, 1987.

Kuehl, John. *Alternate Worlds*. New York : New York University Press, 1989.

Laxness, Halldór. *Independent People*. New York: Vintage Books International, 1997.

Martin, Stephen-Paul. "A Comparative Study of Androgyny in Twentieth-century Experimental Literature." Ph.D. diss., New York University, 1984.

Performers Television Credits (Volumes 1 and 3). Jefferson, NC: McFarland, 2001.

Secrest, Meryle. *Leonard Bernstein: A Life*. New York: Alfred A. Knopf, 1994.

Sendak, Maurice. *In the Night Kitchen*. New York: Harper & Row, 1970.

Sorrentino, Gilbert. *Something Said: Essays*. San Francisco: North Point Press, 1984.

Stermer, Dugald. *The Art of Revolution*. Introduction by Susan Sontag. New York: McGraw-Hill 1970.

Van Vechten, Carl. *The Tattooed Countess: A Romantic Novel with a Happy Ending*. New York: Knopf, 1924.

Vandiver, Elizabeth. "The *Odyssey* of Homer." Springfield, VA: Teaching Co., Lecture 2, 1999.

Ward, William S. A *Literary History of Kentucky*. Knoxville, TN: University of Tennessee Press, 1988.

White, Edmund. *The Burning Library*. New York: Alfred Knopf, 1995.

WORKS BY COLEMAN DOWELL

MEMOIRS

A *Star-Bright Lie*, Normal, IL: Dalkey Archive Press, 1993.

NON-FICTION

"Coleman Dowell." *The Writer*. March 1968, 81.3, 23.

"The Dakota: 'Absurd, Magical, Old Palace.'" Review of *Life at the Dakota*, by Stephen Birmingham, *Courier-Journal*, October 22, 1979.

"Dense and Rich Themes in a Woman's Struggle." Review of *The Suicide's Wife*, by David Madden, *Courier-Journal*, November 5,1978.

"A 'Fierce Intelligence,' Advent of a Major Writer." Review of *Final Payments*, by Mary Gordon, *Courier-Journal*, May 14, 1978.

"From Four Noted Names: One Winner, Three Losers." Review of *Altered States*, by Paddy Chayefsky; *Tuesdays and Thursdays*, by Abby Mann; *Another I, Another You*, by Richard Schickel; and *Madmen Must*, by William Jovanovich, *Courier-Journal*, June 18, 1978.

"Gilbert Sorrentino's *Aberration of Starlight*." *Review of Contemporary Fiction*, 1.1, 143–52.

"At Home with Drosselmeier." *Bomb Magazine*, No. 10, Fall 1984.

"A Handful of Anomalies." *Bomb Magazine*, No. 13, Fall 1985.

"Literary Balcomb Greene." *Review of Contemporary Fiction*, 2.1, 99–100.

"Mary Gordon's Second Novel Absorbs, then Scorns the Reader." Review of *The Company of Women*, by Mary Gordon. *Courier-Journal*, March 1, 1981.

"Meandering Evangelizing from Joyce Carol Oates." Review of *Son of Morning*, by Joyce Carol Oates, *Courier-Journal*, November 26, 1978.

Review of *Men and Angels*, by Mary Gordon. *Courier-Journal*, May 12, 1985.

"Peeks into the Lives of Two Writers." Review of *Selected Letters of John O'Hara*, edited by Maxwell J. Bruccoli; and *The World of Tennessee Williams*, edited by Richard F. Leavitt, *Courier-Journal*, September 17, 1978.

"Pristine Novel, Permeated by Decay." Review of A *Married Man*, by Piers Paul Read, *Courier-Journal*, March 30, 1980.

"A Provincial South Hiding a Touch of the Universal." Review of *The Rock Cried Out*, by Ellen Douglas, *Courier-Journal*, September 16, 1979.

"Scary and Beautiful, a Work Full of Grace." Review of *The Glass Sea*, by Marian Engel, *Courier-Journal*, October 28, 1979.

"'Starlight:' Laughter and Brilliance." Review of *Aberration of Starlight*, by Gilbert Sorrentino, *Courier-Journal*, August 31, 1980.

"Two From North Carolina, Both Regional and Worldy." Review of *The High-Pitched Laugh of a Painted Lady*, by Lewis W. Green and *Dwelling Places*, by Burke Davis, *Courier-Journal*, January 18, 1981.

"Unheralded, a Woman's Grievances." Review of *Willo*, by Karen Snow and *Entropisms* by, Harriet Zinnes, *Courier-Journal*, February 4, 1979.

"Uneasy Memories that Return Eloquently." Review of *Chamber Music*, by Doris Grumbach, *Courier-Journal*, June 10, 1979.

"Van Vechten as Photographer." Review of *Portraits: The Photography of Carl Van Vechten*, *Courier-Journal*, February 25, 1979.

NOVELS

The Grass Dies. London: Cassell, 1968.

One of the Children is Crying. New York: Random House, 1968.
(Reprint, Weidenfeld & Nicolson, 1987).
(Reprint, *Hay un Niño Que Llora*. Barcelona: Ediciones del Serbal, 1988.)

Mrs. October was Here. New York: New Directions, 1974.

Island People. New York: New Directions, 1976.
(Reprint, Normal, IL: Dalkey Archive Press, 1996.)

Too Much Flesh and Jabez. New York: New Directions, 1977.
(Reprint, Elmwood Park, IL: Dalkey Archives Press, 1987.)
(Reprint, Elmwood Park, IL: Dalkey Archive Press, 1995.)
(Reprint, *Trop de chair pour Jabez*. Castenau-le-Lez, France: Climats, 1995. Translated by Bernard Hepffner.)

White on Black on White. Woodstock, VT: Countryman Press, 1983.
(Reprint, London: Serpent's Tail, 1990.)
(Reprint: *Blanc sur noir sur blanc*. Castenau-le-Lez, France: Climats, 1998. Translated by Bernard Hepffner.)

Eve of the Green Grass. Unpublished.

WORKS BY COLEMAN DOWELL

POETRY

"Partridge House." *Ambit* 76, 1978, 23.

"The bird, me, my lady." *Ambit* 89, 1982, 40–41.

SHORT FICTION

"Alte Frau im Garten." Translated by Ruth Landshoff-York. *Frankfurter Hefte* 17 Jahrang, Heft, April 4, 1962, 269–72.

"The Keepsake." (Excerpt from the novel *Island People*). *New Directions: An Anthology of Prose and Poetry* 26, 1973, 88–103.

"The Birthmark." (Excerpt from the novel *Island People*). *New Directions: An Anthology of Prose and Poetry* 27, January 15, 1973, 1–15.

"I Envy You Your Adventure." *New Directions: An Anthology of Prose and Poetry* 28, 1974, 161–68 (Reprinted in *Houses of Children*).

"First Person Biography." (Excerpt from the novel *Island People*). *New Directions: An Anthology of Prose and Poetry* 29, 1974, 142–60.

"I am the Beast." (Excerpt from the novel *Island People*). *Ambit* 61, 1975, 30–38.

"Victor." (Excerpt from the novel *Island People*). *New Directions: An Anthology of Prose and Poetry* 30, 1975, 34–67.

"If Beggars were Horses." *New Directions: An Anthology of Prose and Poetry* 31, 1975, 118–30 (Reprinted in *Houses of Children*).

"Singing in the Clump." *New Directions: An Anthology of Prose and Poetry* 32, 1976, 84–96 (Reprinted in *Houses of Children*).

"The Moon, the Owl, my Sister." *New Directions: An Anthology of Prose and Poetry* 33, 1976, 32–40 (Reprinted in *Houses of Children*).

"The Drought Ends." (An excerpt from the novel *Too Much Flesh and Jabez*). *Ambit* 65, 1976, 25–40.

"Handy." (An excerpt from the novel *One of the Children is Crying*). *Kentucky Renaissance*, ed. Jonathan Greene, 1976, 49–57.

"Her Good Man Gone." (An excerpt from the novel *Too Much Flesh and Jabez*). *Ambit* 69, 1977, 24–32.

"Ham's Gift." *New Directions: An Anthology of Prose and Poetry* 35, May 11, 1977, 5–11 (Reprinted in *Houses of Children*).

"My Father was a River." *New Directions: An Anthology of Prose and Poetry* 36, 1978, 70–81 (Reprinted in *Houses of Children*).

"A Lifetime Proposition." *Ambit* 73, 1978, 33–35.

"The snake's house." (An excerpt from the novel *White on Black on White*). *Ambit* 79, 1979, 17–33.

"*White on Black on White*." (An excerpt from the novel *White on Black on White*). *Conjunctions* 3, Fall 1982, 119–131.

"Prison Visiting." (Excerpt from the novel *White on Black on White*). *Ambit* 88, 1982, 10–19.

"The Silver Swanne." *Ambit* 84, 1980, 6–25.
(Reprint, Grenfell Press, 1983.)
(Reprint, *Conjunctions* 5, Fall 1983, 7–29.)
(Reprinted in *Houses of Children*).

"Wool Tea." *Ambit* 94, 1983, 58–66 (Reprinted in *Houses of Children*).

"The Great Godalmighty Bird." *Conjunctions* 4, Spring 1983, 55–69.

"Eve of the Green Grass." (Novel excerpt.) *Conjunctions* 6, Spring 1984, 189–220.

"Kitty." (An excerpt from the memoir *A Star-Bright Lie*). *Ambit* 100, 1985, 59–68.

"Writings on a Cave Wall." *Conjunctions* 8, Fall 1985, 95–99.

"The Hobo." *ADENA*, Spring 1980.

"Five Prose Pieces: Wool Tea, Cancer, City Sundays, A Lifetime Proposition, Elegy." *Conjunctions* 9, Spring 1986, 216–42.

"The Surgeon." (Excerpt from the novel *Island People*). *New Directions: An Anthology of Prose and Poetry* 50, 1986, 211–21.

"In the Mood." *Review of Contemporary Fiction: Fiction Issue*, 6.1, 99–118 (Reprinted in *Houses of Children*).

"City Sundays." *Harper's Magazine* 274, April, 1987, 34–35.

"Willow Sheridan Rode Voltaire." (Introduced by Maria Vittoria D'Amico.) *Rivista di Studi Nord-Americani*, May, 1994.

COLLECTED SHORT STORIES

The Houses of Children. New York: Weidenfeld & Nicolson, 1987.
(Reprint, First Dalkey Archive edition, Normal, IL: Dalkey Archive Press, 2000.)
(Reprint, *Les Maisons des enfants*. Joelle Losfeld, 1996. Translated by Bernard Hoepffner.)

STAGE PLAYS

Haymarket, 1949.
Gentle Laurel, 1957.

The Indian Giver, 1959.
The Tattooed Countess, (adaptation of novel by Carl Van Vechten; produced New York, 1961), Chappell and Company.
Ah, Wilderness! 1957 (With John Latouche. Adaptation of the play by Eugene O'Neill).
Eve of the Green Grass, 1963 (produced New York, 1965).

CREDITS

Excerpts from the Coleman Dowell Papers are used by permission of the Fales Library, New York University and Dr. Bertram Slaff, Literary Executor for the estate of Coleman Dowell.

Excerpts from the Sumner Locke Elliott Papers are used by permission of the Howard Gotlieb Archival Research Center at Boston University.

Excerpts from the Ruth Landshoff York Papers are used by permission of the Howard Gotlieb Archival Research Center at Boston University.

Excerpts from the Gilbert Sorrentino Papers courtesy of Department of Special Collections, Stanford University Libraries.

Excerpts from the John Howard Griffin Papers are used by permission of the Rare Book and Manuscript Library, Columbia University.

Excerpts from the New Directions Publishing Corp. Records are used by permission of Houghton Library, Harvard University.

Excerpts from the letters of James Laughlin (copyright 1972–1975 by New Directions Publishing Corp.) are used by permission of New Directions.

Excerpts from letters by members of the New Directions staff (copyright 1974, 1975 by New Directions Publishing Corp.) are used by permission of New Directions.

Excerpts from The Carl Van Vechten Papers are used by permission of the Carl Van Vechten Trust.

INDEX